# BENTO BOX
### IN
### THE
# HEARTLAND

My Japanese Girlhood in Whitebread America

Linda Furiya

SEAL

For my parents,
James Ichiro and Teruko Furiya

Bento Box in the Heartland
My Japanese Girlhood in Whitebread America

Copyright © 2006 by Linda Furiya

 Published by
Seal Press
An Imprint of Avalon Publishing Group, Incorporated
AVALON 1400 65th Street, Suite 250, Emeryville, CA 94608
publishing group incorporated

ISBN-13: 978-1-58005-191-0
ISBN-10: 1-58005-191-X

Library of Congress Cataloging-in-Publication Data

Furiya, Linda.
Bento box in the heartland : my Japanese girlhood in whitebread
America / Linda Furiya.
      p. cm.
ISBN-13: 978-1-58005-191-0 (alk. paper)
ISBN-10: 1-58005-191-X (alk. paper)
1. Furiya, Linda-Childhood and youth. 2. Furiya, Linda-Family. 3.
Japanese Americans-Indiana-Versailles-Biography. 4. Japanese
Americans-Indiana-Versailles-Social life and customs. 5. Cookery,
Japanese-Social aspects-Indiana-Versailles. 6. Versailles
(Ind.)-Biography. 7. Versailles (Ind.)-Social life and customs. 8.
Racism-Middle West-Case studies. 9. Japanese Americans-Cultural
assimilation-Middle West-Case studies. 10. Middle West-Race
relations-Case studies. I. Title.

F534.V34F87 2007
977.2'14004956-dc22
  2006030696

Cover & Interior design by Kate Basart/Union Pageworks
Printed in the United States of America
Distributed by Publishers Group West

# Contents

Swallowing Fish Bones

My mother first told me this story when I was six years old, before I knew that the language she spoke was Japanese.

Her personal tale takes place in Tokyo during the 1930s, when she was a young girl. Her neighborhood, she explained, was a jigsaw puzzle of low-story, fragile houses constructed of wood and paper. The homes survived the many earthquakes that shook Japan, yet most burned away like dried leaves when Tokyo was bombed during World War II.

Every day a community of mothers in the neighborhood gathered together to feed their babies a midday meal and to rest from endless household duties and the tongues and ears of nosy in-laws.

While the older women gossiped and watched over the little ones, the younger women made lunch for the babies, who ate softer versions of what their mothers served at their tables—rice, fish, soup, and vegetables.

Often the fishmonger's wife brought a whole fish to broil until the skin charred and cracked on a small outside grill. The mothers slid the flaky, sweet, white meat off the bone with the tap of a chopstick.

Using their fingers to feel for any stray fish bones, they thoroughly mashed, pinched, and poked the tender fish meat before mixing it with rice and moistening it with *dashi* (fish stock). Despite all the care, sometimes a transparent bone, pliable and sharp as a shark's tooth, slipped past scrutiny.

I picture her wearing braids and standing in the distance, quietly observing yet part of the gathering. Now her short hair frames her face like the black slashes of an ink brush. In this story my mother explains how before modern medicine, the mortality rate was high not only for newborns, but even for healthy men, who were struck dead from illnesses that would start as a common cold.

"One day you are in good health, the next . . ." Mom's eyes flicker at this point, like two flints sparking. She snaps her fingers at the swiftness of it all. Back then, mothers needed reassurance that their babies were strong, and eating was an infant's first test of survival. If the baby didn't know how to eat, suck from its mother's nipple, or push out a fish bone, the child wouldn't know how to survive when she grew older.

One day during a feeding, my mother's story goes, the *wagashi-* (Japanese pastry) maker's baby sat still and silent, holding his mouthful of fish and rice.

"Eh?" grunted Obasan, the old matriarch of the group, as she peered at the baby through thick spectacles.

The *wagashi*-maker's wife nervously patted the baby on the back as all the other mothers talked quietly, trying not to stare. Strings of saliva and bits of fish dribbled out of his mouth. His tiny bud of a tongue moved in and out before finally pushing out a small fish bone, the size of a pine needle.

The *wagashi*-maker's wife gushed with pride at her baby's grit for life. Obasan cackled loudly, proclaiming he would live a strong, healthy life, as the other women sighed and laughed with relief. Years later, Mom says, he became a doctor and people credited his success to overcoming the fish bone.

Another time the soba noodle–maker's baby swallowed a small bone. Reminiscent of the first infant, he sat still and silent, but no spittle and bone came out. Instead, he swallowed. Not long after, the baby developed a fever and refused to take his mother's milk. A doctor removed a small bone that had been lodged in his throat, and the soba-maker's wife began worrying about her baby's future. No one was surprised when he died of tuberculosis at the age of ten.

Unlike stories with resolution that I would become accustomed to hearing from teachers and other adults throughout my youth, Mom left the tale at that, leaving me baffled as to its lesson or moral. Growing up, whenever I complained about mistreatment by a friend or the unfairness of some school interaction, my mother repeated her story of the infants and the fish bones. Growing up in the only Japanese family in Versailles, Indiana, I quickly learned that I would have to overcome many fish bones. My very first notion of how different we really were struck me among the pastel-colored molded trays and long bleached wood tables of the school cafeteria.

My elementary school lunchroom was a sweaty, brightly lit place that reeked of hot cooking oil, Pine-Sol, and the yeast from rising bread dough. It was dead quiet when empty, and otherwise it echoed with the sound of children's high-pitched talk and laughter and heavy wood and metal chairs scraping against the tile floor.

I had never eaten a lunch before then without my parents. My two older brothers, Keven and Alvin, ate lunch at school. Mom was a stay-at-home mother. She churned out three meals a day as efficiently as a military mess hall. My father worked second shift at a factory in Columbus, Indiana, where he assembled truck engines. Because he started his shift midafternoon, he ate a hot, filling lunch at home to compensate for his dinner, a cold *bento* box of rice, meat, and vegetables, with a cup of green tea from his thermos.

These lunches with my parents were magnificent feasts made in our tiny kitchen. The size of a hall closet, the small room became alive during lunchtime, like a living, breathing creature, with steam puffing from the electric rice cooker, rattling from the simmering pots, and short clipping notes of Mom chopping with her steady hand guiding her *nakiri bocho* (Japanese vegetable knife).

At the dining room table, Dad and I grazed on cold Japanese appetizers—spicy wilted cabbage pickled in brine with lemon peel, garlic, smashed whole red chili peppers, and kombu (seaweed). Meanwhile, Mom prepared hot dishes—cubes of tofu garnished with ginger and bonito flakes (dried fish shavings). There was salmon fillet, if we could get it, grilled to the color of Turkish apricots on a Japanese wire stove-top contraption; or sirloin, sliced tissue-thin, sautéed with onions, soy sauce, and a dash of rice wine. And there was always a bowl of clear fish broth or cloudy miso soup and steamed white rice.

As I was used to such sumptuous lunches, it wasn't long before the novelty of my school's cafeteria fare wore off and my eyes wandered toward the lunch boxes other children brought from home. From inside the metal containers, they pulled out sandwiches with the crusts cut off, followed by tins of chocolate pudding and homemade cookies.

My best friend, Tracy Martin, was part of the lunch box brigade. Her mother packed the same lunch items every day—a cold hot dog and applesauce. We also ate with Mary, a Coppertoned, baby-faced girl with a Clara Bow haircut, whose mother precut all the food in her lunch box, even her cookies, into bite-size pieces.

I wanted to be a part of this exclusive group, and after much pestering, I was thrilled when my mother relented and agreed to pack my lunches.

When I joined Tracy and Mary at lunchtime, carrying my own lunch box, I studied the girls, who carefully unpacked their containers as if they were unveiling family heirloom jewelry, observing the packed-lunch protocol. I unlocked my lunch box and casually peeked under the lid. My stomach lurched. I expected a classic elementary school lunch of a bologna, cheese, and Miracle Whip sandwich and a bag of Durkee's potato sticks, but all I saw were three round rice balls wrapped in waxed paper. Mom had made me an *obento*, a Japanese-style boxed meal.

I snapped the lunch box lid shut before the other girls caught a glimpse of what was inside. How could this have happened?

"Sandwich?" Mom asked in a genuinely astonished voice when I came home from school that afternoon protesting. "Why go to trouble to make lunch for just plain old sandwich?"

"That's what everyone else brings. That's what I want," I demanded. My desire to emulate my classmates was palpable. My *obento* lunches were a glaring reminder of the ethnic differences between my peers and me.

The agony of being different from my classmates was inten-sified the day Scott Leach pointed out the slanted shape of my eyes. Scott had snow-white hair and constantly dug his pinkie finger deep in his ear. One morning as we stood in the milk line, he turned to me and furrowed his eyebrows, point-ing at my eyes as if they were insect specimens.

"Why do they look like lines?" he asked with a smirk far more adult than his age.

When the other kids laughed, I knew this wasn't a nor-mal question. My throat tightened as if a fish bone were on the verge of lodging itself in my windpipe. I took a step back, bringing my index finger up to my mouth to shush him, only to witness him pull his own eyes back at the corners to more laughter from the classmates in line. Encouraged by the other children's reactions, Scott pulled his eyes back and tilted his head from side to side.

I stood there like a mannequin. I was filled with helpless, choking anxiety. The spell was broken only when the recess bell rang to go back to class. The incident initiated what became open season for teasing me.

A couple of days later at recess, after I won a round at hopscotch, Susie Sillerhorn, a pinch-nosed blond and known sore loser, announced that she had heard my parents talk-ing "sing-songy" in the grocery store. Susie's pal Donna Underwood joined in by pulling back her eyes until they appeared closed and made pinging nonsense noises. The other girls laughed.

Defiantly, I asked why she was doing that. "You should know what I'm saying. This is how your folks talk," she replied haughtily. I didn't know the name of it then, but the feeling this early interaction left me with was my first feeling of injustice.

Still, I wanted their friendship and to be accepted, so silently, but with deep resentment, I put up with friends who called me Chink and Jap. Some innate self-control wouldn't allow me to give my prosecutors the lesson they probably needed to learn, of knowing they were hurting me. Eventually, though, the resentment, anger, and developing drive for self-preservation gave me the gumption to fight back.

My first stand, albeit lame, was against Tracy, who instantly resorted to calling me Jap when we got into an argument about whose tree swings were better. She watched my reaction with calm, steady eyes. Tracy knew the power behind the word.

Unable to think of anything to say, I spurted out the first thing that came to mind. I called her "pizzahead" because of her Italian ancestry. It was weak, like throwing confetti at an opponent, but it was my first stab at fighting back.

At night, I'd lie awake and fantasize about how to get revenge. I imagined that Dad was an undercover agent on a special assignment, a foreign dignitary from Japan. His cover was a factory job in a small Midwest town. I saw the surprised looks on my friends' faces when they realized we weren't who they thought we were. The meanest ones, including Susie and Donna, begged me to be their best friends. I smiled smugly and shook my head. My family was leaving Versailles and I wouldn't be going to school there anymore, I explained. Then I enjoyed their looks of dismay and confusion, just as they had enjoyed themselves when they teased me. A cavalcade of shiny black Cadillac sedans appeared and whisked us away. I waved at my classmates from the rearview window until they disappeared. I hugged my pillow and twisted my bedsheets so hard, wishing my fantasy would come true.

When I believed it couldn't get any worse, a turning point came one afternoon as I waited to use the playground swings. Raymond Neilley, a chubby boy in JCPenney Huskies jeans, pulled his eyes back in the overused imitation my peers favored.

"Chinky, chinky, Chinese," he sang, doing a little dance. For the first time, blinding fury replaced fear. First of all, I wasn't Chinese. I heard the other kids around me snickering as they encircled us and moved in closer. Dread prickled me like a scratchy blanket on a hot day. My mouth was cottony and my palms were slick. I could feel my heart beat quickly, rushing color to my face. Mom's fish bone story came to mind. It wasn't about swallowing or spitting, I realized, but about fight or flight.

"Shut up, fatso," I said, louder than a whisper. I recognized a flash of fear pass over Raymond's plump face, yet he continued to taunt me.

I raised my voice, making it commanding and deep. "I said shut up, you big ball of . . . lard!" I plucked this word out of a conversation I had overheard at the grocery store. It wasn't the choicest of names, but it had a nice menacing ring to it with high potential to damage, like the kind of mud balls my brothers threw when they fought with the neighborhood kids. Inside each firm handful of wet earth was a surprise, a skin-breaking chunk of gravel.

Raymond's darting eyes confirmed I had hit a raw nerve, filling me with giddy power.

Like a bombardier honing in on a target, I unleashed all the anger that I had pent up during the past weeks, screaming "fatso" and "lard" until the other children, like summer cicadas, joined in on my name-calling. Raymond didn't say anything. He stared and tried to figure out how the tables had turned.

After that the other kids thought twice before they teased me. If they tried, I fought back with everything I could get on them. Crossed eyes, crooked bangs, rotten teeth, dirty finger-nails, moles, eyeglasses, and freckles were all fair game.

With the gift of victory, I began to shake the overwhelming need to be like my friends. So what if I played by myself, got the cold-shoulder treatment, or had to deal with whispering behind my back? Nothing, I decided, could be as bad as putting up with the name-calling and the dread of waiting for it to come. I understood now why some boys took a beating instead of accepting daily torment: It was pride. I lost a sense of innocence that first year of school, but from it grew a defined measure of self that would stay with me and emerge during difficult times in my life.

❁

Tracy interrupted my thoughts. "Whatcha bring?" A straw pulled at the corner of her mouth as she sipped grape Kool-Aid from a plastic cup. The fish bone scratched at the back of my throat. I knew what I had to do. I took the apple out of my lunch box with discretion.

"Is that all you have?" Tracy asked.

"No, there's more. I'm just not hungry right now." I avoided her eyes.

Along with the apple, Mom had wrapped in plastic a few cookies among the tightly packed rice balls. The conversation was buzzing around me. I said as little as possible. The apple and cookies stuck in my throat like wet soot, but I ate slowly and purposefully, as if nothing were wrong.

Feigning a stomachache, I left the cafeteria with my lunch box tucked safely under my arm. I looked behind me nervously before I ducked into the girls' restroom.

Huddled in the pewter-gray toilet stall with the medicinal smell of Lysol, I cradled one of the three firmly packed rice balls in my hands. Its seaweed wrapping had the crispness of handmade rice paper. My pounding heart steadied a moment as I imagined Mom shaking salt on the palms of her clean wet hands and then pressing and rotating each ball three or four times until it was uniform. Despite my repeated requests for a sandwich, she persisted with the rice balls. She knew they were my favorite.

Startled by the noise of a toilet flushing in a nearby stall, I took a big bite of the *onigiri*. My teeth ripped through the crunchy seaweed wrapping, through the salty rice, to the surprise center, a buttery chunk of salmon placed precisely in the middle of the rice and seaweed ball. The other rice balls had centers of pickled plum and silky kelp.

It was a secret act that I found empowering and primal, rather than diminishing. I was hungry, and yet there was an odd sense of invincibility, the banishment of fear of what might happen if a teacher walked in on me. I had the sensation that if I left one grain uneaten, something inside me would shrivel up and die. I took big mouthfuls of the rice and chewed as fast as I could until there was no more.

That afternoon, delighted to find my lunch box empty, Mom asked if I enjoyed the rice balls. I told her I did and said nothing else. She continued to make one delicious *obento* after another, and for the remainder of the year I ate cookies and apples with my friends and consumed the rest of my lunch in the stall of the girls' bathroom. The lunch box crowd voted unanimously that my mother packed the lamest lunches in history.

I never told Mom about the fish bones I navigated my first year in school. I also announced that I wanted to eat school lunches again once I got into second grade.

❁

Summer vacation lay before me like a lazy ripple moving across a lake. My brothers and I spent our days digging for crawdads by the creek bed and our evenings catching fireflies as the dew fell. But still, in the back of my mind, the new school year loomed like a dreaded appointment with the dentist.

I decided to talk to my father on a rare Sunday he had off from work. I found him perched at the top of the two steps of our front porch, fresh from a shower. I sat at his feet on the lowermost step. His elbows rested on his knees as he enjoyed his favorite weekend ritual—a cigarette and a bottle of beer before dinner, and the early evening air cast a bluish tint as light leaked away from the muggy summer sky like a drying watercolor. Eager fireflies began their glow dance as the crickets' chirp rose and fell.

Dad had spent this particular Sunday outside, attending to his favorite chores of ripping out weeds from around the azalea bushes, spreading the grass clippings around the tomato plants, mowing and raking the lawn, and all the other yard work he rarely had an opportunity to attend to during the rest of the week.

In the summer, his winter potbelly disappeared from all the garden work. Dad pushed the mower until rivulets of sweat trickled down his toffee-brown face, like overflowing streams after a spring thaw, and his T-shirt clung to him like plastic wrap. He wore leather flip-flops, as he had problems finding shoes to cover his wide, compact feet.

My father had a thick, short torso, with strong legs and a square head. Except for his muttonchop sideburns, he resembled a Buddha statue. He had the same fleshy, long earlobes symbolizing good fortune. In the Japanese culture, gold coins were said to drop from Buddha's ears when pulled. My father's nose was rounded and flat, his eyes like dark lines drawn on paper, and his smile broad.

I gazed across the expanse of our yard and saw our neighbor Mr. Jones drive by on his riding lawn mower. At the start of summer, the police had pulled him over for driving under the influence and taken away his driver's license. His lawn mower now served as his mode of transportation to the liquor store and back. We raised our hands to him in unison, as we did with all passing motorists—an unspoken rule of small-town friendliness.

We sat there a long while before I finally asked him why we were the only Japanese family within a thirty-mile radius. He gave a surprised grunt but didn't respond, instead letting the crickets fill the silence.

"Let me tell you a story," Dad said in English, abruptly and loud, the way people begin to talk when they've already started the conversation in their heads. Then he switched to Japanese.

"A long time ago in Japan there were two daimyo."

I knew that a daimyo was a feudal warlord in Japanese history, but Dad emphasized their great power at the time of his story by telling me that they possessed armies of samurai warriors and houses full of wives and concubines.

"Today there are no more daimyo." Dad cleared his throat and looked thoughtful for a moment.

"This was four or five centuries ago, with many civil wars and constant fighting across the countryside. Our family, the Furiyas, came from one of these kingdoms. Our biggest battle was not about politics, land, or farmers—the reason for many of these wars—but about the heart."

I was conscious of the way I sat up straighter when my father mentioned our family name in such a majestic context. He noticed and continued in a stronger tone of voice.

"Our ancestral father's castle was surrounded by Japanese maple trees like these." He motioned across the yard to a familiar set of trees with deep burgundy leaves and feather-tipped points. He had bought them at a flower nursery in Cincinnati on one of our biweekly grocery trips, and Mom had gone on and on about the rarity of finding a Japanese maple here, of all places.

"In the next valley lived the Maruyama clan, a name that means 'round mountain.' The warlord of this clan wanted to marry a beautiful maiden, but she was already secretly in love with our forefather Furiya, also a warlord. This maiden danced like a sparrow and played an ancient string instrument, the zither, like a lily reed singing. She was a sad and tragic beauty, which was fashionable back then." He gave me a coy wink.

"Both daimyo were willing to go to war to win her. They made a foolish pact that whoever lost would be exiled forever, a fate worse than death in the old days," Dad explained. At that moment, Mom emerged from behind the sliding door to announce that dinner was ready. I didn't know why my father was telling me this story, but I desperately wanted him to continue.

Switching to English and a regular voice, Dad grunted, "Wait a minute. I'm telling an important story to answer an important question." He waved his hand at Mom and she raised an eyebrow before retreating inside.

"Their two-year battle killed an entire generation of villagers and scarred the countryside. It destroyed all the beautiful Japanese maple trees. In the end only one castle remained standing: the house of Maruyama." Dad paused, lowered his head for effect, took a swig of beer, and then stifled a belch.

"The loser had to live out the rest of his life in exile, as agreed. In the public square, Maruyama broke our forefather's sword at the hilt to show his defeat to the world. The Maruyama clan chased Furiya out of the kingdom and gave him only a bow and arrow to survive in the wilderness. He was an outcast across the entire region and should have died. Yet somehow he survived. During the harsh winter, he lived off wild grubs and whole, undigested soybeans picked from deer and horse manure."

I considered that perhaps it was our family legacy to be outcasts and rejects. My hopeful prospects of a peaceful school year in which I would feel accepted became all the more bleak and doubtful.

"Months passed and Furiya lived. One day a farmer approached him to find out what this stranger was doing on his property. When he was close enough, the farmer saw the tattered garb of royalty beneath the peasant's straw cape, and he knew he was in the presence of a warlord. The farmer watched as Furiya withdrew an arrow, the last one in his quiver. Before he sent the arrow into flight, he looked the farmer in the eye and vowed to rebuild his kingdom where the arrow landed. The arrow fell from view into the horizon. The farmer watched Furiya without another word walk toward the arrow until he too seemed to drop over the edge of the sky. And that was the last anyone saw of him." Dad looked off at the dusky sky, dazed, as if he were the farmer watching the lone traveler disappear into the distance.

"That spring," my father continued, "the Japanese maple, long thought to be dead, sprouted shoots through the ashes of Furiya's former kingdom. Maruyama was outraged and ordered his men to dig up the roots and burn them. By some miracle, the roots were harder than gold, and neither a hatchet nor fire could destroy them. The trees grew and prospered long after the rule of Maruyama, a legacy of Furiya's kingdom."

As with my mother's fish bone story, I realized that my father was trying to tell me something in a roundabout way, but impatience got the best of me. Exasperated, I sighed, "But that doesn't tell me why we ended up here. Why did you move here?"

Dad squinted in concentration, the skin around his eyes crinkled like dried figs. He gazed out at the freshly mown lawn, the crimson-leafed Japanese maple saplings, the magnolia and azalea hedges, and the tall blue spruces.

Under the bluish-pink canopy of that summer's evening sky, he answered with a purpose that calmed my doubts and planted renewed hope and unfathomable pride.

Turning to me, no longer storyteller but soothsayer, he said, "Be proud of your name. Remember Furiya means 'falling arrow.'"

"Someday you will also shoot and follow your arrow." He touched a finger to the place where we sat. "My arrow, it landed here."

## Rice Balls (Onigiri) with Four Flavors

*These versatile rice balls make a meal at any time of day. If I have leftover rice, I make the balls and stash them in my bag for a midday snack. They are filling, healthy, and delicious. Here are the four flavors I like most: shredded beef, pickled plum, seaweed, and black sesame.*

> 2 cups white rice, rinsed and drained
> bowl of cold water
> salt
> ½ teaspoon grated fresh ginger
> 1 teaspoon sugar
> 1 teaspoon mirin
> 1 teaspoon sake
> 1 tablespoon soy sauce
> 1 tablespoon water
> 2 ounces beef sirloin, thinly sliced
> 1 pickled plum *(umeboshi)*, seeds removed and shredded
>     into small pieces
> 1 1 inch x 6 inch strip of dried seaweed (nori)
> 1 tablespoon roasted black sesame seeds

Cook rice according to manufacturer's instructions. Place rice in a bowl. Cover and cool until warm to the touch, about 20 minutes.

*For the shredded beef filling:* Combine ginger, sugar, mirin, sake, soy sauce, and water in a small pot and bring to a boil. Add beef slices to the liquid and cook for about 3 minutes until brown. Set aside.

Divide the cooked rice into 4 portions and put 1 portion into a medium-size bowl. Mix beef filling and its liquid into the portioned rice, using a spatula or your hands for better mixing.

Moisten hands in cold water and shake some salt into each hand. Rub hands together. Using your left hand, scoop up about ½ cup of beef and rice. Keep in mind that the rice balls should fit easily in one hand. Using the same motion as in making a snowball, mold the rice between your hands into a ball. Flatten it between your hands into a thick patty about 3 inches in diameter and 1 inch thick.

Mix the pickled plum filling with the second portion of rice and mold the mixture into another ball as described above. Moisten hands in cold water and then salt hands as described previously.

Mold the third portion of rice into a ball. Wrap the strip of dried seaweed around it. Tear off excess seaweed. Moisten hands in cold water and then salt hands as described previously.

Make a fourth ball using the final portion of the rice. Sprinkle black sesame seeds onto a plate and roll the ball over the seeds until it is evenly covered.

Eat balls immediately, or keep at room temperature if wrapped in wax paper or plastic wrap. Refrigerate if not eaten within 6 hours.

Makes 4 rice balls, 1 of each flavor.

The Fish Head Soup Deal

The wonderfully lazy momentum of summer soon shifted to the chill and briskness of fall, and then to the bracing hug of deep winter. It was on a midwinter morning, after a heavy storm that left the hedges and bushes in our front yard covered in snow, that I learned about my parents' arranged marriage. In typical fashion after such snowfall, the sun's brilliance, like polished silver, was accentuated against the turquoise sky.

I sat at the dining room table, where I could see Mom preparing green tea in the kitchen. Dad sat in the armchair at the head of the table, thoughtfully packing loose tobacco into his pipe. During the school week, I rarely saw my father. My brothers and I were at school during the day, and his second-shift job started before we came home from school. School was closed because of the snow, and Dad's presence and the pristine white snowscape outside worked to create a giddy festiveness to the day.

Dad peered out the window, drawing evenly from his pipe, as Keven and Alvin trampled the fresh snow like pillaging heathens, leaving gaping footsteps and broken icicles in their wake.

From where I sat, I admired Mom's profile as she lifted her head to reach for the canister of loose tea on the shelf, her smallish, sloping nose, wide, long forehead, Cupid's-bow lips, and strong chin like those in the illustrations of geisha in Japanese woodblock prints. Unlike the stark whiteness of the Japanese artist's subject, Mom's skin was the color of café au lait. Her almond-shaped eyes and the length of the space between her nose and top lip are family traits, aspects I now see in my own reflection.

Mom dropped dried tea leaves into the small porcelain teapot, which tinkled softly as they hit the bottom. I figured then was as good a moment as any. "What does arranged marriage mean?" I asked my parents. I wasn't addressing the question to either one of them in particular, but it was my mother's surprised expression that conjured the familiar feeling of awkwardness I had started to experience only recently.

This question had been festering in my mind since the day before the snowstorm, during a visit to my friend Tracy Martin's house.

Mrs. Martin was letting Tracy and me view her wedding photo album when she asked me how my parents met. I had responded that they had an arranged marriage, though I had no idea what the term actually meant.

"An arranged marriage? Really, Linda?" Mrs. Martin's carefully penciled-in eyebrows shot upward, and she turned to look at me with a mixture of shock and curiosity.

Her reaction caught me off guard. Uncertain, I responded by nodding my head slowly.

I was just seven years old at the time, very much in the habit of repeating words or phrases I overheard from my parents or picked up from television. Most of the time I didn't understand what I was saying, or the weight behind my words. As I contemplated the strange reaction to "arranged marriage," I realized that perhaps these were words that adults didn't want me to say.

"Mom, what does that mean?" Tracy asked, picking up on her mother's sudden interest.

"It means they didn't choose who they married. Someone else decided that for them." Mrs. Martin said this in the hushed voice one would use in a church.

"Does that mean they weren't in love?"

"Shush now, sweetie," Tracy's mom responded, getting up from her seat and taking the photo album from Tracy's hand before briskly leading us into the other room.

That conversation and the quick way she had shoved us along had left me feeling even more insecure and uncertain, another reminder that we weren't like other families, and that something that had seemed perfectly normal was in fact not normal at all. I had naively assumed that "arranged marriage," a phrase I had heard my mother utter once or twice in my presence, simply meant that my parents had had a traditional church wedding like any other of my friends' parents, with the long white dress and train and multitiered wedding cake.

But now my mother was looking at me in a way that also made me feel self-conscious, once again as if I'd said something wrong.

Now I sat waiting for an explanation, which, by the time I finally worked up the courage to ask for it, felt vital to my understanding of the world as I knew it. I didn't want my parents' arranged marriage to signify yet another difference that distanced me from my classmates. If it were as different as I had been led to believe based on Tracy's mother's reaction, it would be yet another thing that made our family stand apart from the others.

My school life was finally going smoothly. The teasing that had plagued me during first grade had diminished considerably. I had reached a point where I even felt comfortable at times with my classmates, but this seemed precarious to me, as if it could change with one wrong look or one misstep or seed of information. The look of astonishment on Tracy's mother's face when I so casually mentioned my parents' arranged marriage was the same sudden spark of morbid curiosity I saw reflected in my classmates' eyes the year before when they discovered I used chopsticks.

❀

As I sat quietly awaiting the response to the question, there was a loud clatter as the teapot lid fell to the linoleum floor. The noise reverberated through the room like the crack of lightning. Mom hastily picked up the lid, replaced it on the teapot, clicked on the gas stove, and placed the teakettle upon the flames with care.

Across the room, Dad sat puffing on his pipe.

Their silence, tense as a taut rope, was strange to me. It wasn't until I became a parent myself that I understood that my parents were dueling over who would address my question first.

Internally I debated whether I should repeat the question, hesitating as my apprehension from the other day with Mrs.

Martin rolled into place. Steam rose from the teacup Mom passed to Dad. She sat down at the table and blew in her cup before taking a sip. As I grew older, the agonizingly long silences that followed a question like this one would madden me. But there was no hurrying them. Each second ticked by like condensation dripping from a stalactite.

"We weren't in love when we got married because we didn't know each other or hadn't even met." Mom announced this with the same matter-of-factness she would use five years later when telling me that Mr. French, our poodle, had been put to sleep, or when she'd calmly inform me that I wasn't welcome home when I wanted to quit college my freshman year. Her blunt way and poor command of English left me stripped and weak, to the extent that I learned to brace myself before broaching her with any question that held value for me.

"So what was your first date like?" I followed up, since neither of them seemed compelled to answer my question. My parents both burst out laughing, making me feel, yet again, that I was incapable of asking an appropriate question.

"Ho, ho! No dating," Mom whooped. At the time I thought they were laughing at my naiveté, but I have since come to realize that their laughter was a defense against the fact that the Western style of dating was as foreign to them as eating a bowl of cornflakes with milk for breakfast. (Every morning Dad ate a bowl of leftover warmed-up rice and one raw beaten egg with a little soy sauce drizzled over it, and Mom had a bowl of miso soup with rice.) Mom explained in English, stifling a chuckle, "Our first date was when your father picked me up at the airport. This was the first time we met face-to-face. I flew here from Japan to marry him.

"In Japan, love marriages are not popular. Causes too many problems. Good families always use a matchmaker. Very few marry out of love. Everyone knows they don't work. Always end up in breakup." I sneaked a look at Dad. I knew he was listening, even though he had turned to face the window, silently sipping his tea and drawing deeply from his pipe. The grassy aroma of green tea mellowed out the smoky sweetness of tobacco.

As I got older, I found that others would find my parents' arranged marriage fascinating; some even thought the fact that they were still together was quite romantic. But as I sat at our dining room table that morning, wishing my parents were the type to offer more information rather than less, I felt as if my whole concept of marriage were being disassembled limb by limb.

I nodded miserably when Mom asked if I wanted to see their wedding pictures. She disappeared to the basement and returned with a thin leather photo album.

Flipping briskly through the thick black pages, Mom stopped at a big photo showing a younger version of herself and my father. Originally black and white, the picture was touched up with watercolors. My parents had unusually rosy cheeks. Dad was dressed in a dark suit with a skinny tie. Mom was in a turquoise colored sheath and matching jacket. Their wedding bands, white gold in real life, were touched up with yellow. They were sitting close together on a sofa, wearing genuine smiles, not staged camera smiles. When I studied the photograph years later, I detected the intimacy and closeness of newlyweds in their eyes.

Mom held up the album for Dad to see. He smiled and nodded, taking another puff from his pipe. As she refilled

Dad's teacup, she told me that the photo was taken right after they were married at the Justice of the Peace, in the sitting room of the boardinghouse where they were staying.

The afternoon Tracy and I had flipped through her parents' wedding album, Tracy had also dug into the back of her mother's closet, where Mrs. Martin stored her wedding dress in a big department store box. It was carefully packed between sheets of tissue paper and was an eye-blinding white. My parents chuckled again when I asked where Mom's wedding dress was. "Dad had no money. Those were our best clothes, and what you see in this photograph is what we wore in the ceremony."

Whether because he noticed my agitation at this new information, or because he didn't like the way Mom was telling the story, Dad finally decided to tell his side.

He launched into his story in Japanese, cutting through my mom's broken English with his typical assertion of authority. "When I came to America I was not good enough to marry anyone yet. I was a lonely bachelor in my home country. I had nothing. After a couple of years I had a job, a car, and a small savings. I wanted to share all this with a Japanese wife. Someone like me, who spoke Japanese and shared a similar background."

He hesitated and then added sheepishly, "Of course, I also wanted someone who could cook Japanese food. Some Japanese men can marry white women. For me, it would have been too strange, too different. I don't want to explain what tea ceremony is or teach someone how to use chopsticks. The only way to find such a woman was through a matchmaker in Japan. My good friend Mr. Yokohama promised me, before I left Japan, that he would help me find a wife. But it took a long time before I was ready to contact him."

It occurred to me then that it was strange that I didn't know how Mom and Dad had met. In my young mind I knew the two only as Mom and Dad, a matched set like salt and pepper. I had assumed that they had met in Japan and come over together. As my father spoke I was piecing together an entirely new story, one that featured my parents in true form, rather than the fantasy backgrounds I had concocted based on my seven-year-old assumptions about how things were done.

"I had a difficult time coming to America," Dad explained. Even though my father was an American citizen born in California, he was sent to Japan to be raised by his grandmother at the age of four after the death of his mother. He was stripped of his U.S. citizenship during World War II and drafted by the Imperial Army. After being captured by the Russians and held in their POW camp for three years, he returned to Tokyo, where he waited ten years for his citizenship reinstatement.

"I didn't think the process would take as long as it did. I wanted to be ready, so I signed up for English-speaking classes at the Tokyo YMCA. I would need a skill in America, so I chose chick sexing because I heard it was making many Japanese men rich."

During the 1950s, chick sexing, the dividing of one-day-old cockles and pullets, was much in demand in U.S. farming regions. It was a lucrative occupation that allowed Japanese men to work the spring and summer seasons in America and live comfortably during the rest of the year in Japan.

"I even packed a suitcase." Dad chuckled at the memory but then became serious. "I waited ten years. Ten years for my citizenship to be returned." I stared at him in disbelief. A week seemed like a long time to me. I couldn't imagine how it must have felt to wait for something for ten years.

"Did you ever feel like giving up and staying in Japan?" I asked.

"A little, yes. But I tried to keep busy. I refused to unpack that suitcase. To me that would have meant giving up."

A decade older, my father arrived in New York City and reunited with his brother George and sister Jane. All of the siblings, except for the second sister, Sumiko, had been given American names by their parents. Dad had very little money, only $29. The Japanese yen was worth practically nothing, and this was the maximum amount of American dollars the exchange office would allow him before he left Japan.

By then a fast and accurate chick sexer, my father immediately found work in the hatcheries of America's heartland. "I worked hard and chick sexing paid well, but it's a hot, noisy, and dirty job. Feathers everywhere, up my nose and even inside my socks. The more chicks I separated, the more money I made, so most days I sat for twelve straight hours."

For the next several years, during the spring and summer, he drove to chick hatcheries in Michigan, Illinois, Indiana, and Ohio with a bottle of soy sauce and *ajimoto* (MSG) stuffed in the dashboard and a folding worktable, a strong overhead work light, a cloth army cot, and a bag of clean clothes stashed in the trunk of his car.

"Chick sexing all over Indiana, that's how I found Versailles," Dad explained. "Clean air, nice people, lots of hills and trees. I knew I wanted to live here when I first saw it."

Versailles, the town Dad chose, is one of the nondescript farming towns dotting the southeastern heel of the sock-shaped state of Indiana like clusters of white fuzzy pills.

It was only after I left home that I began to see with new eyes the beauty Dad must have experienced the first time he arrived in the region. Large patchworks of farmland make up the picturesque landscape. Verdant rolling hills thick with blue spruces, elms, and sycamores dip sharply into steep valleys, the dramatic cuts sliced by shifting glaciers during the Ice Age. On the top of one of these hills is Versailles, a sleepy town with a county courthouse building flanked on four sides by charming clapboard office buildings, a pharmacy, a bank, a doctor's office, and two local watering holes.

"Once I found where I wanted to live, I grew excited about sharing my life and settling down with someone," said Dad. "I was ready and I couldn't wait to write Mr. Yokohama."

Dad slapped his palms together and tilted his face toward the ceiling as if he were praying. "I wrote, 'Dear Mr. Yokohama, please help me find a Japanese wife. Someone special and who can cook well.' And see, I got your mother." He grinned.

Looking over the rim of her teacup, Mom rolled her eyes at my father. Reverting back to Japanese, she said, "It was at a family reunion where Mr. Yokohama approached me about a possible match. Since he was a friend of my cousin, I had to listen to what he wanted to say."

Setting her cup down in front of her, Mom giggled at the recollection. "When he told me about your father, I laughed in his face. At that time, I was having the best time of my life. I had a good job at a bank. I went skiing and hiking all winter. Every night I went out to eat with friends from work. Give all that up to come to America to marry a stranger?" She sighed as she entwined her long fingers around the cup. "Six months after I met Mr. Yokohama, I opened my mind to the idea of marrying someone who lived in America. I was almost thirty, too old to find a Japanese husband," she admitted. "Mr. Yokohama assured me that your father had a good job and wanted a family and security. I didn't know this James Furiya in America, of course, but I knew Mr. Yokohama, and so did my family. Coming from him, it wasn't a promise, but the truth. This is why matchmaking is good. No lies, no surprises."

Then she continued, looking at my father as she spoke. "If Dad lied to the matchmaker, he loses face for everyone in his family and the matchmaker's family. Dad would never be able to return to Japan. Right?"

Before he could answer, she looked at the clock and jumped up, sloshing her tea onto the table. "Eh, we better go to the grocery store before they close. I need to buy ground pork for the *gyoza* (fried pork dumplings) for tonight's dinner."

At the mention of Mom's preparation of dumplings, one of his favorite dishes, Dad grunted in agreement. He gulped down his tea before grabbing his hat, coat, and car keys as if there were a family emergency to rush off to.

❊

On another occasion, I leafed through my parents' album and found a black-and-white snapshot of Mom in a small kitchen, taken months after she and Dad were married in 1961. She was wearing a kimono. A *noren* (indigo-blue curtain) she had brought from Tokyo hung in the doorway. She stood beside the stove, proudly displaying a pot of simmering sukiyaki. I could almost hear it bubbling, see the tangle of clear cellophane noodles, wilted green onions, cubes of white tofu, and curls of sliced beef jiggling as it boiled in the sweet dark broth. Mom's chopsticks were poised midair over the *yosenabe*, a cast-iron pot whose name means "putting together."

She looked dated in her cat-eye frames and Japanese garb.
Now she wore tortoiseshell-frame glasses, a black turtleneck,
and slim gray wool trousers. As Mom split open a package
of wonton skins and spread the thin squares across a floured
wood cutting board, I studied the snapshot for a long time
before pointing it out to her.

Wiping her hands on the front of her apron, she held the
album up to get a closer look and smiled. "I remember this.
We had just moved into our first apartment next to a doctor's
office. I'm making sukiyaki, our first Japanese meal as a married couple. We were *so* happy to eat Japanese food."

Returning to the counter, she used her fingers as a spoon
to scoop the filling onto the thin wonton squares. "What I
remember the most," Mom said, slicking a few drops of water
around the square to seal the edges like ravioli, "is how long
I went without eating any Japanese food when I first came to
Indiana."

When Mom arrived that chilly, overcast November afternoon in 1961, it was before bridges and freeways connected
the small towns. Dad took the ferry across the Ohio River to
get to the Greater Cincinnati Airport, which at the time was
just a couple of landing strips and a building where passengers
checked in.

Dad wore his best dark suit, smoked more cigarettes than
usual, and fiddled with his felt fedora, taking it on and off. He
had plenty to be nervous about. Finally, he would meet his
wife-to-be in person.

"The flight from Tokyo took over twenty hours. At that
time regular people didn't fly because it was so expensive.
Everyone dressed up to fly, too. I had a special blue plaid skirt
and jacket and a beige wool coat made especially for the trip."

Her first impression of Dad was *mama*—average. "He looked exactly like the man in the picture he sent. I had a round-trip ticket in my purse. If I thought he was ugly, I would have gotten back on the plane."

Years later, I pressed Mom for the thoughts that must have gone through her mind on her last night in Japan. Was she scared, excited, happy? She avoided my gaze and said too quickly and easily that she couldn't remember emotions felt that long ago. When I insisted she try to remember, she pleaded with me to let her be, as if the thought of it drained her of energy.

When I finally gave up, frustrated by my need to understand who she was then, she offered brightly, "I remember what I ate before boarding the plane: *sekihan* (sweet rice with red beans, sprinkled with black sesame seeds). I had the gold heart necklace Dad sent me, and his picture so I would recognize him at the airport. But when I arrived he was the only Japanese person there."

Only then, perhaps because she had made it clear that my prying was futile, she offered a bit of a revelation. From her post in the kitchen where she made meat dumplings, she told me in Japanese, "I did have bad dreams before I left. Some women at work were jealous and said behind my back that I would return to Tokyo after two months in America. I started worrying when I couldn't even find the name of the town on a map. In my dream I came back to Tokyo with no husband, no job, only feeling disgrace. I decided that I would not allow myself to return home, no matter what happened."

Hearing about her fears and doubts gave me the first glimpse into what was at stake. She had left her country, mother language, friends, family, job, everything, for a man whom she had never met in person. Family and friends had already assessed his personality, character, and potential. Taking this step required far more than love; it was more like a leap of faith and a strong belief system that everything would work out.

At the time, my young head was filled with fairytales, mythology, and romantic notions. I couldn't help but feel a blush of pride at the determination behind my parents' union.

As an adult, when I explain my parents' arranged marriage, people presume my mother was a picture bride, and that Dad chose a random stranger from a stack of photographs. For my own peace of mind, I long ago had to rationalize the legitimacy and appropriateness of their arrangement and did so by believing that Dad wasn't looking just for a wife to take care of him, but for someone to share in the dream he sought to build in America.

Mom went on to describe the month before their wedding date, how they lived in separate rooms at the boardinghouse of Mrs. Cizek, a hardworking, Depression-era woman who was well respected in the community. As Mom's sponsor, Mrs. Cizek made certain the couple was constantly chaperoned before they married, even though Dad was thirty-seven and Mom was thirty.

The newlyweds stayed on at the boardinghouse until they found an apartment, which ended up being adjacent to the doctor's office. Eager to move out and start her own home, Mom took to daily mental reviews of the inventory of items in the trunk she had brought with her from Japan, with all the ingredients and tools to start a proper Japanese kitchen. She couldn't wait to unpack her surprises for Dad: a sack of rice from her father's store, dried ropes of gourd strips used in soups and one-pot stews, sheets of dried seaweed, salt-encrusted kelp, fermented miso paste, chopsticks, porcelain rice and noodle bowls, graters, a bottle of soy sauce, rice vinegar, sesame oil, good rice wine, freeze-dried tofu, high-quality green tea, a double-handled wok, and two kitchen knives—one for cutting vegetables and another for cutting fish.

"I missed Japanese rice so badly," Mom remembered. "Mrs. Cizek made rice cooked on the stove and put butter in it! She wouldn't let me use the electric rice cooker I brought. It was her house, her rules. Wastes too much electricity, she said, and rinsing the rice grains used too much water. Poor Dad made me a hot dog and chicken noodle soup from a can for my first dinner in America. I didn't complain, though. What could Dad do? I wanted to cry. Dad was sad, too, and from those early days we knew that we would do everything we could to make the food we loved."

A look of serenity came over her face, smoothing the lines on her forehead. She gazed again at the photo, and I imagined she was slipping back in time to that tiny kitchen with the old-fashioned icebox and tiny white enamel stove.

As if talking to her younger self in the photo, she asked, "What did I expect? Happily ever after? Dad and I were total strangers. After the wedding, when we moved into our new apartment, the honeymoon was over. We argued all the time, testing each other. Sometimes it was hard, other times easy. All part of the marriage deal."

Mom didn't have to spell out the details of their deal. I constantly saw it played out. Because Dad paid the bills, it was Mom's job to take care of the children, sew our clothes, do all the housekeeping, make all the meals, and try to make the money he worked hard for go as far as it could. She was the last to eat so she could serve the meals fresh and hot. If Dad thought the sauce needed more salt, she'd shake a little onto everyone's plate, rather than having us do it ourselves. If Dad mentioned that the meat was undercooked, she'd put it back under the broiler until it cooked to his liking. In a single sitting, she'd often get up as many as five times to get spicy pepper for Dad's pickles, to serve more rice, to serve the miso, to pour tea, to clear the dishes, to refill the teacups. All the while, Dad sat in his chair, not budging until the meal was finished.

❦

As a teenager I felt helpless to say anything in support of my mother. It was clearly defined in an unspoken way that my father was the breadwinner and Mom was the primary caregiver.

As a college graduate making my own living out in the world and experiencing romantic relationships, I came to despise watching the way Mom catered to Dad's every need. I felt a gnawing anger at my father for treating my mother like a servant, at Mom for putting up with it, and at myself for never having said anything. After years of observing this, I couldn't hold back my bottled resentment and began to speak up. I confronted Dad on occasion, asking him why he didn't help Mom or couldn't get something he wanted himself. In the beginning, he gave me a sharp, annoyed look, one that would have immediately shut me down as a child. I returned his look, along with a glare that announced I was entitled to an answer.

At first he ignored me. The second time, he said, "Because your mother does it for me." When I thought about his response, I realized it wasn't his fault and that behavior doesn't change overnight. During later visits, he made a great show of going to the refrigerator to fetch Japanese condiments he needed or getting himself a second helping of rice to indicate that he was trying.

Licking my wounds through two divorces, both of which began as what my parents called love marriages, I began to appreciate the concept of arranged marriages. My parents, after all, were nearing their forty-fifth anniversary. I left Dad alone, thinking, *What do I know about love and marriage in the first place?* Today, Mom still fetches and fusses over Dad, but I don't say anything, as I catch a sense of enjoyment that was probably there all along but that I was never able to detect through my prejudices in the past.

Having stirred up the memories of their early years together, Mom continued to share with me, and she recalled a story of how fish head soup had strained their marriage almost to the breaking point.

With the money Dad had saved up during the lucrative chick-sexing seasons of his bachelorhood, he bought a house and the empty lot next to it. The house was a couple of blocks from the center of town and bordered by lush woods that expanded into one of the state's largest parks, a park whose changing color of the autumn leaves in its thick forests rival the foliage in New England.

At the time, my brother Keven was a toddler, Alvin an infant, and Mom was seven months pregnant with me. My parents dreamed of having a vegetable garden, neighborhood baseball games, cookouts in the sprawling backyard, and flowerbeds in the front.

It was the perfect starter home for a young family. There was only one problem: The entire property was stripped of topsoil, which was part of the reason they got it at an afford-able price. To Mom, this meant more waiting for the long-promised vegetable garden that would provide fresh produce for her Japanese cooking. Planting a garden was Dad's respon-sibility, his end of the deal.

That spring, Dad began fishing in a creek about a half mile from the new house. He caught nothing but thick, bug-eyed, fat-lipped carp. He was thrilled, even so, to have the fresh fish whose head could be used for fish head soup, a true delicacy.

Without notifying his wife it was there, Dad left the live unclean fish in the kitchen sink, contemplating the prospects of soup at that evening's meal. He whistled to himself as he imagined the simple yet rich fish broth simmered with sliced ginger: the flavor-rich head; the cheeks, tiny morsels as sweet and succulent as fresh mussels; and, only if they were popping outward, the eyeballs, intense salty-sweet beads like plump Osetra caviar.

Up to that point in their marriage, Mom had done what Dad expected. But being very pregnant, caring for two tod-dlers, and impatient at the prospect of having to wait months for a garden, Mom was not pleased when she found the live fish flapping in the kitchen sink. Suddenly the deal seemed very unfair.

Dad was puttering around with his gardening supplies when Mom stomped down into the basement, dangling his prized catch at arm's length.

"Who do you think I am, your servant? Why didn't you clean this stinking fish?" Her face was smooth and expression-less, her voice tight. "You plant a garden like you promised, and then maybe I'll consider making the fish soup. If you want soup now, you clean the fish and make it yourself." The fish landed with a wet plop at his feet.

"You have to cook what I ask! You're my wife!" Dad yelled after her as she climbed back up the stairs. She responded with an audible sniff before slamming the basement door behind her.

Dad had stresses of his own. To pay for the house and the growing expenses of a family of five, he took on a full-time job at Cummins Engines, where he put together the engines of eighteen-wheel semis. In addition, during the spring and summer, he continued sexing chickens at the local hatcheries.

He hadn't been neglecting the business of the garden. He had just neglected to inform Mom that the topsoil was not as easy to come by as he had originally thought. Poor planning would ultimately result in a full year's passing before the dirt could be delivered, and even then it would be another season before he could plant.

The fresh carp still needed tending to, however, so Dad cleaned and made the soup himself. He didn't know where any of the tools and ingredients were and was too proud to ask Mom, who rested in their bedroom.

At dinner, Mom chatted cheerfully as if nothing had happened. Dad drank the soup he had made himself, silently, without slurping in his loud, boisterous style. He sucked out the tender cheeks from the fish head, as if giving it a big, sorrowful kiss.

The following summer, Dad caught more carp, which he intended to use for fish head soup. Before putting the fish in the sink and leaving it for my mother to clean and cook, he carefully felt out the situation.

"I caught three fine fish today. They would be perfect for soup," he offered.

In a breezy voice, Mom answered, "It sure would be nice to have fresh green onions instead of having to wait every two weeks to go to Cincinnati." The situation was as clear as premium sake: Dad would have to make his own fish head soup as long as there was still no garden.

Mom stuck to her decision, not just because she didn't have her garden, but also because she was intolerant of overpowering smells and flavors, a characteristic the matchmaker, friends, and family had overlooked in suggesting the two of them as a match.

Mom favored lightly steamed vegetables, clear, bland soups, and white-meat fish—nothing with an odor. She didn't like many traditional Japanese foods, such as *natto* (fermented soybeans), broiled fish (such as mackerel), or even pickled vegetables, which she thought resembled the bits of food collected in the sink stopper after washing the dishes.

Dad, on the other hand, thrived on rich, oily fish, marinated hot peppers, raw garlic soaked with bourbon and ginseng, braised cow organs, and stewed fish parts. The smellier, hotter, more fermented, and more aged, the better.

Despite their incessant bickering, Dad's fondness of eating and Mom's skill at cooking complemented each other like a bowl of spicy rice crackers mixed with sweet fried green peas. Once I saw Mom blush like lovers do when they talk about their amour. "One good thing about your father is that he loves to eat."

She would tell me often, "When you're grown up and start cooking for other people, you'll understand what I mean when I say that some people don't know how to appreciate good food. They put it in their mouth, chew the food, but just sit there, *shiranpuri*." She turned her head away and looked up, showing me her nonverbal way of ignoring someone.

Although Mom refused to oblige Dad with fish head soup, she tried to please him with other cooking. When he wanted more Western food, Mom asked Mrs. Buyo, the American wife of a Japanese friend, to teach her how to make pot roast, spaghetti Bolognese, chiffon roll cake with chocolate icing, flaky crust for pies, and roast chicken with potatoes and gravy. She learned how to make a Thanksgiving turkey and an Easter ham. Mom was an adept student, as long as she had a recipe to follow. Handling a big piece of meat such as beef or a whole fowl was a new concept, since meat of that size was never eaten when she was growing up in Japan.

Not long before carp fishing rolled around again the following summer, the topsoil was delivered and spread. Dad laid down a soft bed of hay over the lawn seeds he had spread throughout the front and back yards. He marked the garden boundaries and planted a small selection of hearty seedlings.

By the end of the summer, the grass had sprouted into a thick carpet and the garden yielded its first harvest. Dad left a peace offering on the kitchen counter—a basket holding small bright red tomatoes, green beans, and green onions—as precious to Mom as rubies and emeralds.

Through the tight tomato skin, she felt the firm ripeness beneath. She felt the velvet skin of the green beans, their slender shapes taut with freshness. She shook the dirt clinging around the onion bulbs. The next time my father caught a carp, she took over for him at the sink. She began scraping the scales from the fish with her Japanese fish knife meant specifically for scaling and gutting.

As the fish simmered, she opened all the windows, turned on the exhaust vent full blast, and clutched a hankie scented with Chanel No. 5 over her nose. That evening Dad happily slurped and stripped the fish's head of every shred of meat, saying it was the best soup he'd ever tasted.

"There were many more fights after that one," Mom said as she bent down to pull out the big cast-iron skillet from the bottom cabinet. It was so heavy she had to use both hands. "But that was the biggest test of our marriage. I still think arranged marriage is best. Family comes first. If we were in love, Dad may have said, 'You don't love me if you don't cook fish,' or, 'You don't love me if you push me to plant a garden.'

"Too much hurt feelings. But what do I know about love relationship?" She laid down rows of dumplings across the well-oiled black surface of the skillet, overlapping the edges evenly like tile on a temple roof.

For a moment she seemed to have lost the bravado she had assumed in telling me the details of her relationship with my father. I felt the doubt in her softened voice and slumped shoulders. I didn't know what to say. I wanted her to share with me. I wished I were twenty years older. All I could do was give her a small smile when she glanced at me, which seemed to snap her out of her second thoughts, perhaps her fear that she had told me too much.

Mom gave a little start when she looked down at the rows of dumplings, as if they had appeared out of nowhere, then shook her head, laughed at herself, and turned her attention back to cooking the *gyoza*.

To make sure the meat filling cooked through, she steamed the dumplings by adding water to the scaldingly hot pan and quickly covering it. The *gyoza* sizzled and popped under the lid. The dumplings' skin surfaces puffed out with steam and hot juice. When she removed the cover, the ginger, garlic, and meat aromas dazzled my senses.

She gave the bottom a good scrape with a metal spatula and then flipped the pan upside down over a platter, revealing a crisp brown top.

I couldn't get to the dinner table fast enough. I dipped the piping hot *gyoza* into a shallow bath of tangy soy dipping sauce. I bit into the crescent shapes—crunchy on one side, soft textured on the other, and juicy hot on the inside. My first bite broke the skin, as should always happen with truly good dumplings, flooding my mouth with the savory ginger and garlic pork filling.

That night, woozy from a stomach filled with dumplings, I drifted off to sleep trying to remember if Mom had answered my initial question about whether she and Dad were in love.

❖

When I lived in China with my baby boy, I came to understand the isolation my mother faced in raising a family in a small town in Indiana. My situation wasn't as extreme in comparison to my mother's situation. I had a small circle of American friends, but because I didn't have command of the language, I felt frustrated and despondent daily. I considered myself a strong and independent woman, and I disliked finding myself depending heavily on my husband, who was fluent in Mandarin.

I found comfort in knowing that I wouldn't be living overseas all my life and wondered how my mother, a free-spirited, cosmopolitan, independent, and athletic woman from Tokyo, had given it all up to become a mother of three, closed off from the rest of the world in rural Indiana, with limited English-speaking skills.

From the time I started school, she told me I had options she never had: an American citizenship, a chance to go to college, a fluency in English she would never possess, more cultural freedoms than she had ever had in Japan. I could do anything I wanted, she said, her eyes sparkling at the thought of it.

In my teen years, I'd smirk to myself when she talked quietly with me about what I wanted to be when I grew up. Many times she encouraged me to dump my small-town boyfriend, go to college, forge my own life, and not be afraid of the challenges that lay ahead. Like any smart-aleck teen, I foolishly believed I had the world figured out at sixteen years old. *You don't even know how to drive a car; what would you know about going to college or pursuing a career?* I'd think, not daring to voice the thoughts that I knew would hurt her.

It wasn't until I was twice that age that I began to understand Mom's sense of adventure, motivation, and self-sacrifice, and to see that she had faced more personal obstacles and struggles in her teens, twenties, and thirties than most people did in a lifetime.

## Japanese Potstickers (Gyoza)

*It's important to thoroughly mix the filling for several minutes so the flavors can be absorbed into the meat. I find squeezing the meat with clean hands the most effective and fun way to accomplish this. Serve the gyoza with a traditional dipping sauce or Furiya's Gyoza Dipping Sauce (recipe follows).*

> ½ pound ground pork
> 1 cup finely chopped napa cabbage
> 2 green onions, chopped
> 1 garlic clove, minced
> 1 tablespoon ginger, grated
> ¼ cup sake
> 2 tablespoons soy sauce
> 1 teaspoon sesame oil
> dash of salt and pepper
> 1 package of 3½-inch-round dumpling wrappers
>   (see note below)
> 1½ tablespoons vegetable oil

In a large mixing bowl, combine well the ground pork, cabbage, green onions, garlic, and ginger for about one minute. Add sake, soy sauce, sesame oil, and salt and pepper and mix well for about 5 minutes.

Place the individual wrappers on a flat surface. Put a tablespoonful of pork filling in the center of the wrapper. Seal the dumpling by moistening the edge lightly with water halfway around the round wrapper. Fold the edges together and press down firmly.

In a nonstick skillet, heat the vegetable oil over high heat. When a small piece of wrapper sizzles in the oil, lower the heat to medium high. Place the dumplings in rows so they are touching closely. When the edges begin to dry, after about 3–4 minutes, add water so the dumplings are one-third covered. Cook until the water evaporates.

Using a spatula, lift the *gyoza* out by rows. Flip the *gyoza* over, brown side up, onto a plate or cookie sheet. Keep warm in the oven. Cook remaining dumplings as directed above.

Makes approximately 30 *gyoza*.

*Note:* Dumpling wrappers are sold in Asian groceries and the refrigerated sections of some supermarkets and are generally sold in 12-ounce packages.

### Traditional Gyoza Dipping Sauce

> 1 part rice vinegar
> 1 part soy sauce
> chili oil to taste

Combine ingredients. Serve with *gyoza*.

### Furiya's Gyoza Dipping Sauce

> ¼ teaspoon Colby's dry mustard paste
> 1 tablespoon soy sauce
> 1 teaspoon rice vinegar

Combine ingredients. Serve with *gyoza*.

# The Hungry Past

**M**y father had a theory on how to get my brothers and me to eat new foods. All we had to do was taste the dish three times, but not at one sitting. By the fourth time, he claimed, our palates would have grown accustomed to the new taste and texture and we'd be ready for a full serving. I can't say that his theory worked every time, but more often than not it nudged my taste buds toward unusual foods, such as salty, gritty-textured *toronako* (fish roe) and strong-flavored, oily *saba* (mackerel). The strategy worked better than the guerrilla tactics some of my friends' parents used, such as expecting their kids to finish a heaping plate of liver and onions, as though they inherently enjoyed the stinky dish.

It was my father's father, Jinnosuke, who inspired this method and who, Dad claimed, taught him how to eat. Not the mechanics of eating, such as how to use chopsticks or cut meat with a dinner knife, but the spiritual aspect of eating thoughtfully, mindful of the source, and pacing oneself as in meditation or praying. Dad learned from his father, and passed down to my brothers and me, an appreciation of eating as a smorgasbord for the senses, a boost to the spirit, a conduit of memories. According to family lore, my grandfather had such a seductive, ravenous way of eating that anyone sitting with him at the table who saw the way he savored each morsel, the expression of pure pleasure he wore, would suddenly feel hungry. In the same way that you might feel calmed by a person who's deep in meditation, by the expression of peace showing in his or her sitting posture and face, my grandfather inspired people to appreciate food. In my family, this was considered the ultimate compliment.

It never occurred to me as unusual that Dad called his own father and mother by their first names. Jinnosuke was my blood grandfather, but unlike my friends, who showered their silver-haired elders with endearing names such as Pap-paw or Grandpappy, I felt indifferent toward Jinnosuke's spirit. This indifference was molded by the heartwrenching stories Dad told my brothers and me about his own tragic youth.

My grandfather was an elusive apparition who passed in and out of Dad's conversations. Dad described him with the reverence and respect one would use to describe a fallen hero, but his stories were spiked with undertones of resentment and a kind of longing so strong, it was like an ember that could never be extinguished.

In some people, the sight and feel of a bauble or a certain scent in a room can set off a string of memories. For Dad, it was always food—the setting of a meal or its sensual characteristics—that struck a chord of nostalgia.

The summer after I turned eight was unseasonably cool, as if spring and its rains had decided to stay a while longer. It was the perfect weather to enjoy *yakiniku* (grilled meat) and cook it on the electric griddle.

Open windows let out the smoke and the rich aroma of the thin-sliced grilled sirloin and assortment of vegetables: eggplant, squash, onions, and mushrooms. The fun of eating *yakiniku* was cooking our own meat to our liking.

Under Dad and Mom's watchful eyes, my brothers and I were each designated a square area of space on the long griddle and a plate holding a stack of thinly sliced sirloin and vegetables to cook and eat as we pleased. It was a very busy affair as five pairs of chopsticks crisscrossed to lay down, flip over, or pick up the seared meat and vegetables.

It was not until the second or third batch of grilling that the pan was perfectly seasoned with the meat juices, producing a beautifully seared surface to cook on. The beef, its cobweb of fat and red-striated meat spreading out like a scarlet gossamer lace handkerchief, shivered and shrank on the hot pan. Tendrils of smoke and the smell of charred beef lingered in the dining room.

It was a rare meal where everyone was present. When Dad had a day off from work, his relaxed appearance at the foot of the table, usually empty at most dinners, put us all in a jovial, lighthearted mood. That night, even Mom, who often remained in the kitchen cooking and serving food through the end of dinner, was seated at the table, good-naturedly teasing and joking, indulging in rice wine from a traditional square cedar sake cup. Because we cooked our own portions, she had done all the slicing of vegetables and meat ahead of time.

Dad peered at the tough, shriveled meat I had taken off the pan. He shook his head disapprovingly.

"Good that Jinnosuke not here to see this." He waved his chopsticks at my meat, the dirty gray hue of an old washcloth.

"I like it this way," I retorted. It didn't occur to me that he thought I was ruining a good piece of meat. My parents chastised us for the usual things, such as not covering our mouths when we coughed, but rarely for our style of eating, as long as it wasn't wasteful or terribly unappetizing to watch.

He glanced again at my beef, now reduced to the color of gray asphalt with a floppy consistency. "Nothing made Jinnosuke sadder than overcooked meat."

Ignoring his comment, I dipped the beef in my bowl of sauce, a piquant mix of soy sauce, green onions, minced ginger, and my favorite, a good squeeze of fresh lemon juice. To prove to Dad that it was fine, I ate it. The once-pink marbled tissue of sirloin resembled a crisp brown autumn leaf. The meat flavor was nonexistent, and I was tasting mostly the rich, savory dipping sauce, in which the most dominant taste was the clean, spicy notes of grated daikon radish that reverberated from the tip of the tongue to the back of my throat.

Dad ate all his meals with vigor and passion, as if each were his last. He hated eating in a hurry as much as his father despised overcooked meat. Instead, Dad lingered over every sip of wine or bite of food throughout the duration of a meal. He paused between bites, resting his chopsticks across his rice bowl as he decided which delicacy he would taste next. Dad admired the whole meal placed in front of him and then studied each dish, appreciating its appearance and aroma. He may have eaten a dish a hundred times, but he approached each meal anew, as if he had never before tasted what lay in front of him.

It was his habit to hold his rice bowl with his left hand, his thumb at the rim and his middle and fourth fingers holding the base; he used chopsticks with his right. The rice bowl worked in unison with the chopsticks as he carried each morsel of food from vessel to mouth.

As he enjoyed the special foods—the first vegetables of summer, or a nicely cooked piece of fresh fish, or homemade tofu—he'd close his eyes to better focus his senses on the experience. Sometimes when he opened them, his eyes would shine as if he had just experienced a thrilling roller coaster ride.

Before making some more meat, I added eggplant and mushroom to my section of the tabletop griddle as Dad recalled Jinnosukes scolding his older brother George for wolfing down his food, rather than pacing and appreciating such aesthetics as the minty aroma and dainty fronds of the single *kinome* (young leaves of *sansho* or Japanese pepper) sprig sitting atop the soy sauce–simmered potatoes. Jinnosuke often reprimanded the house cook for not turning and salting the pickled cabbage as carefully as he had shown her.

As I reached for a couple of slices of meat, Dad, who was no longer able to bear watching me cook, reached for my stack with the length of his chopsticks and said, "Back in Jinnosuke's day, *yakiniku* was very expensive. Not everybody could afford to order beef in a restaurant, especially rib eye. When I was your age, Jinnosuke told me that meat should barely be cooked on each side. Taste better this way. Let me show you."

At our table, eating *yakiniku* could be competitive among us siblings. Meat was snatched from another person's plate when one wasn't looking, and unwanted vegetables were snuck onto other sections of the griddle. I knew Dad wasn't taking my meat, so I sat back in my chair, enjoying the attention as he added the meat to the griddle.

"Must be very hot," Dad continued, holding the palm of his hand over the griddle's surface to check the heat.

"Grill one side. *Jaa!* Not too long time. Like that." He imitated the sound of sizzling meat.

"Don't wait, don't hesitate, just turn it over. *Jaa!*" Dad flipped the steaming piece of meat into my sauce bowl. Unlike my wilted piece, the full-bodied taste of the beef coated my mouth with flavor, the same way the tannins of fine red wine would when I was old enough to appreciate wine. The slight tang of rare meat remained after I'd swallowed. From then on, *jaa-jaa* became my way of cooking *yakiniku*.

At the dinner table, my father was in his element. It was there, during college and later in life, where the boyfriends I would sometimes bring home with me would ask him to share stories of his colorful past. Although flattered by their requests for details, Dad chuckled uncomfortably, giving in only after several minutes of coaxing. Out of politeness, he'd give them the short version, just enough to satisfy their curiosity. But his most spellbinding stories were the ones he told unprompted to my brothers and me over dinner.

❉

When I was eight years old, every day after school from my bedroom window I would watch the melancholy, inky-blue sky fade to complete darkness as fall welcomed winter in its place.

The first frost of the season was expected that night. In the vegetable garden, the last few remaining *hakusai* cabbages were draped in plastic, an indication that our meals would be heavy with the sweet, hearty leaves.

On a cold evening, the perfect end to a meal was a bowl of *tamago gohan* (rice and egg porridge). The rice porridge was my comfort food, like chicken noodle soup was for my friends. Japanese mothers fed their children this porridge when they had a cold or were recovering from the flu. The essential flavors of the porridge came from the rich broth that remained after chicken-*nabe*, a one-pot chicken and Chinese cabbage dish.

It was unusual for Dad to cook, but chicken-*nabe* was his specialty, and the ingredients and dark wintry weather at hand suited this meal. Like the *yakiniku*, chicken-*nabe* is a communal meal prepared at the table, where those joining in can help themselves to the cooked chicken parts and *hakusai* cabbage as they please.

The clay pot sat atop a butane-heated tabletop burner that kept the broth, precooked poultry, and vegetables piping hot. We ate in happy silence, savoring the tender chicken and silky cabbage, dipping it in a lush, lemony-salty soy dipping sauce. As Dad prepared to make the porridge, the meal was just starting for me. I watched Dad, as if he were catching goldfish with a handheld net, slowly drag a slotted spoon across the golden broth to strain the remaining bits of chicken and cabbage. When it was clear of the meat and vegetable, Dad turned up the blue flame of the gas stove, bringing the broth to a rapid boil before adding the fresh steamed rice to the pot. Like Italian risotto, the rice porridge required long constant stirring to prevent scalding. It was the rhythm of the stirring that seemed to put Dad in the mood for storytelling.

Dad was in the habit of picking up a conversation from months before as if it had been a topic of conversation earlier that very evening. "Jinnosuke made a good living off of his jewelry and watch-repair business," he said out of nowhere. At this, Keven stopped tapping his rice bowl with his chopsticks and Alvin wiped a bit of cabbage he was about to fling on me onto his napkin.

He spoke in Japanese, allowing himself to speak without stumbling for the right word or losing his train of thought while concentrating on putting sentences together.

I could hear the rice grains splashing in the pot as Dad swirled them around with a wooden rice paddle. Within minutes, the grains would plump up with hot liquid.

He stopped for a moment and turned toward us. "Before all his good fortune, though, in the late 1890s, when he was still in his twenties, Jinnosuke arrived in the port of Oakland. He moved to Sacramento, which had the second-largest population of Japanese in the United States after Los Angeles, and opened a small watch-repair shop downtown. Later, as his business grew, he opened a jewelry store."

"Was he married to Mume yet?" I asked, eager to learn more about my grandmother. This was before I knew of my father's habit of calling his parents by their first names, and so, for me, Mume meant "Grandmother" in Japanese.

He held up his finger in a way to indicate that he was coming to that part.

"By the time he was forty, younger than I am now," Dad said, touching his chest, "he had a thriving business, a family, and a big house—all the things a person dreams about when coming to America.

"There was a time around 1908 when Japan and America made a pact called the Gentlemen's Agreement." He stopped a moment to gently tap the wood spatula against the side of the pan before setting it in the spoon rest. "This pact restricted the entry of Japanese and Chinese laborers to America. The government thought these immigrants were taking away jobs from American citizens. There were no women for these men to marry because only Japanese women with husbands were allowed in. Mume and thousands of other Japanese women came into the country as picture brides."

"What's a picture bride?" I asked, impatient for him to tell me more about my grandmother.

Dad gave me a look that was reserved for me when I asked too many questions too quickly. Again, he held up his finger.

"These laborers couldn't afford to go to Japan to marry, so their families sent pictures to them and initiated the matchmaking process that way. The women coming over on the ship and the men who went to meet them had pictures of each other to recognize whom they were meeting.

"Of course," Dad continued, looking away, "this became a business, and sometimes another woman other than the one who was promised would show up."

"So Mume was Jinnosuke's picture bride?" Keven asked, twirling one chopstick through his fingers.

"No, no, Mume came over as a picture bride, but she didn't like the looks of the fellow she was promised to and turned down his offer of marriage. This was courageous for a twenty-year-old Japanese woman back then. Then she decided to stay in San Francisco." Dad stopped his story to add a couple of ladlefuls of broth to the thickening rice. I stayed at the table, deep in my own thoughts about my independent-minded grandmother.

Talking about her conjured the antique photos of Mume I had seen in the old family photo albums many times. There was one taken in a photographer's studio. My grandmother's voluptuous hourglass figure was clothed in a high-collared ruffled Gibson girl blouse; she wore a long dark skirt that touched the tops of her lace-up boots.

I had seen that photo so many times that I had memorized every detail of her expressionless face, the way she leaned against a table, a gardenia entwined in her fingers. She did not smile, as was the custom in photos back then, but there seemed to be intelligence—even secrets—behind her black pinpoint eyes. When I first saw the picture, I felt relieved and proud that she was dressed in Western clothes, that her hair was twisted in an Edwardian-style updo. I never once saw any photos of her wearing a kimono. From what I knew about her headstrong character and unconventional ways, it seemed appropriate for a contemporary woman such as she was to go against what was expected, to defy traditions.

Through the coming years, as I entered adulthood, I would become more and more fascinated with the enigma of my grandmother Mume: Her life in Northern California after the years she left the man she was promised to marry and before meeting Jinnosuke, and the way she and Jinnosuke met, are still a mystery even to my father.

My father told me what he knew: "Their history together began in 1916 when Jinnosuke, who was thirty-five years old, married Mume, ten years his junior. Uncle George was conceived soon after their wedding, followed by Jane, Sumiko, and then me—in 1923. Those ten final years of Mume's life were the happiest for Jinnosuke."

Unlike his contemporaries who scrimped and saved every cent for the endless possibility of hardship that could befall immigrants in the new country they chose to call home, Jinnosuke freely spent his money on his family.

As I waited for Dad to stir the rice and continue his story, another sepia photo I had gazed at many times came to mind. It showed the happy, privileged life my grandparents had lived. The words "Christmas Day 1923," the year my father was born, were scrawled in ink across the bottom of the picture. I wondered if the slanted cursive was Jinnosuke or Mume's handwriting. It was a candid family portrait, rather than the usual stiff and serious sittings so popular back then. It was shot in the parlor of their house and clearly featured a windup record player, wicker stroller, and dolls surrounding a Christmas tree so tall it touched the high ornate ceiling. The photo captured a mustached Jinnosuke dressed in a suit, doubled over laughing. Uncle George, then six, wore a jacket and short pants, and Aunt Jane, age five, was in a stiff-collared dress, also laughing. Mume had an amused smile on her face, her hair twisted and pinned up, a long, lustrous string of pearls around her neck.

"I was four years old when Mume died," Dad said, repeating a fact I already knew. "I don't remember it happening, but my brothers told me that Jinnosuke almost lost his mind. His life changed. All our lives changed."

Dad stirred in silence, leaning his weight over the stove, taking care that the rice did not stick to the bottom of the pot. It appeared that his mind was focused on the making of the rice porridge, but I knew he was lost in his memories.

Mume died at thirty-three of complications from pneumonia. My father had another photo of Jinnosuke that stands out in my mind. He was standing behind the jewelry counter of his store. The inside of the shop was shot from far enough away to see the beams across the ceiling. Jinnosuke wore a tweed vest, dark wide tie, and white shirt with the sleeves rolled to the elbows. He appears small in the spacious, dark, wood-paneled room. It was clear that it was taken after Mume's death. His eyes lacked the brightness and playfulness I saw in other photos. His mouth, straight as a line, looked as if it would crack if he smiled, the corners turned down like a basset hound's. Many times I tried to contemplate the depth of the loss he must have felt after his wife died, a tragedy that prompted him to separate his family. George and Jane remained in California with Jinnosuke, while the two youngest children, my father and his sister Sumiko-chan, were sent to Japan to be raised by their grandmother, Jinnosuke's mother.

Mom brought Dad two eggs in a small bowl. Before she stepped away to begin washing the dinner dishes, she rested her hand on Dad's shoulder for a moment. He didn't acknowledge this gesture, and it could have passed undetected, except that his shoulders straightened. I could tell from his satisfied grunt that the spatula scraped clean when he dragged it along the bottom of the pot, indicating the rice mixture was ready for the final ingredient: eggs. Carefully, Dad broke the eggs into the small bowl and, with a long pair of kitchen chopsticks, beat them to a bubbly yellow foam. He slowly trickled the egg batter over the rice with one hand and stirred slowly and evenly with the other. I knew the rest of the story, that Jinnosuke couldn't take care of his four children without his wife. The older two were more self-sufficient, but the youngest were sent to live with my great-grandmother.

Dad seemed tired all of a sudden. He turned off the burner before placing the lid on the pot. The rice porridge had to sit for a few minutes.

While we waited, Dad leaned back in his chair for a moment, then forward on his elbows. "I remember when I left Sacramento by boat. It was a big boat and I was by myself. I stood at the rail, just crying and crying." I learned at another time that the two youngest siblings weren't sent over together. Sumiko arrived months later, and Dad had to make that trip over first, alone.

My brothers and I exchanged looks, our shock reflected in each other's faces. This was part of the story we hadn't heard.

"In Japan, I lived in the countryside in a town north of Mount Fuji for five years when I was nine. My grandmother couldn't afford to care for Sumiko-chan and me, so we moved to Tokyo to live with our new parents who adopted us. I missed the fresh air and view of the mountain. That was the best place for a boy to be. But that was a long time ago."

When Dad said "adopted," I glanced over at my brothers. They wore masks of nonchalance. We would all perfect this facade of being emotionally unfazed and unmoved as we grew older, but I knew they were as shocked as I was.

"Mom, the rice is finished!" Dad yelled from his seat. As Mom stood at the table, spooning out the thick rice porridge using a wooden rice paddle, I saw her look at Dad before asking if he was okay.

Dad quickly nodded his head, cleared his throat, and lifted the lid. His eyes closed just as a puff of steam blurred his features for a second. "When I moved to Tokyo, my name became Ichiro Shimura. No longer was I called James Furiya. My new parents were civil servants of the Japanese military. They could not have me using my American name. The other boys at school found out I came from America and bullied me around. I learned judo, and that put an end to the teasing."

My father looked at me and abruptly asked, "Do you know what time I had to get up when I was your age?" His sudden use of English startled me.

I shook my head but did not answer. My brothers and I leaned into the table, our bowls of porridge in hand and our heads drawn together so we could eat and listen at the same time. Mom handed Dad a bowl before starting on her own.

Falling back into Japanese, he answered his question without prompting me to speak when spoken to. "Four o'clock every morning. The first thing I had to do was go to the well and fill up two pails with water. The wintertime was worst."

He looked down at his hands. "I couldn't move my hands, they were so cold, and sometimes the skin cracked and bled. At the house, I'd heat the water and make breakfast for the family. If I had to wash clothes in the morning, I needed to get more water, back and forth to the well."

Shifting his attention to his porridge, he said, "The rice needs a little salt." Mom reached across the table for the shaker, sprinkled it generously into the rice mixture, and then gave it a couple of stirs.

"If you were adopted, didn't that make you part of their family?" Keven interrupted.

"No, it was different in Japan at that time than it is here and now. Adoption was the same thing as being a servant," he explained matter-of-factly, responding to my brother's question in English. The attitude toward children during my father's youth was different from what it is now. It was a fact of life that if a family couldn't afford to support a child, or if the home situation changed, orphanages or well-off families were a place to send them.

"One of my responsibilities was washing all the corridors of the house," my father continued. "First with water, then dry it with a towel, and afterward rub it with *okara,* the leftover soybean fiber after it's made into tofu. I wrapped it up in a cloth and used as a cleaner. Then I followed with linseed oil. If you didn't rub the oil into the wood well enough, the wood felt sticky. I had to rub the wood for a long time. It was a big house, too." Dad made fast swiping motions with his hands as if scrubbing an invisible surface.

Maybe he was trying to protect himself, or maybe us, by continuing with these details in English rather than his more articulate Japanese. But he didn't realize how the details told in his choppy English actually made the story more shocking. His blunt, simple style of storytelling stirred the imagination more than any vivid descriptions could.

"Sometimes I had no time to eat breakfast, just enough to clean up the house and go to school." Dad pushed rice into his mouth.

"One morning I used too much oil and needed to rub it in longer. I thought I was finished. When my stepfather inspected it, he got very angry at me. I was on my hands and knees, and he yelled at me, 'Still feels sticky, keep rubbing!' He pushed his stocking foot on the floor, then kicked me hard.

"It was early morning and I was already tired and hungry, but I rubbed down the corridors again. I was late getting to school, so my teacher made me stay late that afternoon. This made me late getting home. Boy, my stepfather was angry. As a punishment, he made me sit like this for two hours." Dad put down his rice bowl and chopsticks and got down on his hands and knees on the floor. He sat on his calves and ankles, the traditional way Japanese women typically do.

Standing up shakily, he said, "I can't do this now. Too painful. My legs go numb. But at the time, if I moved, my stepfather hit me on the head with a bamboo stick." He slapped his hands together, then quickly cowered and covered his head as if deflecting imaginary blows.

Holding his head high, he squeezed his fists closed and a brightness came into his eyes. Angrily Dad hissed, "Still, to this day, I hate that man."

As he shook his fists at the recollection of it, Mom said softly, "Poor Dad," in a way that made me know she had heard this story before.

My eyes turned down, I stirred and blew on the half-eaten rice porridge, even though it was already cooled, for something to do. Then, holding the bowl to my mouth, I scraped heaps of rice in with my chopsticks. These simple, normal motions felt exaggerated and awkward. The silence blared in my ears and remained after our rice bowls were empty. Putting my chopsticks down, I asked Dad if he ever saw his father again, more to fill the empty space than to know the answer. I expected the answer to be no.

Dad slurped down his bowl of porridge with five swipes of his chopsticks. Handing his bowl to Mom to refill, he answered, "Yes, after I had been gone for almost ten years, Jinnosuke moved back to Tokyo with Aunt Jane in 1936, before the second Sino-Japanese War. Uncle George came back, too, but returned to America to dodge the draft in Japan. He was eighteen or nineteen by then. I was fourteen. Jinnosuke had made a small fortune from Seiko watch company. They bought an invention of his, a timer for new washing machines. He took me out to eat sukiyaki."

"Jinnosuke took you out to dinner?" Keven asked in surprise. He was old enough to understand the shock and irony of hearing about a father having dinner with a young son he had sent away years before and who was, by then, practically an indentured servant to his adopted family.

"Yes, he always took me to dinner—*unagi-ya* (grilled eel), tempura-*ya*—whenever he came to visit me. Remember, I told you, he loved to eat."

Dad seemed to hesitate before saying, "By then, I didn't call him Father anymore; I called him Uncle."

I caught my rice bowl before it toppled to its side. "You called your own father Uncle?"

Dad answered my question with his typical void of emotion and said evenly, "Since I was adopted by another family, he was no longer my father. I called him Uncle because that's what they did back then."

I learned later that my grandfather eased his guilt about sending his son away with gifts from California, such as a pound of white sugar, a new transistor radio, and a pair of skates—luxuries children would never have received at that time.

The question that occurred to me at that moment was why, if Jinnosuke were living in Japan at the same time as his youngest son, didn't he take Dad back into his home?

I asked this and sat in anticipation as Dad looked down for a moment, as if the answer could be found in the weave of the carpet. I wondered if he had ever considered the question before. He shrugged his shoulders. The apparition of Jinnosuke appeared on Dad's face. I recognized the resigned sadness captured in the photo taken at the jewelry shop. I thought of daffodils, a tenacious flower. If trampled, or if a torrential rain shower beats them down, they bend as if on the verge of snapping, but then slowly they straighten back up. And that's exactly what Dad did. He set his shoulders, straightened his back, cleared his throat, and in a strong, unfaltering voice, he said, "It was too late, I think. He couldn't take care of me."

## Japanese Barbecue *(Yakiniku)*

*Often confused with* teppanyaki, *in which meat, seafood, and vegetables are cooked and served at a restaurant's table grill,* yakiniku *is the home version. A good flat nonstick electric frying pan works best. Otherwise, you can use a butane gas tabletop burner and a nonstick frying pan. Ask your butcher to slice the beef sirloin as thinly as possible (1/16 of an inch). Stay away from lean cuts of meat. If you plan to cut it yourself, freeze the meat for 10–15 minutes for easy slicing.*

    1 pound of tissue-thin sliced beef sirloin
    shrimp
    scallops
    sliced eggplant
    sliced mushrooms
    sliced onions
    sliced zucchini
    Jinnosuke's Dipping Sauce (recipe follows)
    2 fresh lemons, halved
    soy sauce

Serve the raw meat, seafood, and vegetables on separate decorative platters (all the meat on one platter, all the seafood on another, and so on).

Place the electric frying pan in the center of the table, where everyone can comfortably reach. Diners cook their own ingredients, dipping them into the sauce right off the pan.

At the table, serve the *yakiniku* with Jinnosuke's Dipping Sauce, the halved lemons, and soy sauce.

Serves 4.

## Jinnosuke's Dipping Sauce

*There are countless varieties of dipping sauces; you can even buy bottled ones. I prefer this dipping sauce recipe for its citrusy bite, a mouthwatering combination when paired with the seared meat, seafood, and vegetables.*

> 1 cup daikon, grated
> 5 green onions, chopped
> 4 teaspoons ginger, grated

In four small decorative serving bowls, place a 2-tablespoon mound of daikon, a sprinkling of green onions, and ginger. Serve with *yakiniku.* Set aside any left over as reserve.

# The Sleepover

Just shy of turning eight, I believed Tracy had it all. The fixtures in her life—the blond June Cleaver mom, the bedroom spun in pink and white, and the red barns of the family farm—were as pristine as the settings of Grandma Moses paintings and Little Golden Books.

In my mind, she lived the life of the true all-American girl. She even looked the part, with her strawberry-blond hair hung in ringlets like ribbons on a wedding bouquet. During harvesttime, her father let her steer the farm tractor up and down the fields. Every spring, her family flew to Bermuda, which was unusual in a town where a long drive to Tennessee's Smoky Mountains or the white sands of Myrtle Beach, South Carolina, was the usual vacation plan.

When I slept over at Tracy's house, I was wowed by the grand indulgences that didn't exist at my home. If Mr. Martin wasn't home for dinner, we went to the basement freezer, where boxes of frozen dinners were stacked among the plastic-wrapped segments of half a butchered cow. A bottle of Big Red or RC Cola emerged from wooden soda crates stacked in the mudroom. Mrs. Martin allowed Tracy and me to eat from table trays in front of the television.

As with most of my classmates whose families lived on farms, Tracy's grandparents lived right next door to the Martins' white-shingled house; her aunts, uncles, and cousins lived only a short distance away. Because I had no immediate family nearby, I was fascinated by the closeness of Tracy's family—especially her grandparents.

Tracy's grandmother was as strong and agile as the farmhands who helped during harvesttime. She'd chase after us in her grassy back yard, hairpins flying everywhere, her panty hose bagging around her ankles. When she encircled me in her warm, jiggling arms, the pleasant smell of talcum powder, burnt coffee, and bacon filled my nose. She'd exclaim, "I got my little chickadee!" and I'd squeal with such delight that Tracy's grandfather, in his worn overalls, habitual toothpick dangling from his lips, would saunter to the screen door, peer out, and ask in his low voice, "Everything awright, Ma?"

It wasn't just the proximity of family and the affection openly showered on Tracy that I envied, but the open cow pastures and old red barns where she was allowed to run wild without the constant watch of an adult. Even before we were eight, Tracy and I came and went as we pleased, climbing the tall old maple tree with branches as thick as the arms of a favorite uncle, swinging from a rope in the hayloft, gathering warm eggs as the protective rooster looked on nervously, or sneaking into the empty grain elevator to watch owls nose-dive for mice.

Later I'd find out that the farmhands and uncles working in the fields kept and eye on us as they worked.

Being with Tracy allowed me to tap into my girlish side, an act denied me growing up with two older brothers. By the end of the day, we'd tumble, exhausted, into her Cinderella pink-canopied four-poster bed, part of a matching set of mirrored dresser, bureau, and desk ordered from the JCPenney catalog. Before finally drifting off to sleep, we'd point out constellations in the pale blue and pink glitter sprinkled across her ceiling.

In the morning, Mrs. Martin, her head wrapped in a colorful scarf, would scuff around in her housecoat and terrycloth slippers, sipping coffee, as Tracy and I, still in our pajamas, balanced bowls of cereal on our knees as we sat on the floor watching Saturday morning cartoons. By late afternoon, my ears strained for the sound of the gravel crunching under Dad's truck wheels as he steered up the Martins' gravel driveway, signaling that my reprieve was over. Lack of sleep combined with my excitement about the rare freedom from my parents gave way to a stab of dejection as I realized that I had to go home and that this lifestyle was not mine.

One Monday morning after a weekend sleepover at the Martins', I ran into Tracy at the school lockers. She looked past me and screwed up her mouth at the corner. *Maybe she is having a bad morning,* I thought, the smile fading from my face. "Hi," I said, but Tracy just shrugged her shoulders and looked away, holding her books tightly against her chest like a shield. This wasn't just Tracy having a grumpy morning. My stomach muscles tightened and a wave of nausea came over me. Without another word, she headed to homeroom.

In class, I tried to catch her eye, but she looked straight ahead at the blank chalkboard.

I didn't hear a word the teacher said that morning as I racked my brain trying to figure out what was wrong, replaying in my mind the events of the weekend sleepover—the conversations, the playing—mentally dissecting each moment for an occurrence I might have missed. It had been a typical visit, no different from any other.

At recess I found her skipping rope by herself in one corner of the gym. I approached her, my heart pounding against my chest. The butterflies in my stomach turned into a full-on stomachache. I hated that I felt that I was somehow at her mercy, that this act signified that I needed her friendship. Unlike many girls, I actually didn't need to be part of the group. For me that meant more people who might turn against me, more people to have to potentially defend myself against. A part of me felt the urge to walk away and be done with her friendship. The other part—the stronger part, it turned out—pushed me to put my pride aside and ask her what was wrong. She stopped jumping and put her hands on her hips. She tilted her head so that her bangs fell into her green eyes. "How come you've come to my house a hundred times and never invited me to your house once?"

Her question took the steam out of my resentment. The thing I most dreaded had caught up to me.

I don't know how long I stood there, not saying anything. It was rare for me to invite friends to my house. Mom encouraged me, but I always refused, feigning disinterest. It's not that I didn't want to have friends over. I did. I just didn't want them to see how different my home life was from theirs.

In the late 1960s, the Midwest was a homogenous plain of people with little diversity. Many sections are still like this, but television and overseas commerce have brought ethnic diversity. When I was a child, the only Asian food on our local grocery store shelf was dusty cans of La Choy brand chop suey. Being different or sticking out wasn't something I wanted. I wanted to be like everyone else.

The differences reflected at my home were glaring. We had to take our shoes off at the door. My parents spoke a foreign language. In our kitchen, a wok was poised on the burner instead of a cast-iron skillet. A jelly jar housed chopsticks. A bottle of soy sauce and a shaker of *togarashi* (mixed red peppers) were coupled with peanut butter and strawberry preserves. I wanted to keep these details within the walls of my home.

It wasn't only the cultural differences that I feared would be exposed. Deep down, I was afraid my parents would do or say something to embarrass me.

The more I visited Tracy's home, the stronger my feelings were that I should avoid inviting her over.

At my house, we sat just inches from each other, yet my parents conversed with raised voices. They weren't arguing. This was the way they spoke. My brothers and I thought it was funny, but in the end, we had to speak just as loudly to get a word in edgewise.

Other times, Dad yelled at Mom from the dinner table, over the sizzling food frying in the wok and the roar of the exhaust fan.

Invariably, his mouth would be full. "Mom, *gohan suo chodai* (bring the rice vinegar)!" he'd order. Sitting next to him, I had to cover my head to avoid the shower of rice grains flying from his mouth.

Mom would invariably yell back, "I already gave you rice!"

"No, I need rice vinegar! Rice vinegar!"

During my visits to Tracy's, I placed her and her parents on a lofty pedestal. When Mr. Martin was home, dinner was a civilized affair. Paper napkins covered their laps. They took quiet sips from water glasses and then gently set them down on coasters. The family discussed the day's activities in low voices. The noise level never grew high enough that you couldn't hear above cutlery tapping against a plate, Mr. Martin's swallowing, or Mrs. Martin's jaw clicking.

Of course, they ate like everyone else, but I had convinced myself that they were somehow better. I was terrified by the idea of how Tracy would react to my family, and I wondered if she would use what she saw against me if she ever got mad at me. I was leery and distrustful of her, even though she was my best friend. At that fickle age of eight, we could be like sisters, playing in solidarity one minute but enemies the next. I feared that possibility.

This distrust and the need to protect myself would be something I took with me as I grew up. It became a chip on my shoulder that grew to the size of a log that crushed the pride in my ethnicity. It took many years, and moving many miles away from Versailles, Indiana, before I felt an inkling of pride in my Asian identity. It would be decades before I got to the point where I believed that I was educating people through my difference, rather than revealing a weakness.

And although Dad's style of eating embarrassed me in front of people outside my family, in private I understood and admired his unrestrained enthusiasm and enjoyment. It was something to witness the pleasure he exuded through the meticulous care he took in stripping meat from every inch of a bone. He inserted whole chicken wings and baby pork chops into his mouth. He wrapped his lips around the bone that would hang out of his mouth, using his tongue to maneuver it and nibble at it with his teeth. With crab shells, he'd spend minutes sucking and picking the meaty reward out of a tiny piece of shell. When he was done, the pile of spotless bones and shells stacked on his plate resembled the clean, bleached bones of lost steer strewn across the desert, like those in old Western movies.

It was difficult to believe that Tracy would share Dad's philosophy that forks and knives couldn't do a better job than fingers and chopsticks. He believed that scraping the bottom of a soup bowl with a spoon for the last drop was a waste of time when it could be finished off more easily by tilting the bowl to his mouth.

I was always aware that my table manners were less than adequate, and I wasn't confident enough to wing it. When I ate at Tracy's house, I made a mental note to start eating a few seconds behind everyone else at the table. I started doing this after I embarrassed myself at another friend's house, where I sucked up a big tangle of spaghetti Bolognese in one big loud slurp in the same way I ate Japanese noodles at home. My friend's mother looked at me in awe. "Lordy," she said, chuckling heartily before showing me how to use the big spoon next to my plate to twirl the noodles. The rare times I did have a friend come over for dinner, I'd insist that Mom order a take-out pizza so I wouldn't have to worry about my family's dinner-table etiquette.

I couldn't anticipate what Tracy would think if she knew any of this, but I did know for certain that unless I invited her over soon, I would lose her friendship for good.

That night I asked Mom if Tracy could spend the night, prefacing the request with the suggestion that it would be okay if she didn't want to bother with it. But Mom said it was a wonderful idea, and that she liked Tracy very much.

❀

The week before the sleepover, I brooded around the house, imagining every worst-case scenario. What would she think about the Japanese calligraphy framed and hanging prominently in the living room? Or the baby-size sake cups and bottle displayed in Mom's curio cabinet? At the last minute, in an act of desperation, I tried to anger Mom in the hope that she would punish me by taking away the sleepover privilege. But I was unsuccessful.

When Friday night finally arrived, I gave an inner sigh of relief when Dad had to work the entire weekend and wouldn't be able to join us for lunch the next day. But it wasn't long before I saw Mom drizzle soy sauce on Tracy's noodle casserole without asking her first. Tracy's eyes widened, but she didn't protest, and she ate all of it.

I cringed when Mom set up her bed earlier than usual. Dad snored so loudly—a long, hollow sound that shook the floors—that it drove Mom to sleep on the living room sofa on a foam mattress fashioned with a fitted sheet secured with safety pins.

Of all nights, she chose this one to make up her sofa bed before Tracy and I had gone to sleep. That Mom and Dad didn't sleep in the same room like other parents was just another thing that made us different. The space where Mom set up her bed was the only place in the house where we could sit in front of the

TV. I suggested we climb onto the mattress and under the blankets as if it were the most normal thing in the world. I watched Tracy's expression carefully, but she didn't appear to mind that we were watching television curled up with my mother on her makeshift bed on the couch. I was sure she was taking mental notes that she'd share with everyone at school the next week.

For our evening snack, Mom poured us each a small glass of cola and counted out four small cookies each. Mom was a stickler when it came to sugary snacks and drinks. She doled them out like a sergeant in a food line. After we brushed our teeth, Tracy and I crawled into bed, where we giggled and played with a pen flashlight until Mom poked her head in and sternly told us to go to sleep.

Before Tracy's visit, I had asked Mom not to make a big production of breakfast. I told her we were just as happy eating cold cereal and milk in our pajamas. She scowled and said that she didn't like that; it was too sloppy. But that's what I did at my friends' houses, I informed her. She replied with a shrug. Thus, Mom hustled us out of bed the next morning and made sure we got dressed for breakfast. Slow-moving and bleary-eyed from having stayed up most of the night, we groggily sat down to a breakfast of bacon, eggs, and toast. A small vase of daisies from our garden adorned the table.

After breakfast Tracy and I milled around in the living room. Tracy's mom wasn't picking her up until midafternoon, and I had no idea what we could do in the meantime.

I was about to suggest going to the town waterworks plant, just a block away, where we could watch the truck barrels being filled, when I saw Tracy pressing her face against the glass door of a cabinet holding *katachi* (Japanese knickknacks). Mom passed by with an armful of clean folded towels.

"Do you want to see better?" Mom asked.

Tracy nodded her head vigorously.

Mom slid open the glass doors carefully and took out a pair of miniature wooden lion-head puppets that slipped over her hands like mittens. One was lacquered bright red, and the other black with red markings. Both had a big tuft of long black hair sprouting from the crowns of their heads and cheeks. The wide wooden mouths clacked open and closed. She put the puppets on and shook their heads, making them appear to dance.

"On New Year's holiday, these lions dance, chasing away evil spirits," she explained, letting us put them on our hands.

From a corner of the shelf, Mom pulled out a green brocade scroll wrapped several times with a heavy dark-blue cord. She unrolled the yardage of stiff rice paper that showed scrawls and curlicues of Japanese calligraphy.

"Before I left Japan, my family and close friends wrote a short message of good luck." She translated a few of the passages to English and smiled. She reached for an intricate carving of a bear holding a fish in its mouth made from a rare wood from Akasaka.

"Akasaka," Tracy repeated. "Where's that?" She reached for the carving, holding it up close to her face to examine it more closely.

"A place in Japan, near Tokyo, where I grew up."

"What's Japan like?"

"Hon ... it's like ... hard to say, but I can show you," Mom said, taking out a photo album from a drawer.

Mom pointed to a photograph of herself in her twenties. In it, she wore a thick wool sweater, a scarf tied around her neck, and tailored dark pants. She cradled a camera in her lap; a majestic mountain scene graced the background. "This was taken in the Japanese Alps. My nature photography class took trips into the mountains, where we would camp, climb, and take pictures."

She showed Tracy another photo of herself dressed in ski clothes, wearing long wooden skis and holding poles. Behind her was a steep hill spotted with trees buried under snow that resembled armies of monstrous snowmen. "I loved to ski so much I went every weekend. Sometimes I went with strangers," she said, laughing at her recklessness.

"During the season, I would leave work at the bank on Friday nights and take a train all the way up to the mountains. Standing room only sometimes. My coworkers and I stayed in the company cabins. Skis were made of wood back then and were quite heavy. We'd hike up the mountain in the early morning with our skis on our backs, then spend the afternoon skiing down."

"Do you go skiing now?" Tracy asked.

Mom laughed. "No, never. No time to play like when I was younger."

Sensing a longing, Tracy asked, "Do you miss it?"

"Sometimes." Mom nodded.

A blue paper crane fell out from between the pages. "What's this?" Tracy picked it up and examined the folded bird closely.

"It's origami," I answered in a know-it-all tone. With each of Tracy's questions, I felt myself growing more invisible. I resented that I hadn't asked Mom those questions first. That I had never asked those questions. I saw how little I knew about Mom's life before she married Dad. I didn't know the stories behind the objects in the display case. They had been there for as long as I could remember and were permanent fixtures in our house, and yet I knew nothing about where they had come from. Before that moment, I had never thought of Mom as having a history or a life before becoming a wife and mother.

"Can you show me how to make this?" Tracy asked Mom eagerly. I opened my mouth to speak, but nothing came out. Mom was connecting with Tracy in a way I never had. Jealous of their bond, I glared at Tracy. I fumed silently and contemplated telling them both that I was the sole reason she was there in the first place.

While Mom went to gather the origami supplies, I worked up my most haughty voice as I told Tracy about the rabbits, frogs, boxes, hats, and swans Mom and I had made together.

Mom returned, not with the thin, solid-colored sheets we usually used, but with handmade *washi* paper. From it she folded some tiny paper hats for our Barbie dolls and some swans and cranes.

Keven and Alvin came around in search of food. In midfold, Mom looked up. "I forgot about lunch."

She looked at Tracy and asked, "Do you want to try a special omelet?" Despite Tracy's strong rapport with Mom, I found myself worried again about what her impression might be of Mom's interpretation of a Western dish.

A few nights a week, Mom made Western food. Our table was set with plates, napkins, and silverware instead of the Japanese rice bowls and chopsticks. But those dinners always felt like a false front, with the distorted touch of a child's tea set.

Mom tackled learning how to make Western food at Dad's suggestion. They concluded early on in their marriage that it would help them fit in and ease their use of essential, hard-to-get Japanese ingredients. Mom couldn't read the English cookbooks, so Dad asked the American wife of a Japanese friend to teach her how to make some dishes. Aunt Nora had been the cook for a wealthy family in Cincinnati, and she taught Mom how to make moist meat loaf, juicy chuck roast, and flaky piecrust.

It took years for Mom to master the techniques. Many times she attempted whipping up Western dishes without a recipe. It wasn't that she didn't know how to cook; she simply didn't know how what she was preparing was supposed to taste.

Pan-fried potatoes seemed easy enough: Just fry some thinly sliced potatoes in an oiled skillet until they brown. But instead of the crisp-on-the-outside, flaky-on-the-inside tuber side dish she had in mind, the potato starches, stimulated by the heat, glued the slices together. Since she didn't cook the potatoes long enough over a high flame, the outsides got brown, but the middle parts remained raw and crunchy. My brothers and I masked the texture with lots of ketchup and gave each other supportive looks. We often nibbled on Mom's experimental meals, but we longed for the nights when she cooked what she knew.

She devised a solution for reusing leftovers and vegetables that had been in the crisper too long: Chop them up and fry them in the wok and then give them a squirt or two of various condiments and spices. Once she stir-fried shredded cabbage, chopped onions, and some limp carrots and greens, and then she added sugar, ketchup, and the inevitable squirt of *tonkatsu* sauce (a sweet, savory bottled sauce made from fruit and spices). Last, she added cooked spaghetti to the hodgepodge and stirred it up in the wok. She was oddly proud of the chunky sweet-and-sour mixture she called tomato spaghetti, even though the only tomato in it was the ketchup.

But Tracy did not know anything about Mom's concoctions and answered an unhesitating yes to Mom's offer of an omelet. I felt my jealousy flare up like a fever. Frustrated, all I could do was cross my arms and fume.

As the wok heated, Mom diced garlic, green onions, green peppers, and leftover chicken. Her cleaver went *rat-tat-tat* like a snare drum. The vegetables turned bright and glossy upon being tossed in the hot oiled wok. Mom's spatula banged against the pan like a bell as a mouthwatering aroma filled the kitchen. She tossed in several cups of cooked rice and a handful of frozen peas before adding the chopped chicken.

Mom cracked and beat a half dozen eggs. She swirled the wok over the flame with one hand while pouring the beaten eggs in with the other. The egg mix bubbled and clung to the side. When the edges looked dry and curled away from the iron surface, she spooned a generous portion of the rice and vegetables into the center and flipped one side of the omelet over to the other to complete it. Before serving it to Tracy, she gave it a good drizzling of *tonkatsu* sauce.

The corners of Tracy's mouth turned down at the sight of the brown sauce. "It looks like chocolate," she said, trying to sound optimistic.

"Try it. Sweet like ketchup," Mom said. Tracy smiled at that.

The more Tracy hesitated, the more sauce I squirted over my own omelet. "We use this almost as much as ketchup," I commented smugly.

As Tracy cautiously dipped her finger in the sauce, I started on my portion of the omelet, making sure I placed a bite of everything on my fork the way I liked it. Mom's rice omelet was one of her adaptations that was actually delicious—the perfect sampling of fluffy egg, tangy sauce, crunch of green peppers, aromatics of ginger and garlic, and unique charred flavor that can be created only by a hot, well-seasoned wok. After that first delicious taste, I didn't care anymore about what Tracy thought.

I couldn't read Tracy's expression, but one forkful turned into another, and then another, until her plate was empty except for streaks where she had run her portions along the plate to sop up the last of the *tonkatsu* sauce.

Tracy's mom arrived promptly after lunch. Mom and I waved goodbye from the front door as Tracy cradled her folded paper creations and described the lion puppets to her mother as they walked back to Mrs. Martin's car. I breathed a sigh of relief that the sleepover was officially over and that my home had made a positive impression on her.

❀

The following Monday at school, as I'd expected, Tracy was eager to tell our friends about the sleepover at my house. She went on and on about the great-tasting omelet with the sweet brown sauce, the knickknacks in the glass case, and the paper-folding. She had brought with her the paper crane Mom showed her how to make. Instead of making it sound freakish, she spoke with the enthusiasm of someone who had spent the weekend at Disney World. She looked me straight in the eyes when she announced she couldn't wait to be invited back.

What Tracy didn't know was that after she went home, I was left with a gnawing insecurity and jealousy. I moped around Mom, fiddling with the dangling chain on the small reading lamp as she straightened up the living room. I began badgering her with silly questions, such as whether she liked Tracy better than me, or if she thought Tracy was more fun and interesting than me.

"No," she answered, "but Tracy shows more appreciation than you do. You should try to learn from that." I flinched. Deep in my heart, I knew she was right, but I remained indifferent and unbudging.

The stories Mom had told Tracy and me the morning after the sleepover haunted me. There was so much about her that I didn't know. Digging around the closet in the basement, I came upon the photo album Mom had shown Tracy and me. In the picture, Mom wore a big smile. She was wearing a hat, coat, and gloves and clutching a bouquet of flowers.

Hearing me rustling around in her things, Mom came from the washer and dryer, where she was folding dish towels, to see what I was in to. I looked up from the album I was studying as she stuck her head around the corner.

This was my chance, my chance to show my appreciation and interest. I had so many questions, good probing questions that Tracy would ask if she were there, questions that Mom would have enjoyed being asked, such as where the picture was taken and what she was doing at the time. But I didn't ask any of them. I held my tongue and continued turning the pages, studying each photo.

I'd learn later the photo was taken at the airport in Japan right before she boarded the plane to America. In the years to come, I repeatedly asked myself why I didn't act on the impulse to ask my mom about her life. I could feel Mom was waiting for me to ask, to show my interest, to turn a corner. But I just couldn't bring myself to do it. The opportunity slipped by like a passing breeze.

My heart sunk when I heard her wordlessly move out of the room and back to her folding. A few minutes later I heard her climb the stairs, each footstep perfectly paced in a rhythm like a slow-beating drum. I tucked the photo album carefully beside another one, holding all the family baby photos, in the closet and silently followed Mom upstairs.

## Japanese-Style Omelet

*My mother's omelet makes an excellent late-night supper—hot, filling, and full of flavor. Be sure to use the tomato ketchup. This misunderstood condiment adds the perfect amount of tomato sweetness and tanginess that you can't duplicate with paste or sauce. Tonkatsu, the brown tart sauce drizzled on top of the eggs, is sold at any Asian supermarket. My favorite brand is Bull Dog.*

### Fried Rice

> 2 teaspoons vegetable oil
> ½ medium onion, chopped
> ¼ cup frozen peas
> ¼-inch-thick slice of ham, diced into ¼-inch pieces
> 1 cup cooked rice
> 2 tablespoons tomato ketchup
> dash of salt and pepper

### Omelet

> 2 teaspoons butter
> dash of salt and pepper
> 4 eggs, beaten
> *tonkatsu* sauce

*For the fried rice:* In a medium-size sauté pan, heat vegetable oil over medium-high heat. Sauté onions and peas; add ham, cooked rice, ketchup, and salt and pepper. Mix well. Transfer to a medium-size bowl and set aside.

*For the omelet:* Rinse out the sauté pan and return to the stove top. Over medium-high heat, melt half the butter.

Add a dash of salt and pepper to the beaten eggs and stir. When the pan is hot, pour in half the egg batter. Reduce the flame to medium. Gently swirl the egg batter so it evenly coats the pan's surface. When the edges pull away from the pan and the center begins to solidify, add half the fried rice to the center of the egg. With a spatula, fold one-half of the egg over the center. Do the same with the other side, at the same time lifting the edge of the pan to help flip the omelet over. Allow to cook for an additional 30 seconds.

Repeat with the remaining egg batter and fried rice. Serve immediately with *tonkatsu* sauce.

Makes 2 omelets.

The Green Cooler and Wasabi

When I was eight years old, Dad left the house in our red pickup and returned behind the wheel of a new station wagon. In the back was a big green Coleman cooler, given as a promotional gift that came with the car. With a sheepish grin to answer Mom's smirk of annoyance, my father somehow was able to convince her that the big-ticket purchase was perfect for summer vacations.

The combination of the new car and cooler, Dad told Mom, had cinched the deal and would put an end to their fresh-fish worries. Mom nodded her head, slowly warming to the idea, particularly the part about the fresh fish.

Fresh fish, so fresh it's eaten the day it's caught, is a vital part of the Japanese diet, the way meat and potatoes are to Midwesterners. Both my parents devoted their time, heart, and energy to maintaining their Japanese diet, not simply because they preferred the taste of it to Western food, but because it connected them to their culture and all they had left back in Japan.

During the 1970s, ethnic grocery stores hadn't arrived at the level of popularity that they would enjoy decades later. My parents had to make do with their ingenuity, often making their favorite foods from scratch. Mom mastered preparing *udon* noodles that tasted as though they were made at her favorite noodle house in Tokyo.

Planting vegetables helped tremendously. In my father's back-yard garden, Western vegetables such as juicy, sun-ripened Indiana tomatoes and sweet corn, grew alongside an abundance of Asian produce, such as bok choy and daikon.

For years my parents went without items like *yuzu* (an intensely strong Japanese lemon), ponzu sauce, real wasabi root to grate into the paste known as wasabi, and *panko* (Japanese breadcrumbs), but never without the basic staples: tea, rice, soy sauce, *ajimoto* (MSG), kombu (dried kelp), and katsuo (dried fish flakes) for dashi (fish broth).

The worry that these dry goods would become unavailable ran so deep that Mom had her sisters in Japan mail them to her twice a year. By the time the package reached us, the box was always battered and pasted with exotic postage stamps, scribbles, and red markings. We'd gather around as Mom carefully lifted out the newspaper wrapping, smoothing and laying aside each page to read later. The smell that emerged hinted of sandalwood incense, dried fish, citrus, and tobacco, leading me to imagine the aroma of my relatives' home. In return, Mom always sent gold-boxed Godiva chocolates, Pepperidge Farm crackers, a bottle of Tabu cologne, and Cutex nail polish.

Dad was consumed by his fresh-fish cravings. We lived in a meat-eating town where pork constituted seasoning, whether it was a couple of slabs of bacon cooked with canned green beans or bits of ham in pea soup or bacon grease baked in cornbread. The only fish I'd eaten outside the home was so pan-fried it was rendered tasteless. My father's desperation was what had ultimately led him to convince himself that the scum-eating carp fished out of nearby Lathery Creek was an adequate substitute.

Maybe it was the game-fishing TV shows on Sunday mornings, with glistening fat fish fighting the line and arcing in the air, but that summer he got the idea in his head that Florida was Mecca.

Keven, Alvin, and I were thrilled about vacationing to Florida. We tuned in to *The Wonderful World of Disney* every week. Disney World had just opened in Orlando, and I pictured myself visiting Cinderella's Castle and meeting her face-to-face, just like at the beginning of the program.

As my brothers and I were deep in our own dream of the upcoming vacation, Mom and Dad were imagining fresh grouper, snapper, crabs, and shrimp. As it turned out, we wouldn't make it to Disney World until a future trip. The focus of that summer was to obtain fresh seafood. We headed south from the glacier-cut hills and rivers of Indiana, through the rolling horse country of Kentucky, and down through the forests of Tennessee. We stayed overnight at a Holiday Inn in Georgia. Long after it was dark, the air remained stifling, like a blowing furnace in a windowless room. The next morning, we reached the salty sea breezes and moss-covered banyan trees in Panama City, Florida's "Redneck Riviera."

Dad checked us into a beachside hotel room that had a small kitchenette. There was no vacation from cooking for Mom, who had packed a cardboard box with Japanese condiments, our electric rice cooker, and a sack of rice—enough for a whole week.

Our room had a view of the ocean. Dad got it at a good price, since we were there during the off-season when the weather was at its hottest and muggiest.

Every evening during the first days of our holiday, we dined at the local shrimp shacks and fish houses. I loved the zesty crab Louis, the crunchy fried coconut shrimp, and the tender shrimp cocktails and batter-fried grouper that came with a small metal bucket of rémoulade and cocktail sauce. Dad concluded we were paying too much for the seafood we were eating, and after watching people drop crab cages off the piers, he got a notion that it would be easy enough to catch his own crab for the whole family.

Despite the fact that swimming in the ocean, taking long naps in the afternoon, reading in a hammock, and taking long walks on the beach were all hallmarks of vacation, my father was a man who worked two jobs, and it didn't take too long before he got antsy. Dad said that lazing around all day wasn't enough to get his appetite going.

After getting it in his head that he would catch his own crab, Dad took Alvin and me to one of the bait and tackle shops near the pier, which was about a quarter-mile stroll from the hotel. Stepping into the semidark, wood-paneled store, we were greeted with the friendly scent of balsam, salt air, fish, and plastic. On the shelves and walls hung multiple-size nets, nylon flies, hooks, ropes of beef jerky, and varnished fishing poles. Following the salesman's advice,

Dad bought a rectangular wire-mesh trap and a tub of raw chicken livers, the crabs' bait of choice.

Once we got to the pier, Dad found a spot among the other crabbers. Dad was right; these folks did make catching crab look effortless. They sat back in lawn chairs with coolers filled with sandwiches and cold drinks. Some listened to baseball games on transistor radios and others had their noses in books, but most just looked out onto the beige sand and transparent blue water, wearing the same blissful expression I was used to seeing on people back home sitting in front of a burning fireplace.

Dad set up his cage and waited. I bit my tongue to keep from asking how long we had to stay at the pier. Dad dug in his pocket for some change so Alvin and I could kill time checking out what was available at the food stand.

On our way back, my brother and I saw a group of people gathered on the pier; there was no sign of Dad. I felt light-headed from a wave of fear that washed over me. Something was wrong. Pushing our way through the forest of tan legs, I heard a woman yell, "Whatever you do, don't pull it off! His finger will come off with it!"

We found Dad inside the circle of gawkers with a large crab's pincer attached to his bleeding thumb. Dad yelled "Oucha!" and violently slammed the blue crustacean's body against a pier post in an effort to get it off.

At the sight of my father in pain like this, I screeched and dropped the soda I'd just bought. After several determined thumps against the pier post, the pincer broke off from the crab, which scrambled back into the water. My father's blood dotted the pier's wooden floor. I had been holding my breath without realizing it and finally exhaled. I felt an urge to cry, but I stifled it the best I could, knowing that it would upset Dad more than help him. With the excitement over, there was good-natured laughter as the crowd dispersed. Some ventured to the edge of the pier to catch a final glimpse of the tenacious crab, but most returned to their posts to check on their submerged cages.

Calmness returned to me as Dad settled into a lawn chair offered to him by one of the crabbers. Alvin and I huddled around him, my soda long forgotten. A woman wearing sunglasses asked where he was from.

"I come from Japan, but my family," waving his injured hand at Alvin and me, "live in Indiana."

Cheers arose when others heard this. It seemed many of the older crabbers were retirees from the Midwest.

Encouraged by this, Dad began telling his story about how he had made his way from California to Japan and then to Indiana. I knew how involved he would get in the story, so I quickly asked if Alvin and I could go back to the hotel. He nodded. Set free from the waiting game, Alvin and I made our way back, leisurely collecting sand dollars and starfish along the way.

When my father returned later that afternoon, slightly sunburned and with a white hankie, stiff from dried blood, wrapped around his injured thumb, he burst into the hotel room proudly bearing eight live crabs scratching at the sides of the green cooler. He had also bought a pound of fresh shrimp from a fish market near the bait shop. Mom would join Dad and eat a little of this later on that night, but the fresh seafood feast was agreed upon between my parents as being my dad's affair. That night, we all went to the seafood restaurant, but Dad ordered only a glass of beer and nibbled on oyster crackers.

While Mom readied us for bed, the smell from the kitchenette was spicy and moist from the Old Bay Dad used to boil the crabs and shrimp. My father had transferred the crab and shrimp to a bucket to fill the cooler with ice for his food once cooked. He'd gently submerged several bottles of beer into the cooler as well.

As we crawled into bed, I heard paper crackling as he spread sheets of newspaper across the small porch.

"Go to sleep," Mom whispered, tucking me back between the sheets when I tried to climb out of bed to join Dad.

"Let Dad enjoy himself. We must leave him alone," she said drowsily.

I looked toward the window. The full moon lit the porch and I saw my father's silhouette as he sipped his beer and dipped into the cooler for crab and shrimp. Between the breaking of the surf, I heard the snap and crack of crab shells. This was what he had been waiting for all along.

❁

During those early years, my parents monitored their Japanese food supplies carefully. We had the Asian vegetables from the garden, but the worry of running out nagged at them. Mom checked and rechecked her stock of dried Japanese foods and kept constant lists of items she needed. The tension of watching the supply dwindle was like waiting out a tornado alert.

When inventory got low, my parents relied on a complex network of mutual Japanese friends and acquaintances to find the supplies they needed. Mom learned of a store called Soya Foods, which sold homemade tofu and a limited selection of Japanese ingredients in Cincinnati, more than an hour's car ride from our house. Until it closed in the late 1980s, my parents, often with my brothers and me in tow, visited Soya Foods almost every other week. The car would be filled with laughter and talk on the drive to Soya Foods. Mom and Dad's excitement was contagious. The green cooler was loaded into the back of the station wagon, filled with bags of ice Mom had prepared during the week. All this was done in advance and with careful thought given to the transport of the fresh items home from the city.

Tucked among the warehouses in the industrial part of town, Soya Foods was more a tofu-production plant than a grocery store. The bell above the metal door heralded our arrival. The proprietress, Mrs. Yamaguchi, peeked from behind the wall of paperwork on her desk. Pushing back her salt-and-pepper frizz of hair, she quickly shuffled from behind her heavy, cherrywood desk, muttering repeatedly in a husky voice, *"Irrashimasen!"* (Welcome!), and then busied herself pouring hot green tea into thick earthenware mugs. Her husband, Mr. Yamaguchi, was punching numbers into a calculator. Upon finishing the tallying of his figures, he lifted his head, grunted, and nodded at Dad, who waved from across the room after setting down the green cooler.

A warm muskiness of boiling soybeans rising from the vats permeated the store. On the wall near Mrs. Yamaguchi's desk was a Japanese calendar that contained scenic photos of Mount Fuji, groves of cherry blossoms, and fireworks exploding above a summer festival. I'd stand at the wall, flipping through the images and observing everything going on in the store.

On this particular shopping trip, Dad made his way over to Mr. Yamaguchi as he finished his accounting. Dad took the metal chair and mug of green tea offered to him. As Mom took care of the shopping, Dad would discuss the Cincinnati Reds' baseball season with Mr. Yamaguchi, a heavyset man with milk-white hair and silver-rimmed glasses who had the habit of leaning back and resting his arms on his chair as if he were holding court with royalty. Like a lithe squirrel jumping from branch to branch, Mrs. Yamaguchi followed Mom through the store as she selected dried noodles from the tall gray shelf of Japanese ingredients and spices. During other visits, when shipments had arrived, Mrs. Yamaguchi stayed at her desk or stocked the shelves until Mom was ready to check out. There were no other customers in the store that day as she leaned her bony frame against the painted steel shelving to watch what Mom selected, occasionally making comments about the item.

"Fresh?" Mom asked in Japanese, holding up a plastic bag of dark-brown paste.

"Yes, miso paste moves very fast. A lot of items leave the store the first day we get them. We have lots of customers, but some are funny," Mrs. Yamaguchi replied, straightening packages of dried noodles on a shelf.

"Funny in what way?" Mom asked, taking the hook, knowing Mrs. Yamaguchi's love of gossip.

"Oh, Mrs. Sato, do you know her? Probably not. She's been in Cincinnati for about ten years. She's so tight she brought back a half-eaten block of tofu and said it was not good."

"*Honto?* Really?"

"It's true! Now when she comes, we give her a smaller block of tofu." She spread her spidery fingers on her hip.

"Mrs. Sato explained to me that she must be careful how she spends her money. She needs to save enough to send her daughter to an Ivy League school. Only her daughter is five now," she said, shaking her head. "I tell her I know what she's talking about because we're trying to pay for our son's medical school tuition . . . now!" she roared, laughing.

"Then I say to her, we won't be in business long if customers like you return eaten tofu, claiming it's bad." She scrunched her face as she filled the coarse, white cloth bag Mom had brought from home with rice grains.

Mr. Yamaguchi finally heaved his bulky frame from his chair to fill a plastic bag with water before slipping in a firm cube of tofu as big as a pound cake.

After Dad paid for the food and Mom carefully packed the green cooler with the perishables, Mr. Yamaguchi reached for a small green and pink box of Botan rice candy, a peach-colored, soft, glutinous sweet, and handed it to my brothers and me, holding a finger to his lips as if it were our secret.

Soya Foods was a boon to my parents, but there were many close calls when our pantry was nearly emptied of precious bonito flakes and dried seaweed for fish stock. Mom occasionally made expensive overseas calls to her sister, Akiko, to find out when the last package was mailed.

Akiko would always insist that a package was on the way. Even though she mailed us packages regularly, Mom would insist she read back the address she had. Mom would then deduce that the parcel was either lost in the mail or held up in customs.

Carefully eyeballing the remaining fish shavings and kombu, she'd calculate exactly how many ingredients remained before doomsday. *It isn't as if we would starve,* I thought, but I didn't dare say so to Mom, knowing Japanese ingredients were far too important to her. We had other food, just not Japanese. I can't remember our ever having run out before. Looking back at how my parents carried on about it, I see the dreaded possibility was also an element that brought a jolt of excitement to their lives. If they ever actually did run out, I would imagine it would have been a fear actualized, and that Mom simply would have carried on and made something else until the ingredients were replenished.

Japanese home cooking had become the only daily thread my parents had to their culture. Even I knew that Japanese food symbolized something greater than sustenance. It was like a comforting familiarity that assured them they could make it through the daily challenges of living in a country not their own. A simple bowl of perfectly steamed rice or ramen noodles in hot broth could do wonders in keeping homesickness at bay, lift the blues deepened by the adjustment period of learning new customs, and stir the appetite to eat.

It wasn't until I was in my thirties and living in Beijing that I really began to understand what my parents must have gone through. On the days I was most homesick, a grilled ham-and-cheese sandwich or a homemade milkshake did wonders to boost my flagging spirit.

The closest we ever came to actually running out of Japanese ingredients was during one Indian summer several weeks after school began. Mom was planning a dinner party that summer for several of my parents' Japanese couple friends. Mom had used more of the fish flakes for the dashi than she had planned. The higher-grade green tea was running low as well. A package from Tokyo was not expected for another two months. The situation seemed hopeless when Dad received a letter from Mr. Nagashima, an old acquaintance from Japan who had just moved to a suburb outside of Chicago.

Mr. Nagashima's writing was that of the characters that graced the blue airmail stationery and thin onionskin paper I saw my mother write her personal correspondence on.

My father read aloud:

I was pleased to hear from our mutual friend, Mr. Buyo, that you were living with your wife and children in Indiana.

My company transferred me to Chicago six months ago. It has been a smooth adjustment for my wife and daughter, but we understand the difficulty of getting good Japanese food. Mr. Buyo told me about your predicament. It must be especially hard for you, living out in the country. I don't know how Mr. Buyo can eat Western food every day, but I hear his wife cooks well.

America is a big country, but Indiana is not far from Chicago, right? I wanted to share with you the location of some very good Japanese grocery stores and restaurants we have found here in Chicago. We make a trip to this area of town every weekend to buy food and eat sushi. I highly recommend you come and see for yourself!

Signed,
*Heiro Nagashima*

Mom and Dad decided the situation was dire enough that Dad should take the following weekend off to drive us all to Chicago. Every night that week, after coming home from work, Dad mulled over his road maps, planning out the best route for the six-hour drive. Mom wrote and rewrote a detailed grocery list, compiled from her favorite cookbooks. She noted the necessary as well as the hard-to-find items.

The night before the trip, Mom and Dad contemplated the thrill of the food that lay ahead like two kids anticipating Santa's arrival on Christmas Eve.

"Do you think the sushi will be as good as Mr. Nagashima claims?" Mom ventured.

"He's an old friend. I trust his opinion. Maybe the restaurant will have *hamaguri* (clams)," Dad said.

"No, this is not the season. I hope they have *unagi* (eel). I don't know if I should get the grilled *unagi* or sushi," Mom said.

"I haven't eaten raw *maguro* (tuna) in . . . I can't remember, it's been so long. I bet it will be so fresh that the fish is still moving." Dad smacked his lips at the thought. "I'm getting hungry just thinking about it," he said, rubbing his stomach.

"But it's hard not to think about it, *ne?*" Mom added. "Oh, *unagi* or sushi?" She became wistful again. Early the next morning, Dad took the green Coleman cooler out of storage and packed it with *nori-maki* (salty rice balls), Shasta soft drinks, and water for the trip. He packed just enough so that we'd empty it and be able to use it to haul home all the refrigerated items and seafood.

Mom got my brothers and me out of bed hours before sunrise to get a head start on the six-hour drive. I'd soon fall back to sleep and wake up to music on the radio and the smell of coffee as Mom poured Dad a cup as he drove. Surrounding us were the flatlands of northern Indiana, so different from the lush, rolling hills of the southernmost regions.

Wasting no time, Dad drove directly, like a missile zeroing in on its target. We made our way to Clark Street, the area Mr. Nagashima described in his letter.

Clark Street was in the inner city, where train lines rattled overhead. Paper and overflowing garbage cans littered the streets. It wasn't the best part of town. Mr. Nagashima had warned us not to go there after dark. The sushi restaurant he referred my parents to was hidden behind a dark metal door in one of the nondescript buildings crowding the block. Although the restaurant lacked windows, it was well lit and tidy.

Mom looked around, nodding her head approvingly at what she saw. The surroundings reminded her of the *sushi-ya*, a type of restaurant in Japan that serves only raw fish. Dad ignored the tables and chairs in the dining area, motioning us to sit at the bar. Although it was the weekend, the bar seats were filled with mostly Japanese who had likely also made a special weekend trip in for lunch from the suburbs. The lunchtime crowd was turning over, so we easily found barstools for all of us.

Taking their seats, Mom and Dad immediately began eyeing and discussing the variety of fish displayed in the glass refrigerated case in front of us. Behind the bar stood three chefs. Each of their stations displayed thick white, pink, red, and white-striated fish fillets, tangles of octopus, and small plastic bowls holding bright orange fish roe the size of pinheads and pearls.

After eating a yellowtail *nigiri-zushi,* a rectangular slab of yellowtail tuna atop vinegar rice, Mom fanned herself with the beverage menu and dabbed at the tears running down her face with a napkin.

Concerned, I looked at Mom. "Why are you crying?" I asked. When she didn't answer me, I pressed, "Is it because you haven't eaten sushi in such a long time?"

She choked with laughter when I said this, still unable to collect herself.

Dad, listening in on the one-sided conversation, laughed too. "She ate too much wasabi," he said, pointing to the small mound of green paste.

Mom had served wasabi at home, in the dipping sauce for cold soba noodles, with dumplings and other dishes, but like a sip of beer, it was off limits to us children.

I turned my focus to the tuna *nigiri-zushi* Dad ordered for me. Despite my deftness with chopsticks, the architecture of the rice bed and the fish topping was awkward to grasp with my sticks. I flipped the entire piece into my dish of soy sauce.

The tight ball of rice disintegrated in the dark liquid puddle. Trying to recover, I stuffed the sliver of fish in my mouth, eager to get it right the next time. The slick, cool texture of the fish and the saltiness of the soy sauce made me gag. To Mom's dismay, I let the chunk of fish fall out of my mouth.

"Linda!" Mom hissed, sopping up the soy sauce spots on the counter. Our sushi chef gently told her he would cut the fish thinner.

"Try again," the chef said to me in Japanese, with a wink. "This time, use your fingers. Instead of dipping the whole thing in the soy sauce, turn it upside down and dip only the fish part. Not too much, though. You want to taste the fish."

His method worked much better. The dab of soy sauce enhanced the subtle, clean flavor of the fish and its butter-smooth feel in my mouth.

I watched as Mom mixed soy sauce with the wasabi paste to produce a thick, green-black paste. Its apple-green color and puttylike texture made it all the more attractive to me. "Too strong and spicy for an eight-year-old," Mom said when she noticed my mischievous interest in the spicy paste. I had tasted and enjoyed all the other foods they initially described as too strong-tasting, too spicy, or something I wouldn't like. *Why should wasabi be any different?* I wondered.

I glanced at my brothers' soy sauce dishes and saw that they had wasabi mixed in theirs as well. Ignoring Mom's warning, I slipped my slice of fish into her sauce while she was busy ordering an assortment of sashimi (sliced raw fish).

*What's the big deal?* I thought as I chewed the fish and rice. A few seconds later, heat prickled at the base of my throat and what felt like hot gas rose quickly into my sinuses, blasting them like dry heat from a radiator and triggering a flood of tears. I squeezed my eyes shut until it subsided. I opened my eyes and looked around me, certain I hadn't experienced the explosion alone. I caught the chef watching me with an amused sparkle in his eyes.

Mom knew exactly what I had done when she heard me sniffing and saw my watery eyes. She shook her head and told me, "I said it was hot."

I took a deep breath. It felt like drinking in cold winter air after being cooped up in a too-warm house all day. My eyes glittered and my head swam in the aftermath of the wasabi fire. But finally I received my payoff as the delicious marriage of tuna and mustard kicked in. After that episode, I was more respectful of wasabi, but with each visit to the sushi restaurant in the following years, I acquired a taste for the fish and radish paste combination that would eventually become a lifelong craving.

Our original plan to check into our hotel after lunch and visit museums changed when my parents realized that the markets Mr. Nagashima recommended were better than they had imagined. The stores were no bigger than our small-town grocery store, but compared to the shops in Cincinnati, they were like sprawling supermarkets. They had sections selling Japanese sweets, books and magazines, and even soaps and shampoos.

Dad looked concerned as he surveyed the fish selection in one of the stores. The fillets of sea bream, whole red snapper, mackerel for pickling, trout, smelt for tempura, salted salmon for broiling, fish roe, and several pounds of shrimp were fresh and inviting, but not cheap. Mom plucked at her bottom lip as she mentally costed out the price of lunch, the hotel room, and buying groceries. Turning to Dad, she whispered in his ear and he whispered something back. They went back and forth like this several times.

My parents decided that, rather than spend the night in a hotel, we would drive home that evening. Keven, Alvin, and I didn't mind, especially when Mom bribed us with a bag of rice crackers, one of our favorite snacks.

With Dad pushing the shopping cart, Mom diligently perused the aisles with her long grocery list in hand. She didn't have any difficulty finding what she wanted, as all the labels were written in Japanese, and if she couldn't find a specific item, she was able to ask the clerk her questions in Japanese.

My parents were easygoing and unhurried in the small Japanese market. It was one of those rare occasions when I heard their true voices without anxiety. Most of the time Mom was self-conscious of her heavily accented English. She spoke as little as possible when shopping in the stores at home. Often a young stock boy or an older clerk became wide eyed or was struck speechless by her accent, or they'd answer her loudly, as if she were deaf. If she couldn't find an ingredient, she'd often leave rather than ask for help.

My father didn't fare much better. If the butcher misunderstood him, Dad would take a cut of meat he didn't want, rather than attempt to clarify his request. But here, Dad and Mom were graceful and fluent, unobstructed by language, like seals, slow and cumbersome on land but fast and fluid in the water.

Soon Mom's cart was filled with *haruame* (spring rain) cellophane noodles used in sukiyaki, devil's tongue jelly for one-pot fish stew, a crackly bag of dried wood ear mushrooms, agar-agar (seaweed gelatin) to make tea sweets, packages of dried seaweed from prepackaged toasted strips, salted seaweed bits to put over rice and use in miso, and a raffia-encased drum of Japanese rice wine.

❁

The cooler was soon overflowing with seafood and other cold items. The knowledge of their presence put my parents at ease as Dad wove his way out of the city and onto the highway. The deep-blue sky and fading sunlight blinked in and out through the skyscrapers. As my brothers and I munched away loudly on our rice crackers, I had a hard time believing that we had arrived in the city just that morning.

We arrived back home after midnight. Mom and Dad stayed up well into the morning, unpacking the groceries from the green cooler. They took time to unwrap each kind of fish from the butcher paper and rewrap it in plastic wrap, and then in layers of aluminum foil to stave off freezer burn. Each packet was dated and labeled. The cooler was rinsed, wiped dry, and placed on the supply shelf in the basement, between the canning supplies and potting soil, ready for the next food-shopping excursion.

## Charred Whole Fish with Grated Daikon

*I love the clean taste of rainbow trout. In addition to cooking the fish under the broiler, there is a stove-top gadget you can find in Japanese hardware stores that clamps the fish between two metal screens, making it easy to cook over a stove-top flame. I always look for medium-size fish, about 10 inches long, and have never had any problems with undercooking.*

> 4 rainbow trout, gutted with heads and tails intact
> 1 daikon, grated
> zest of 1 lemon
> soy sauce

Turn on the broiler.

Place the fish on a foil-lined baking sheet. Place under the broiler until the fish begins to smoke and the skin chars and cracks. Flip the fish over and broil as instructed above. Remove from heat and place on serving dishes.

Place the grated daikon in a decorative bowl. Sprinkle lemon zest over the daikon. To eat the fish, add soy sauce and grated daikon directly onto the fish.

Serves 4.

Character Building

It was when I was nine that I began to take notice of my Mom's letter-writing ritual. Once a week, never on a particular day, but often an hour after I got home from school, she sat at the dining room table to compose letters to her female friends and family in Japan. Arranged in front of her were a stack of blue airmail stationery, a ballpoint pen, and a cup of green tea. While she wrote, she kept her head down and still. The ballpoint pen tip made a fast clicking sound when she pressed it against the paper as she raced to put down her thoughts.

Sometimes the clicking would stop for a stretch of time; I'd peek and catch her with her head raised, her eyes staring up at nothing, perhaps replaying a moment she was putting into words or recalling a memory.

She always seemed happier and lighter after her letter-writing. She would whistle while cooking dinner; she smiled more easily, the way women do after talking on the phone to a friend.

When correspondence arrived for her, she seldom ripped it open and read it immediately. Instead, she waited for a quiet moment, as if savoring an exquisite chocolate bonbon, before she carefully slit open the thin envelope with her antique sterling silver letter opener, spread the stationery out, and read each character with care and attention. These letters carried news from overseas about family deaths, births, marriages, lies, infidelities, divorce, and mental illness.

After reading the letters to herself, she'd read them aloud to Dad when he came home from work late at night. Dad had never met her friends and family members in person, but after a decade of hearing every detail of their existence, he must have felt as though he knew them all his life. Sometimes, if there were particularly exciting news, Mom shared the letters with me, too.

"Suzuki-san writes that she's buying a house," Mom told me one afternoon as I sat at the kitchen table doing my homework. She scanned the onionskin paper as if it held some secret inscription.

Before my mother left Tokyo in 1959, at the age of twenty-nine, Suzuki-san was her mountain-climbing companion. Their most memorable trip was a photography/mountaineering course they both enrolled in that took them high into the Japanese Alps. By day they hiked and took pictures of the moonscape terrain, and at night they gazed at stars the size of diamonds with carats in the double digits.

"Hmm . . ." Mom seemed to be looking for a clue. "That's how she wrote it. She's not married. How can afford to buy a house? Very expensive to buy a house in Japan."

Without the nuances and subtle signals exchanged in face-to-face conversation, it was difficult for Mom to decipher the meaning in some of the letters she received. She knew she wrote this way, too, wanting to divulge information the way she would in person, yet feeling restrained by the limitations of word on paper. Through the years, she developed the art of reading between the lines and picking up on the subtle cues in her letter-reading.

I could tell when a letter arrived from her closest friend, Oshima-san, by the way Mom's face lit up when she saw the return address. My favorite stories were the ones about their friendship. She and my mother met while working together at a bank in Tokyo. In the mid-1950s, the two went to Paul Anka and Neil Sedaka concerts and watched American movies such as *Giant* and a rerelease of *Gone with the Wind*.

There were times when Mom longed to pick up the phone and hear her family and friends' voices, but overseas phone calls were expensive and a luxury reserved for emergencies and special occasions such as New Year's Day. New Year's Day was a holiday we celebrated with the same importance with which my friends at school celebrated Christmas.

When my friends talked about the Christmas gifts they received, I didn't mention the presents I got from relatives in Tokyo that we opened on New Year's Day. In fact, I never told my friends that New Year's Day was a more important holiday for us than Christmas. I never mentioned or tried to explain the details and history of Oshogatsu (the three-day-long Japanese New Year celebration that consists of eating, drinking, and resting). I never told them that the Japanese New Year wasn't about counting down the seconds to midnight and singing "Auld Lang Syne."

Despite the secrecy I maintained around this time of year, I loved the Japanese New Year, which began with a soup of clear dashi (fish broth) with a couple of coin-size pieces of *mochi* that were consumed at breakfast. In Japanese tradition, a New Year meal without this glutinous, slightly sweet rice would be comparable to Thanksgiving without a turkey. It symbolizes good fortune and prosperity, and eating *mochi* is as essential a part of the New Year ritual as cleaning the karmic closet by visiting friends and bringing gifts to family.

As most of the people in Versailles slept in after a late night of partying, my family, still in our pajamas, bit into warm, gooey *mochi*, giving it a good pull away from our lips until it created strings like taffy.

An unbroken piece represented good luck for the rest of the year; if it snapped apart, bad luck. My family would laugh when the sticky rice broke in any one of our mouths. It was all in fun, but when it happened to me I couldn't help but fall for the superstition and try again with a second, bigger piece.

The significance of this holiday and its popular *mochi* grew more important to me as I got older, especially when Mom explained its role in her past. During her childhood, the days preceding New Year grew more and more festive; it was a busy time at her father's rice store. Large amounts of rice had to be made into *mochi* in a process called *mochi-tsuki*. Using over-size wooden mallets, my grandfather and his staff pounded the grains of rice in huge wooden mortars to the consistency of saltwater taffy.

Mom described being awakened by the thumping sound of the mallets hitting against the sticky rice and the grunt-ing of "*Yoisho! Yoisho!*" or heave-ho, as her father and his staff worked around the clock to fill all the *mochi-tsuki* orders.

Mom would make a special dinner for this holiday, part of which was served in three-tiered lacquered boxes called *jubako*. In Japan, Mom explained to me, the wooden boxes helped preserve the food that was made ahead of time so wives didn't have to cook during the holiday.

One box held chewy *gomame,* a sweet and salty combination of tiny dried sardines coated with a sweet glaze. Dad loved to eat them with sake or beer. The middle section held *inari-zushi,* deep-fried tofu pockets filled with vinegar-flavored rice. In the bottom box were *kampyo* (dried gourd strips) wrapped in a *maki-zushi* (roll sushi), alongside a rolled sweetened egg *maki* (roll) called *datemaki.* Before bedtime every New Year, we were allowed a bowl of rich, sweet *zenmai* (roasted *mochi* in red bean puree).

The grand finale of our New Year celebration was when Dad made calls to family in Japan. Because of the difference in time zones, it was one of the only occasions that my brothers and I were permitted to stay up late. By midnight, I'd become so sleepy that I'd rest my head on the dinner table, doing my best to keep my eyes open so as not to miss the important calls.

Dad would bring the phone to the table. Slowly, he'd dial the numbers, referring to the page in his battered black address book as if it were the first time he'd ever made a phone call. After the series of connecting clicks, Dad would yell into the phone, *"Moshi, moshi!"* (Hello! Hello!)

The connection was always bad, and my parents spent most of the five-minute call yelling into the phone, repeating the same things several times. Although brief and distorted with static, the calls were worth every minute to Mom, who always hung up last and beamed for days after hearing the voices of the people she loved who were half a world away. For the rest of the year she'd make do rereading the letters she kept in an empty Godiva chocolate box.

The more I guarded this secret of how my family celebrated New Year, the more sacred and precious it became to me. It was a part of my life I wasn't eager to share with the outside. I couldn't risk the chance that it might be tainted by ignorance. I had already learned from experience. Thus, the older I became, the more my naive desire to educate my friends dwindled. There had been other Japanese holidays that held meaning for my mother, which she transferred to me—such as Girl's Day, when old, fragile Japanese dolls, which were passed from generation to generation, were put on display in households. Foods with soft pastel hues, such as salmon and pink-tinted *mochi* with sweet red bean filling, were served to observe the holiday. As a young girl I had shared these traditions with my friends, thinking they would be awed by their uniqueness. Instead, I was met with furrowed brows saved for weirdos and outcasts. I quickly came to regret my openness. I didn't want my family's special holidays to be spoiled or made fun of because their meaning was lost on people who didn't understand them.

❊

One June morning when I was ten years old, Mom received a letter from the Cincinnati chapter of the Japanese American Citizens League, a civil rights organization. The letter announced that the league was organizing a chartered trip to Japan the following summer.

That summer marked almost fifteen years since Mom had last seen her family. During those years there never seemed to be a good time or enough money for her to go back. Plane tickets were too expensive, and my brothers and I were still too young to be left at home unsupervised. At the time, it was inconceivable for Dad to take off from work to visit Japan.

From the time I started elementary school, Mom started making extra money sewing and doing alterations in town, mostly for schoolteachers and women who worked at the courthouse. She put every cent she made into her savings account, keeping an eye on the amount as it grew in the hope that she'd be able to use it to return to her home country for a visit. By the time the Japanese American Citizens League trip rolled around, Keven would be fifteen, Alvin thirteen, and I would be eleven—old enough to have a neighbor check in on us in the evenings when Dad was at work.

Mom would be free to go to Tokyo and enjoy herself, but it was still a year away. There was still the current summer break to get through. My brothers and I had come to that awkward in-between age when entertaining ourselves during the summers was becoming increasingly difficult. There were no organized activities or day camps to go to, or even a public pool where we could cool off and hang out. The Versailles Lake, where we swam as toddlers, had grown polluted and algae-ridden and had been nicknamed Lake Urine. After swimmers, including Keven, contracted nose and ear infections, the beach was permanently closed.

Mom, like most of the mothers in the neighborhood, let her children run free. We had reached the age where she didn't care what we did as long as we stayed out of trouble and came home for lunch and dinner when called.

Some days I'd ride my bike under the white midafternoon sun to the town library. The two-room building was hushed, empty, and cool. I'd settle myself into one of the red, high-backed armchairs and read for hours before choosing the three books I was allowed to check out on my card. I'd often devour them in two days' time, even less during those long lazy summers.

It was during one of my visits to the library, not long after Mom got her letter about the trip, when I found a book about Japan in the modest international section. Though I don't remember the actual title of the book, I can still see the bamboo "oriental"-style print on the cover. Black-and-white 1950s photographs that depicted the life of a typical Japanese family fascinated me. The pictures were foreign, yet comforting and familiar at the same time. In some ways I felt a kinship, the way I would were I looking through old family albums; on the other hand, I looked upon them with the same curious interest I would have had I been looking at a book on the Amazon River's Yanomami tribe or matadors in Spain.

The Japanese family presented in the story sat in a small tatami room, a room lined with straw mats in which no shoes are allowed. Usually there is a low table around which people can sit on the tatami mats or on floor pillows. Pairs of zori (Japanese sandals) were aligned neatly outside the room's shoji sliding doors. The mother, father, daughter, and son wore traditional cotton *yukata* and sat on the floor around a low table. The father sat cross-legged, reading the paper. The mother concentrated on pouring tea into delicate cups, and her children studied.

Another picture showed the children leaving for school dressed in uniforms, with leather rucksacks hanging from their backs. Yet another showed how the family slept in a tatami mat room on thick futons, with roll pillows under their heads.

As I studied the book, I realized that I knew nothing about Japan except what Mom and Dad told us, what I saw in the magazines they traded among their friends or in movies such as Jerry Lewis's *Geisha Boy*, about a magician's high jinks when he goes to Tokyo to perform with the USO and befriends a little Japanese boy.

Although Mom had not said so, I knew that I would stay behind with Dad, Keven, and Alvin while she was away. It hadn't occurred to me before that day in the library that it should be any other way. But something changed in me as I sat there drinking in the visual details of that family's life. I felt a growing excitement in the pit of my stomach. I recognized this feeling as pride. It was at that moment that I became determined to accompany my mother to Japan.

When I got home, I decided to try to imitate what I had seen in the library book. I put on Dad's old green linen robe, one he never wore, and made an obi belt out of a burgundy silk scarf I found in the back of his dresser drawer. For *tabi*, the special white socks with a slot for the big toe, I wore a pair of white cotton socks and shoved my feet into a pair of red rubber flip-flops.

A lovely smell of cooked pork and ginger came from the kitchen as I preoccupied myself with my kimono. Mom had made our supper earlier, probably with the intent of keeping my brothers and me from mooching bites of her *nikuman*, bread dumplings with minced pork and vegetable filling. More snack than dinner, they not only were tasty and filling, but they resembled edible pouches with their twisted, pinched tops.

Mom sat alone at the dining room table as I pieced together my outfit. The aluminum steamer that contained the *nikuman* sat in front of her. This was one of the cooking tools included in her trunk of cooking equipment and ingredients. A haze of steam clouded her face when she lifted the lid. When I peeked in on her to see what she was doing, I watched as she used long Chinese chopsticks to lift out a tennis ball–size dumpling. Lately she had been eating more home-style Japanese dishes, such as *oyako donburi* (chicken and egg over rice), *okonomiyaki* (Japanese-style pizza), or ramen noodle soup. It didn't occur to me until I was older and developed an understanding for homesickness that perhaps the prospect of visiting Japan had heightened a yearning for certain foods.

Mom caught my gaze as she peeled the square of wax paper from the bottom of the dumpling. The paper prevented it from sticking to the metal pan. I liked to dress up, sometimes like a genie, other times like a cowgirl. She didn't say anything, but from her long glance I knew she was wondering what I was wearing.

I don't think she made the connection that I was pretending to wear a kimono until I took a cushion from the dining room chair next to where my mother sat and took it into the front room and began practicing kneeling at the coffee table. Mom, meanwhile, idly dipped the meat bun back and forth in a dark puddle of *wagarashi* (hot Japanese mustard) and soy sauce before sinking her teeth into the fluffy white exterior.

I managed to sit up straight on my knees for a few minutes before crumbling under the pain shooting up my calf. Mom, still eating, thrust her chin forward as oily juice dribbled from her mouth. The trail of juice signified that the dumpling was a good one, that inside the fluffy casing the meat filling had burst on the first bite like a cherry tomato. I heaved myself up, using the coffee table for leverage.

After she finished her dumpling, rather than reach for another, she wiped her chin daintily and set her chopsticks across her plate, an indication that she was finished for the time being. She walked over to the coffee table to show me how to correctly lower into and rise from the kneeling position. "I haven't sat like this in years," she told me, but she moved with grace and ease. Like a pipe cleaner, she bent her body down into a squat. Perching her weight lightly on the balls of her feet, she shifted her weight forward onto her knees, then neatly tucked her feet under her.

"With your feet like this it doesn't hurt so much, but you still need to practice sitting for as long as you can." She patted her lap and demurely folded her hands across it, the way someone who had done it thousands of times would do.

To rise, she reversed the motions, leaning her weight back on her knees, then pushing onto her feet.

I gave it another try, but my toes were numb and my ankles and calves felt as though they were being pricked with needles. Each day for a week, I dressed up in my kimono and practiced kneeling up and down and sitting on my knees for as long as I could bear.

Mom worked on her sewing while I practiced. I was hoping that if she saw how hard I was practicing, she would consider inviting me along on her trip. I'd learned from experience that if I came out and demanded what I wanted, Mom would immediately say no—a knee-jerk reaction she employed out of a belief that my brothers and I would become spoiled if she acquiesced. I didn't want to destroy my only chance of going to Japan, so I decided I wouldn't ask her directly, but would wait and hope that she would offer it if I behaved myself.

Seeing me in my rendition of a kimono inspired Mom to share a story about her father's love of collecting kimono material. After the war, when the only clothes they had were threadbare and material was hard to get, he made garments from the material he had stockpiled.

"In Japan, when young women graduate from high school, parents must buy their daughters a real silk kimono. It costs around ten thousand dollars!"

I couldn't imagine owning anything that expensive. Mom explained that a traditional kimono required several special undergarments, pads, and slips, and that the actual garment was basically composed of a contrasting lining that was worn beneath the thick outer layer and discreetly revealed itself only as the wearer walked. The waist was wrapped with an obi and a stay and sash to hold the belt in place—all made of the finest silk. A handbag, fan, hair ornaments, and the geta (wooden sandals) were also necessary accessories. Mom had two silk kimonos, an orange-and-gold one from her high school graduation, and a deep-purple one she had bought with money she earned while working at the Tokyo bank.

"Does this look like a real kimono?" I twirled around proudly in the living room.

Mom's eyes softened and her mouth scrunched up at the corner. "No, kimono is not a bathrobe."

I wanted to go to Japan with her so badly that I couldn't stop myself from blurting out, "Will you take me to Japan with you next year?"

"I'll think about it," Mom said with an amused smile.

The elation I felt was short lived. Mom didn't have to say so out loud for me to know that she could dangle the trip in front of me for an entire year, with her "I'll think about it" answer being swayed by how good I was that year. For several days things went well. I did everything as carefully as possible.

I couldn't have foreseen, however, that helping Dad make his yearly elderberry wine would jeopardize my seat on a plane to Tokyo. Yet not even a week after I had made a promise to myself to be on my very best behavior, I saw my chances evaporate on a particularly sticky summer weekend.

For the previous two summers, during what seemed to be the hottest weekend of the year, Dad had decided to recruit my brothers and me for the task of helping him make his wine. We had to don long-sleeved shirts, long pants tucked into our socks, and thick work gloves. He then sprinkled yellow sulfur powder, smelling of rotten eggs, around our shirt necklines, wrists, waistbands, and tops of our socks to thwart chiggers and ticks. This was the last thing we wanted to be doing on a scorching-hot weekend, but Dad insisted he needed all the hands he could get. For weeks before, he'd have monitored the rainfall and sun and would have taken periodic visits to check the size and plumpness of the elderberry patches until they were at their peak. That was what would determine elderberry-picking day.

It was arduous work. The elderberry patches were deep in thickets of wild sticker bushes, poison ivy, and bramble on the side of the county roads. I trudged through ditches that were havens for long-legged spiders, gray stinkbugs, and sausage-size tobacco caterpillars. After Dad clipped off the branches, we lifted them over our heads to ensure the berries didn't get jostled off. Since I was the shortest, tall nests of stickers tore at my clothes, face, and hair.

Dad didn't own a truck, so we used our station wagon, which he also used to cart off trash to the dump and cart in manure to fertilize the garden.

The work didn't end there. After dinner, we had to pull the berries from the sprigs. The ripe, deep-purple fruit didn't come off easily. Dad watched over our shoulders and critiqued our handiwork as we sat hunched over our baskets.

"Linda, too many still on. Keven, take your time. Go slower and you won't smash so many. I don't want rotten berries."

After a long day of searching, clipping, and pulling, Dad had what he wanted: five bushels of berries to produce five gallons of juice. On Sunday, Dad smashed the berries with a two-by-four wood plank and then strained the pulpy mixture through cheesecloth.

That evening, when Alvin and I found ourselves alone in the basement, we decided that we wanted to feel the juice and pulp through our fingers as we had watched Dad do. Alvin put his hand in the trash can full of juice.

"It feels squishy," he said with a laugh.

I reached down to feel the deep-purple thickness just as he jerked his hand out, splashing a large stain down the front of my new white sleeveless top that Mom had hand-appliquéd just days before.

I gasped in disbelief as I stared down at my shirt.

"Alvin, look what you did!" I glared at him. For one second the horror in his eyes matched mine, but then he broke out in a peal of laughter.

"Mom's going to kill you," he laughed, doubled over.

"You did this!" I screeched. "You have to help me!"

He responded to my plea with deaf ears and more laughter.

I snuck upstairs to my room, thinking I would first attempt to wash the stain out myself, but Mom caught me in the bathroom, trying to scrub the stain out with a bar of soap.

She grabbed the shirt from my soapy hand and opened it to reveal the Rorschach inkblot of a stain. She wore the same surprised look of someone opening a present, except the exclamation that followed was not one of happiness, but of pure anger. Her eyebrows arched straight up like the hump on a camel's back, her eyes widened, and her mouth opened into a perfect *O*.

"I just made this! This stain will never come out!" she shrieked. All I saw when I peeked up at her were the large whites of her eyes, like eggs cooked sunny-side up. The mirror and windows were steamed up from the hot water coming from the sink, but it felt as if it were her wrath encapsulating the tiny bathroom like a dragon's breath.

"This is why you're not going to Japan with me! This is why you won't get a kimono! You don't know how to take care or appreciate anything!" I didn't dare look up at her for fear that she would strike me. I glanced out the window, but it provided only a reflection against the darkness outside and I was forced to watch the image of my mother shaking the sopping wet blouse.

I wanted to tell her I'd take care of the kimono and that I was sorry, but I couldn't get the words past the guilt and the lump that had formed in my throat.

That night I couldn't sleep, knowing I had destroyed my chance of going to Japan. But I also knew that if Alvin hadn't ruined my shirt, something else would have happened. A whole year was an impossibly long time to behave perfectly. Still, I wanted to go so much that I resorted to saying a prayer. My parents weren't churchgoers themselves but decided early on that they wanted my brothers and me to be exposed to the community and spirituality of a local church. Mom and Dad insisted that we each go every Sunday until we were thirteen, after which point we could decide whether we wanted to continue attending. My current situation called for desperate measures, and appealing for divine intervention seemed like a last resort. It left my mind feeling pure and uncluttered, as if the whole situation were somehow out of my hands.

"Dear God," I prayed, "Mom's going to Japan next year and I want to go so badly. Please, please, please give me another chance. I promise I'll pray every night, and not only when I want something. Amen."

The next day, neither Mom nor I mentioned the previous night's scene, and we acted as if nothing had happened. Mom's volatile moods were like this, coming and going like summer cloudbursts that break with crashing thunder and bolts of lightning.

I didn't dare conjure those storm clouds by mentioning the Japan trip again. Mom had made up her mind and there was no changing it. She was stubborn that way. I still hadn't even been able to apologize or explain what had happened, but I didn't think that any of that would have mattered. Blaming my brothers was not a tactic that my parents appreciated, and so we learned to assume responsibility for the consequences of our actions at a young age.

I sulked around the house that afternoon. The air outside was still and hot like a sauna. I didn't feel motivated to ride my bike to the library.

With no place else to go, I went upstairs to the second floor. Since Keven had moved to a new bedroom off the basement, my parents had turned the open area he once occupied into storage for old clothes, a random coffee table, and hardcover and paperback books. Stacks of outdated *Better Homes and Gardens, Popular Mechanics, National Geographic,* and *Life* magazines lined the plywood bookshelves. The older issues were tied up with twine into tight bundles.

I peered across the room at the small window that glowed at the end of the unfurnished space. I didn't switch on the overhead lights. There was something comforting and soothing about the semidarkness and the soft smell of mothballs, plastic, and musty papers hanging in the air.

I sat down on the varnished hardwood floor, within reach of Mom's old sewing notebooks and embroidery books. I couldn't read any of them, as they were all written in Japanese characters, but I leafed through them anyway.

I then opened Mom's pattern books and found Japanese models with stylish pixie haircuts like Audrey Hepburn's in *Roman Holiday.* I was happy just flipping through the pages, not looking for anything in particular, just looking for anything that would catch my eye and allow my mind to wander for a little while.

Once I got bored with that, I caught a glimpse of something tucked between a copy of *Treasure Island* and a book on plumbing: two brown workbooks, one called *Learning Hiragana* and the other, *Learning Katakana.* Hiragana and katakana are the basic Japanese characters taught to children before they learn kanji, the multiple-stroke characters.

Uncle George had sent us the books after we had visited him in New York City. He had decided that since we kids were living out in the boondocks, as he put it, we needed to learn to read and write Japanese or we'd lose our Japanese identities. Despite his kind efforts, the books had been sitting, spines uncracked, for almost three years.

The issue of whether we should learn to read and write in Japanese had come up before, when I was much younger.

My parents were invited to dinner parties with other Japanese and Japanese American families living in Cincinnati. After one such dinner, the men sat around the den, watching a game on television, and the women gathered in the living room, warming their hands around small teacups, nibbling sugar cookies, and comparing which children spoke and read Japanese.

The discussion spurred a debate among the adults on the necessity of sending their children to the Japanese language school held every weekend in Cincinnati. I was playing hide-and-seek with the rest of the kids. Frantically searching for a place to hide, I had dashed through the living room when one of the older women pulled me aside. She asked if I spoke Japanese. Out of breath from running, I looked around at the other women, all looking at me expectantly, before I told her no. At the time, she was asking me this in Japanese. I was too young to explain that I understood Japanese but couldn't speak it.

I had seen this older woman several times before. She wore her short hair streaked with gray and white, like Cruella DeVille in the Disney movie *101 Dalmatians.* She had lived in Cincinnati longer than anyone at the party, but she spoke in a strong accent, as if she had arrived in America that very day.

Speaking to me in a stern tone in Japanese, she said that I should want to study Japanese. I looked around uncomfortably, pulling my arm away, not knowing whether I was in trouble.

Still holding onto me firmly, she continued along the same line of questions. Why didn't I study Japanese at the language school in Cincinnati? I had never thought about it. I knew that my brothers and I didn't go because it was a two-hour drive. She finally let go of my arm. I looked at Mom, who didn't seem at all affected by what she was saying. I didn't understand at the time that the woman was trying to make a point to her audience.

My parents spoke to me in Japanese, but I answered in English. I knew that some of the kids at the party went to the language school, but I had never heard them speak Japanese. I was about to answer that I didn't know when Mom finally intervened.

"Why does she need to speak Japanese?" Mom asked. She sounded cheerful, as though she hoped to take the edge off the tension.

The woman wore a sour look that pulled down the corners of her mouth like a sad clown's. "Because she is Japanese. It is important to keep our culture and language alive here in America."

Mother waved her hand and asked, "Why spend the time and money if she doesn't use it or isn't interested in learning it?"

"She may not appreciate it now, but later, when she's grown up, she will thank you," answered the woman. I looked back and forth between them. The hide-and-seek game disbanded as the other kids trickled into the living room to see what was going on. I didn't realize that Mom and the lady were talking about me as a stand-in for any one of the children, in whose interest all the adults were invested. I basked in the attention, having no idea of the broader implications of the conversation.

"I appreciate your opinion, and if you come and pick her up and take her to school, I will appreciate you all the more,"

Mom responded, making the other women snicker into their teacups. The old woman excused herself in a huff.

At the time, what Mom said about her children not wanting to learn Japanese was true, but as I sat there among the old books in my brother's old room, I suddenly did care. My hair was damp with sweat and stuck to my forehead and temples. I sat cross-legged on the floor, flipping through the pages of the workbook, studying the rows of Japanese characters. Some were soft and curvy, like slashes suspended in midair, while others were sharp and pronounced like fishing hooks. One character resembled an upside-down *4*, another, a fat *E* tilted on its side; still others looked like decorative *U*s and frilly *Z*s. A dozen empty squares, space for practicing, filled the pages beside each character. At the end of each chapter an exam was provided to test memorization skills. I recognized some of the characters from Mom's books. *Why not memorize the characters?* I wondered. What did I have to lose? I had the whole summer ahead of me.

The air upstairs felt unbearably hot, so I took the books downstairs to my room, where the air-conditioned coolness smelled like cucumbers and vanilla. I flopped on my bed and read the first chapter.

Mom peeked her head in to tell me that *General Hospital,* my favorite soap opera, was starting. I was memorizing the vowels, *A, I, E, O, U,* and filling in the blank blocks.

"That's good," she said, pointing to my *U,* a snazzy-looking half heart topped with a slash-styled hat.

I didn't have long-term plans for studying the characters, but each time I finished a chapter, I had learned five more characters. Characters formed words, and then words formed sentences.

It took me less than a month to memorize all forty-six of the hiragana characters. The more I studied and memorized, the more I read from some of the books Mom and Dad had. I learned to write my name in Japanese.

I read Mom's grocery list. *Bi-fu*, beef. *Pan*, bread. *Ka-re*, curry powder. I read the reminders she stuck onto the refrigerator. "Monday get dry cleaning," one note read. Unlike English, where all letters are from the twenty-six letters of the alphabet, written Japanese is a combination of hiragana, katakana, and kanji characters. It took me some time, but I got to the point where I could make out most of her writing. Because the kanji characters were more complex, I was able to skip over them but still understand the meanings of sentences, similar to the way I was able to skip over longer words when I learned to read English. Mom's handwriting, small deliberate chicken scratches, was fluid and distinctive like a fingerprint. My writing, done with the care and caution of a beginner, looked large, inflated, and jerky by comparison.

I progressed to reading the Japanese condiment labels on bottles that sat on the dining room table, short notes Mom left for Dad, and advertisements in her Japanese magazines. I loved the feeling that I was welcomed into a whole other world when I read Japanese.

A week or two after the school year started, Mom came into my room. Some days before, she had tested me on my memorization of the characters, using the same method that my teachers had used when I learned the multiplication tables in the third grade. Like a teacher, she had written an "A+" in red at the top of my notebook paper when she finished. As she perched on the edge of my bed, her eyes shone and she smiled. Feeling suspicious, I sat up as she fingered the ruffles on the edge of my bedspread. Mom never came into my room unless it was to put away my laundry, vacuum, or stand over me when I was in trouble.

"Dad and I talked about this and have decided that since you learned hiragana and katakana this summer, as a present I'll take you with me to Japan next year," she informed me.

I didn't know how to respond. I wanted to throw my arms around her, but I knew she wasn't the affectionate type, so I fought back the urge. Instead of doing anything, I just lay there, frozen.

"Well, aren't you happy?" Mom asked curtly, interpreting my reserved behavior as disinterest.

"Y-y-yes," I stammered. *I should have hugged her,* I thought to myself. "I mean, no, I'm happy. But I thought you said no was no."

Using the controlled, infuriatingly even voice I associated with the way teachers and ministers' wives spoke, she said simply, "I changed my mind."

Mom stood up. Before leaving, she added, "Remember, you're going because you studied. If you forget your characters, I may change my mind again."

A part of me refused to fully accept this reward. I had learned the hard way that Mom changed her mind on a whim, and I knew most certainly that I couldn't stay out of trouble for a whole year.

It was an unreasonably long time to be good, even though I wanted to go on the trip with all my heart. I gave Mom a weak smile. The characters I learned that summer stay with me to this day, but at the time all I considered was how impossibly long a year was.

## Steamed Buns with Meat Filling (Nikuman)

*These savory buns are surprisingly easy to make. Kids love them for breakfast and snacks. Don't hesitate to serve them as an impressive appetizer. Made ahead of time, the buns can be frozen. Microwave for 2 minutes, and it makes a quick lunch on the go, Shanghai-style.*

### Buns

2 teaspoons + ½ teaspoon rapid-rise yeast
1 teaspoon + 1 tablespoon sugar
1 tablespoon + 1½ cups all-purpose flour
¼ cup + ½ cup warm milk
1 tablespoon shortening
dash of salt

### Filling

½ pound ground pork
1 tablespoon soy sauce
1 tablespoon sake
dash of pepper
¼ teaspoon salt
1 tablespoon sesame oil
3–5 shiitake mushrooms, diced
1 tablespoon minced ginger
2 green onions, chopped
3 raw shrimp, shelled, deveined, and minced

## Dipping Sauce

1 tablespoon soy sauce
2 tablespoons rice vinegar
¼ teaspoon grated ginger

*For the buns:* In a small bowl combine 2 teaspoons yeast, 1 teaspoon sugar, 1 tablespoon flour, and ¼ cup milk. Mix well and let stand in a warm place for 20 minutes or until bubbles form at the surface.

In a large bowl, combine the remaining yeast, sugar, flour, shortening, and salt. Using the fingers of one hand, stir the dry mixture while gradually pouring in the contents of the small bowl and the remaining milk. Knead the mixture for about 2 minutes. Transfer the dough into a clean floured bowl; knead until the dough's surface appears smooth. Place in a bowl under a damp cloth. Place the bowl in a warm place and allow to rise 1–2 hours or until the dough has doubled in size.

*For the filling:* While the dough is rising, mix the ground pork, soy sauce, sake, pepper, salt, sesame oil, mushrooms, ginger, green onions, and shrimp for 5 minutes. Cover and refrigerate.

Remove the dough from the covered bowl and knead for 5 minutes on a floured board until the surface appears taut and smooth. Roll the dough into a cylinder about 2 inches in diameter. Cut the tube in half and each half into 6 pieces. Lightly dust each piece with flour. Keep the unused dough in the bowl under the damp cloth until ready to use.

Using a small rolling pin, roll the dough into 4-inch disks. The center should be slightly thicker than the outer edges. Place 2 tablespoons of filling in the center of the disk. To seal the top, gather 4 sides of the disk and then pinch and twist the ends together firmly. Set the buns on squares of wax paper or line a steamer with whole lettuce or napa cabbage leaves. Space the buns so they are not touching. Bring the water in the steamer to boil. Cook the buns in the steam 15–18 minutes, covered. Do not lift the steamer lid.

*For the dipping sauce:* Combine soy sauce, rice vinegar, and ginger.

Serve immediately with dipping sauce.

Makes 12 buns.

# Motherland

I was ten the summer Mom and I arrived at Haneda International Airport, about thirty minutes outside Tokyo. It was late evening and a storm had preceded us, leaving behind the clean aroma of rain and the sweet strong smell of petrol. The long flight had dried out my sinuses, and the jets' sudden sharp winding screech rattled my eardrums, already weary from the roar of the plane's engine. The airplane's artificial environment drained my senses in a way I'd never experienced before.

After passing through customs, Mom's eyes lit up and her face relaxed with relief as she recognized faces from the wall of strangers greeting us as we exited the terminal. There was a man with a similar smile to Mom's, and an old woman beside him. It was Mom's half brother, Takeo, and her stepmother, Obachan, which meant "grandmother" in Japanese. I didn't know this during most of my Tokyo stay. I assumed it was my step-grandmother's real name, since everyone referred to her as Grandmother the same way Dad called my mother Mom.

We walked parallel to them—they were on one side of the barricade and we were on the other—motioning to meet at the end of the crowd, four people deep, where it thinned out and where a few drivers were holding signs with the scrawled names of their passengers.

Even though the trip was intended as a reward for teaching myself hiragana and katakana, it had been a challenging year. A poor report card and mishaps with my brothers nearly jeopardized my travel plans.

"There are other people waiting to buy your airline ticket," Mom constantly threatened. Despite my wrongdoings, whenever I thought my chances were up, Mom would boost my morale by revealing her growing excitement. She'd sit down with me at the dining room table and jot down our itinerary and excitedly describe to me the people we would see.

Her travel fever was contagious. Eagerly, I'd lean forward, elbows on the edge of the table. I studied the days and activities she had written out in her scratchy handwriting and imagined what it would really be like. I had nothing to go on. Mom claimed that the books I had looked at in the library were outdated. "Those pictures are from the postwar," she told me. "The economy and lifestyle is more modern," she insisted.

❁

Standing there in the hubbub of the busy airport, I took that moment to acknowledge that I was finally in Tokyo. I didn't understand it fully, but even at that young age I knew that the visit that lay ahead of me would instill in me strength and pride in my ethnicity. *Remember all of this. Don't you forget any of it,* I told myself sternly.

During my visit, I had several moments of striking clarity. One of the most moving was seeing Mom meet her family for the first time after an absence a decade and a half long. Since she'd been away, her father had suffered and died of stomach cancer. When she last saw them, her sister, Akiko, half sister, Sachiko, and half brother, Takeo, wore high school uniforms. Now they were married with young children of their own. Takeo had taken over the family rice store. Mom's friends from her job at the bank were married, and some even had grandchildren.

Unlike Americans, who openly hug and kiss their families, my mother, her half brother, and stepmother never touched, just bowed very deeply many times.

I hadn't understood the nuances and meaning behind bowing until I saw my mother bow to her family. I had seen my parents bow when they met Japanese acquaintances for the first time. In public, it seemed hasty and fast. But there, in the middle of the airport, Mom held her bow low and deep. With her head down, I could hear her speaking in a slow, rhythmic, and formal Japanese, saying that a long time had passed since they had last seen each other. In the split-second pause with her head and eyes facing down, hands to the side, I could feel the closeness and familial love radiating from her, magnified by the years of separation.

Soon Uncle Takeo and Obachan bowed in front of me. I wished Mom had briefed me on how to do it properly. Although I wanted to stop, I self-consciously kept bending at the waist. The one thing I remember Mom telling me was that it was considered impolite to be the last one bowing, but I finally gave up trying to figure out how to come up at just the right time.

On the walk to Uncle Takeo's car and during the drive to Tokyo, Mom chatted nonstop. I had never seen Mom so exuberant and happy. She spoke in rapid-fire Japanese in such an unabashed way that I had to look over at her to make sure she was my mother. At that age I wasn't interested in grown-up conversation and couldn't speak Japanese fluently enough to keep up. But on our way into Tokyo that first day, I listened as if seeing my mother for the first time, straining to understand as much as I could.

During the next days, I would see a side of Mom's demeanor that I had never witnessed at home. At home, she was constantly alert, like a skittish doe in an unfamiliar meadow. Her bearing was rigid and angular, as if she were bracing herself for some unknown impact. Upon arriving in Tokyo, her harsh exterior melted, leaving a state of total relaxation and giddy happiness that bloomed more each day, the more settled she became into all that was familiar—her family, the house, food, culture, and emotional support.

This was my first experience with how loaded and emotionally charged "coming home" can actually be. I would gain a greater understanding of these emotions when I returned to Versailles after working and living away from my parents, and learned how returning to the place of my childhood brought my past and present full circle.

That evening in the car on the way into the city from the airport, I was aware of every move and listened closely to gauge every conversation. In the rearview mirror, I watched as Uncle Takeo's head turned to the side to comment on what Mom was saying. Obachan, petite and smallboned, her arms and legs folded in her seat as if it were a chair, nodded, grunted, and occasionally hawed, her way of laughing, at what was said.

It was a touching scene made even more surreal by the fact that they were talking with the type of familiarity and ease I would have expected if Mom had been gone for only a long weekend, rather than years.

Obachan was in her late sixties. I felt drawn to her as my elder. Her brown eyes sparkled with wisdom, and I wondered what miracles and atrocities they had witnessed. Sitting between her and Mom, I would have never imagined the time I would come to spend with Obachan during my visit, or the influence that visit would have on me then and in the years to come. All I was aware of was her welcoming smile.

Obachan caught me staring at her and looked directly into my eyes and asked in Japanese if I was hungry.

"Not too hungry," I replied in English. At this, her eyes grew big. Her jaw dropped open.

It was second nature to answer questions addressed to me in Japanese in English, as I always did with my parents. "Ahh!" she exclaimed. Her face expanded into a smile.

She nodded her head. Mom laughed at Obachan's reaction to my English and told her stepmother how I had suffered a bout of airsickness in the plane when we experienced severe turbulence passing over the Pacific. I looked away, embarrassed that Mom had told her this.

I felt better when Obachan clucked deep in her throat and gently muttered *"kawai soni,"* the Japanese equivalent of "poor thing." She dug into her silk drawstring bag until she found a small sack of natural mint candy.

She held one out to me, saying it would soothe my stomach. Obachan's face was long, and the skin sagged and wrinkled like an elephant's. The elasticity of it amazed me, how it stretched up and across her face when she smiled, then down like a deflated balloon. Her eyes danced like two glass beads in the sunlight. All these features were further exaggerated by her shock of short white hair, so coarse that her two-inch-long strands stood up on their own after brushing.

I took this all in as the white, sugar-crusted candy dissolved in my mouth. The residual queasy sourness I still felt after getting off the plane finally subsided. Long after my stomachache, I sucked on those refreshing lozenges during my stay in Tokyo. For years afterward, Obachan would send me a bag with every New Year package.

As we sped along the highway, billboards and signs flashed large red, blue, yellow, and green neon Japanese characters. From my vantage point they were like long streamers of liquid color, made bolder against the solid wall of darkness of the buildings they were mounted on. The excitement of our arrival wore off as the fatigue of jet lag set in.

I was so intent on listening and paying attention that I was surprised to see that I had dozed off. I woke up to the bright streetlights of the city. Mom talked on as Uncle Takeo steered us around the hairpin curves of the narrow streets, shiny and spotless like polished silver.

Uncle Takeo parked along the street in front of the rice store, where, like in the other neighborhoods we had passed, the majority of structures were one- and two-story buildings housing mom-and-pop businesses.

Once we were out of the car, I followed him down a narrow corridor between two buildings. Mom and Obachan walked slowly behind as Obachan elaborated on neighbors and businesses that had come and gone since Mom's departure. A light in the entryway flicked on and the front door swung open. All of Mom's immediate family crowded the doorway. One woman looked just like Mom, only with much paler skin and a rounder face. It was her sister, Akiko. I recognized two of the other women from photos, too: Mom's pretty half sister, Sachiko, and Uncle Takeo's wife, Eiko, who had a wide nose and a square face.

"Come in, come in," my aunts beckoned me in Japanese. As I stepped out of the entryway and into the foyer, Aunt Akiko and Obachan both gasped and rushed forward. I froze in place.

The entire group of them were yelling, waving their hands, wildly pointing toward my feet as if they were on fire. I was embarrassed to realize that I was about to step up without removing my shoes. Their nervousness turned to laughter and sighs of relief when I slipped out of my shoes and into the entryway.

Inside there was more bowing and questions. It was past midnight, and Uncle Takeo excused himself to go to bed. He had to make rice deliveries to restaurants in the early morning and wanted to get a few hours of sleep.

It was afternoon back in Indiana, and Mom and I were like roosters at the crack of dawn. Suddenly I was wide awake and sleeping was the last thing on my mind. Obachan, a night owl, gave us a tour of the store and house.

Mom knew the layout of the house she had grown up in. The building had undergone renovations and additions through the years, but it still possessed the unique character-istics of pre–World War II Japanese architecture: the exposed ceiling beams, the fragrant dark-wood detailing, the tatami floors, and sliding doors paneled with silk cloth or thick rice paper. These features whispered of the past, contrasting with the microwave atop the refrigerator and the washer and dryer.

As we entered each room, Mom stared at all the details as if seeing them for the very first time. Obachan talked and pointed out the changes that had been made since Mom was there last. Mom absently nodded her head in a way that told me her mind was preoccupied.

At the time we couldn't have known that five short years after our visit, many of the traditional Japanese homes and charming rustic storefronts such as my uncle's would be razed by modernization. Skyscrapers and condominiums would replace these structures across Tokyo's urban terrain like tenacious dandelion weeds. Even my Uncle Takeo would tear down the antiquated wood and paper facade of the family rice store and build a modern concrete-and-glass storefront and condominiums above the store.

In the wood corridors we wore slippers, which were removed and left outside the tatami room before we entered. Obachan and Mom moved easily in and out of the house shoes without looking down or disrupting their conversation. I stumbled around in a large adult pair until I finally gave up and walked around in my bare feet.

Obachan led us through a small room with a TV, which led to the rice store. The entrance was a glass and aluminum sliding door, which she opened and beckoned us through, leading down into pitch blackness. She muttered to herself as her arm disappeared into the dark room. I heard her scratch the walls for the light switch before the fluorescent overhead bulbs stuttered on.

The rice store was a finished concrete space, divided by a metal counter and a small refrigerator with a glass door, displaying canned soft drinks and beer. At the back of the cash register stood a rack of colorful plastic bags: salty snacks such as dried cuttlefish, rice cracker mixes, and dried salted plums. They reminded me of the Slim Jims and salted cashews sold at the grain co-op back home.

Along the back wall stood a tall machine with a huge metal cone used to funnel grains into empty sacks of rice. On the walls were soda ads of pretty-in-pink teenage pop singers with protruding eyeteeth smiles, the Japanese epitome of cuteness.

So many things caught my eye, and I felt proud that this was my family's business.

Before switching the lights off, Obachan pointed out the newly purchased electric cash register. When a purchase got too complicated, she said, she still used the abacus.

After we exited the store, she locked the door and gave it a good tug to make sure it was locked.

As Mom and I waited for Obachan to secure the store, I looked around the dining room. Appliances were stacked in unusual places. A washer and dryer unit stood in the hallway. Crowded inside the room were a dinner table for six, a refrigerator, and a glass dish cabinet. A microwave sat on top of the refrigerator. A coffeemaker, toaster oven, and blender sat on top of the dish cabinet.

I did my best to wear a neutral expression as Obachan showed us around. I was surprised by how small, cluttered, and cramped the house was. The belongings of a household of three generations seemed to be displayed out in the open. There appeared to be little storage; clothing was stacked in big, clunky armoires that dominated the tatami rooms. The kitchen resembled the galley of a small sailboat. Obachan bid us *owane-suminesai*, good night, as we headed to an apartment in another wing of the building. It was one of two that Uncle Takeo rented out to college students. It consisted of a living area tatami room smaller than my bedroom, a blue-tiled squat toilet in a phone booth–size closet, and a doll-size kitchenette.

Although Obachan couldn't have understood me anyway, I waited until we were in the privacy of our own room to tell Mom how I couldn't imagine living in their house, a place so small and confining.

Even the big American suitcases we brought dwarfed the room. As she unpacked our clothes, Mom told me the tatami room served as the living room, bedroom, dining room, and study all in one. In fact, she continued, this apartment, with its private toilet and kitchen, was only a block from the subway line and walking distance to Tokyo University, so it was a great find for students.

"But where do the people take their baths?" I asked.

"Down the street at the public bathhouse," she answered, as if it were obvious. I didn't know this was a common practice in Japan and that the bathhouses were clean, large, and comfortable. The only thing that came to my mind were the dirty, insect-ridden stalls I associated with shower rooms at public pools back home.

Fortunately, we would be using the family bathroom in the main part of the house. I had expected the same style of shallow tub I bathed in back home, where I could lie down but had to squat as low as possible to submerge myself in water. So I was pleasantly surprised to see a deep, white square tub the size and depth of a Jacuzzi.

Joining me, my mother showed me the ritual of Japanese bathing. First, she instructed me to pour some of the bathwater over myself with a wooden scoop that had a long handle on the end. The water felt scalding hot, but I gingerly lifted a leg into the heated tub, as if climbing over a fence. I inched my body in little by little, getting accustomed to the heat and the depth, and sat on a built-in ledge that submerged me up to my chin. Mom enjoyed a hot bath and stepped into the tub without pause.

We soaked in silence together for a while. Mom then explained how washing outside the tub kept the water inside the tub clean, saving time and water because the tub didn't have to be refilled every time a person bathed. She motioned for me to climb out of the tub and sit on the low plastic stool sitting right next to the rim. There she scrubbed me with soap lathered on a long terry-cloth towel.

Using the long-handled scoop to rinse myself off, I climbed back in for a final soak while Mom repeated the cleaning ritual on herself. Once again sitting next to me in the tub, she leaned her head back from her own position on the side of the bath, closed her eyes, and gave a long relaxed sigh.

As long as I can remember, both my parents, no matter how busy their schedules, always found time to take a leisurely bath at the end of their day. It would take me years after my trip to Japan to understand that the Japanese bath I experienced during my trip wasn't about getting clean. I learned later that the public bathhouses and hot springs were a social gathering of friends, families, and neighbors before plumbing made it a private luxury.

As an adult, I would pursue my own Western style of bathing with bubbles, salts, and beads, which Dad jokingly disparaged, saying that a bath should be taken only in clean, hot water. He explained how in Japan, the act of disrobing symbolized leaving the associations of daily life behind and the water represented purification. All this culminated in a state of relaxation and contemplation.

When I was finished with my bath, Mom replaced the tub's plastic top to retain its heat for the next bather.

In our small room, the soft drumming of rainfall and the familiar green smell, combined with the warm bath and jet lag, made me stumble with sleepiness and fatigue.

I couldn't wait to crawl between the covers of our bed, but there were no beds in our room. I was about to ask Mom about this when she opened a tall sliding door and pulled out two thick cotton futons, a couple of lightweight blankets, and small bolster-style neck pillows.

A cool fresh breeze blew through the room. In the distance I heard the haunting sound of wind chimes as I was about to tell Mom I was happy to be there. I pulled the blanket up to my ears instead and fell asleep.

❋

I awoke to the sound of crackling paper and Mom's back to me as she rummaged through one of the suitcases.

"I've spent more money on *omiyage* (gifts or souvenirs from where one has been) than on the airplane tickets for both of us," Mom mumbled to herself. Before the trip, Mom insisted that she couldn't bring back anything but the very best. The art of Japanese gift-giving is still a complex, expensive part of the culture in which the quality of the gift signifies the giver's respect toward the receiver. Anything less would be viewed as cheapness on her part. She bought Coach handbags, Chanel No. 5, and Godiva chocolates for her sisters. For her half brother, Rémy Martin cognac, Levi's blue jeans, Marlboro Reds, and an eelskin wallet. Because Mom was afraid she might overlook someone, such as a friend's husband, she bought several cartons of American cigarettes and three bottles of Johnnie Walker Black at the duty-free shops. These were viewed as gifts that showed some status.

Downstairs in the dining room, over a Japanese breakfast of miso soup, steamed white rice, leftover meat from the evening before, and green salad with a curl of Kewpie brand mayonnaise, Mom gave out the gifts she had brought.

Sitting around the table proved to be the best time to study my relatives unnoticed. Uncle Takeo was a handsome man. He had pronounced cheekbones and upturned eyes. His thick blue-black hair was like a bunch of jagged exclamation points that he tried to control with strong-smelling hair tonic, which only gave it a shiny, spiky appearance.

He and Aunt Eiko had been married by arrangement two years earlier. She possessed a young girl's charm with her shoulder-length wavy hair tied in stubby pigtails and her girlish way of giggling when nervous and happy. She wasn't long-limbed and willowy, like most Tokyo women, but big-boned and strong. She and Uncle Takeo had a baby girl named Nao-chan, who gurgled and pounded her tiny fists against Eiko's chest like a *taiko* drum.

During the first week of our trip, Mom reacquainted herself with her home city. Most days, we left the house mid-morning and met one of her former work and school friends for lunch. Other afternoons we shopped at department stores where bowing greeters stood dressed in pastel-pink suits, matching pillbox hats, and short white gloves, and where elevator girls pushed the buttons and announced the wares on each floor.

The basements of Tokyo department stores were devoted to foodstuffs that included pickled vegetables, rice crackers, grilled seafood, fancy tea ceremony sweets, and rice balls made with all types of fillings, such as pickled vegetables, different kinds of fish, and pickled plums. Gorgeous French pastries resembling oversize pieces of costume jewelry were displayed in lighted glass cases.

For *omiyage* (gift-giving) there were fancy rice crackers and dainty cookies, each individually wrapped in simple plastic, or in a covering as fancy as handmade paper and then stored in an elegant canister. Dozens of types of preserved seaweed glistened from wooden buckets. Even common household items such as soaps were displayed in decorative boxes as though they were expensive imported chocolates.

I was overwhelmed by the variety and the different items to look at, smell, and taste. The people who gave out food samples were dressed in elaborate costumes and occupied each corner as they plied customers with trays of samples. A Napoléon Bonaparte lookalike brushed baguettes with goose-liver spread, and a woman in a full kimono offered fish pickled in rice-bran mash. It was an unforgettable sensual food carnival that left my stomach full and my head spinning with the choices.

One afternoon, on the way to an old friend's house, Mom showed me the bank where she worked before coming to the United States. It was a typical staid financial building with a spiraling ceiling, marble floors in the lobby, ornate iron grid details around the stairwell, and decorative wall sconces on the ceiling.

Mom had tallied corporate accounts when she worked there, counting millions of yen. They didn't have electronic calculators at the time, so she used a yard-long abacus. I was familiar with the shorter one she used at home for the household accounts, her fingers flying like a concert pianist's.

Looking over at Mom in her stylish short haircut, white linen sheath dress, and white Capri sandals, it was hard to envision her hunched over an abacus with stacks of currency around her. At times, walking together, I saw a flash of the independent single working woman she had been before moving to America and marrying Dad.

If we walked down a quiet lane or busy thoroughfare, Mom retraced her old steps and described what she remembered, such as the ringing bells that once alerted neighborhood housewives to the approaching knife-sharpening vendor, or the location of a favorite *oden* (pieces of fish, fish cake, and vegetables simmered in broth) restaurant or a traditional stationery store. Sometimes she became bewildered, and she scratched her head and looked up at the street names and signs, searching for a store or business that no longer stood where she remembered. She would try to hide her disappointment, but I knew she thought that Tokyo wasn't the same city she had left years ago, and that she might feel as if she had missed the changes while she had been away.

We spent our days exploring, visiting, and shopping, and we'd ride the subway back to the house in time for dinner with the family. We'd exit at the Hakusan subway station and retrace the very steps she'd taken when she lived at the house where we were now just visitors.

I enjoyed joining the crowd of people on their way home. In step with the pace of the commuters, I could almost convince myself I too lived there. The transportation system, the network of subways, trains, and buses, had grown vastly since Mom rode it fifteen years earlier, its lines spreading across the city like ivy, and she was relieved to find it was more clean, fast, and efficient than she remembered.

Dinner would be waiting for us back at the house, but there were a few times when we didn't have the willpower to ignore the smoky fragrance as we passed the yakitori seller. Skewers of juicy chicken meat and slightly charred green onions were lined up side by side over the red embers of a makeshift hibachi. One evening, we bought a couple of skewers to eat on the way home, our stomachs growling.

"Every day after work, vendors set up stands selling all types of food outside the subway, not just yakitori," said Mom. "Some sold grilled sticky rice or fish balls. When I was your age, I bought sweet pastries before supper. I was a picky eater at that time and got away with not finishing my supper. Father never figured out that I had already eaten sweets," she said with a conspiring twinkle in her eyes.

In all of my ten years, I never felt as happy as I did that evening, strolling along the busy sidewalk, pulling tender chicken nuggets and sweet green onions off bamboo sticks with my mother, our heads turned sideways and forward to prevent the juices from staining our clothes. My mother and I were close, but we had never spent this much time together. At home, my life revolved around school and friends, while my mother's life revolved around Dad, the housework and cooking, and taking care of my brothers and me. There in Tokyo, it was just the two of us. I languished in the way she confided in me like a girlfriend. She was sharing her city with me, and I knew that in many ways she was seeing it anew through my eyes.

As we finished our savory snack on the last block before we reached home, we stopped at a small Shinto temple. It was slightly bigger than a hall closet and tucked away from the main street.

We had passed it many times, but this particular time the lush greenery amid the seamless, stark gray concrete drew me in. I had seen elevators bigger than the plot of land the temple stood on, but in it were the same religious symbols as the large ones we had seen in other neighborhoods. We stepped past the *komainu*, a pair of dog statue guards, and through the entrance-way of red painted *torii*, an unadorned gateway topped with two bars that symbolized entrance onto sacred ground.

As a sign of respect and cleanliness, we washed our hands at the small fountain before entering the temple. On a bam-boo wall, a battalion of moss-covered stone deities banished the world outside. I thought it was strange that the Shinto statuettes were dressed in miniature hats and capes made of red cloth like dolls. Mom whispered that this temple had been here as long as she could remember.

Strung between the temple columns were *shimenawa*, rice straw ropes plaited with white paper, used, it was said, to keep out impurities, both spiritual and solid. To this day, priests wave wands of this rope in purification rituals to bless new property, such as a home, an office, or a car.

I inspected a wooden board lined with pegs upon which were hung index card–size panels of wood with handwritten messages. Mom said people came to these shrines mostly for superstitious reasons and to have wishes granted—to get good examination grades, good jobs, a rich spouse, or good health.

The smoke from the incense urns hung motionless in the humid air. The worshippers who preceded us, an elderly couple, must have requested complex wishes, as joss sticks—usually lit one stick at a time—smoldered in fat bundles.

I knew Mom had a superstitious streak, but I never knew how much so until she gently pulled me into the thick of the smoke. I covered my mouth with my hand and closed my eyes as she fanned the smoke on me. She believed it held protective powers.

Before we left, she threw a coin into the offering box, bowed deeply two times, clapped her hands twice, then bowed deeply again and said a short prayer. I did the same, though I didn't know the meaning behind what I was doing. I watched Mom with fascination. I had never seen her pray before, even though she and Dad insisted I attend Sunday school until I was thirteen.

I mimicked what she was doing, sneaking glances as she prayed. She tucked her head deep into her hands held in prayer position, her eyes closed tightly. I wondered what she was praying so intently about. I know now that she was connecting to her spirituality in this place, this country where she grew up.

She lifted her head and opened her eyes, looking refreshed, as if she had taken a long nap. Smiling, she said to me, "Let's go home."

❁

At the start of our second week, we rode one of the sleek, blue-and-white, high-speed bullet trains, whose clean futuristic lines resembled something out of a science-fiction movie. Our destination was Hakone, a resort town famous for its hot spring baths. Before we left the station we bought *obento* (flat boxed lunches) and cold drinks sold at food kiosks on the train station platform.

As the bullet train zipped silently past the bucolic countryside at 125 miles an hour, I nibbled from the lunch box set on my lap like an open book. There were six small sections in the *bento* box, each one as eye-catching and flavorful as the next.

I didn't know which I liked the most, the salty grilled salmon surrounded by pickled gingers in a spectrum of reds and pinks; a salad of cellophane noodles, wakame (seaweed), cucumbers, and shiitake mushroom; or the braised green onion and rare beef rolled in *tamagoyaki* (thin Japanese-style omelet) and tied with a band of nori.

The train pulled into Hakone station at midafternoon, the perfect time for a bath, Mom told me with a mischievous smile, as if we were about to do something decadent. Oshima-san, Mom's old friend from the days she worked at the bank, met us at the *ryokan*, the traditional Japanese inn where we would stay. She was funny, enthusiastic, and always up for travel, ski-ing, hiking, or shopping, according to Mom. Her dazzling gold tooth shone with the brilliance of sun reflecting off water.

Tucked in a lush valley surrounded by picturesque rock formations, groves of trees, and rolling hills, the *ryokan* was in the traditional tatami style, with no Western furnishings. Mom told me that people from the city came here to soak in the famous therapeutic volcanic hot springs and enjoy *kaiseki*, the multicourse Japanese dinner with seasonal ingredients and intricate presentation of regional ingredients.

After we settled in our room, we put on blue-and-white cotton *yukata* robes (a light, cool kimono worn in summer) patterned with the clan insignia of the hotel and light wooden geta (wooden sandals). The sandals made cheerful *clop-clop* noises as we headed for the hot-spring pool. I didn't understand why my mother and Oshima-san, who by now were laughing and joking loudly, were excited about taking a bath, but I was happy that they wanted me to come along.

The bath area felt like the open outdoors, even though it was inside. Surrounded by slate and built into the ground, the shallow tub was as large as a swimming pool. Nude women sat in the tub or leaned back against the wall, using their hand towels as headrests. Open stalls ran along one wall, each with a mirror, a small wooden stool, a spigot with a separate handle for hot and cold, a metal basin, and a cake of soap where women washed and rinsed.

Suddenly I felt very self-conscious. Mom told me that if I was shy, I could hold my long washcloth in front of me.

Mom sometimes forgot that I understood Japanese. I overheard her say to Oshima-san, "Why is she embarrassed? She's just a child."

Oshima-san chuckled and said, "She's getting to that age now." Mom sighed at her friend's observation. Oshima-san had a daughter about to graduate from high school.

In my first week staying with my family in Tokyo, I'd gotten the hang of taking baths Japanese-style. Here at the *ryokan* I took my time and went through the relaxing motions of the ritual bath. Like the other women, I washed and soaked and got out to cool down and sunk back into the pool to warm up.

By the time we returned to our room, it was early evening; we were still in our cotton *yukatas*. Maids had opened the doors to a simple porch that overlooked a wooded area. Sunshine streamed through the plumage of leaves and branches and made brilliant patterns of light that flickered and twinkled at the whimsy of the breezes. Like a musical box, water gurgled from a nearby stream. Oshima-san brought out a package wrapped in a blush pink and red *furoshiki* (decorative cloth) and handed it to me. I untied the knotted silk and spread out the cloth. Inside was a stiff cotton *yukata*. It was so beautiful that I sat there speechless, staring at the oversize pattern of red, orange, and yellow zinnias. A matching red obi (sash) made of spun silk and pair of natural wood geta (wooden sandals) with a red velvet cord for toes completed the outfit.

As I tried on the *yukata*, Mom and Oshima-san, with damp hair that framed their flushed faces, fussed with the drape of the kimono and tugged and straightened the line of the fabric before winding me in the obi.

I looked at myself in the floor-length mirror, turning in different directions so I could see the full effect. This was the kimono I had dreamed of. I would no longer have to pretend by wearing Dad's old bathrobe.

I saw love in Mom's eyes when she looked at me, and a touch of bittersweetness, perhaps a longing to have shared a similar experience with her mother before she died.

Wearing my kimono, I sat on the floor the way I had practiced for a year. I sipped orange soda and fanned myself with the sandalwood-scented paper fans. Since arriving in Japan, I had felt total freedom and none of the doubt and hesitancy I often experienced at home. It was like visiting an opposite world, where forks weren't available at restaurants and I would get odd looks when I spoke English in public.

But I wasn't yet mature enough to truly appreciate the aesthetics of my surroundings. I spent that evening with my mother and Oshima-san waiting for something to happen, as opposed to enjoying the moment, something that Mom and Oshima-san had clearly mastered.

I didn't gaze long enough at the color of the leaves or the shade of the sky as the sun verged on setting. Instead I watched the changing expressions on Mom and her friend's faces, the long, comfortable pauses in their conversation, their state of relaxation after the bath, and the glow on their cheeks from small glasses of beer they sipped as I drank my soda.

"*Shitsureshimasu,* excuse me," chirped a woman who slid open the door. She wore a shimmering gold brocade kimono and a stunning obi with tangerine-orange and bamboo-green swirls. In an elaborate series of motions, she set a lacquered tray of drinks on the floor outside, stood up, entered the room, knelt down next to the tray, and slid the door closed. Then she picked up the tray and brought it to our table.

In her spotless white *tabi* (socks), she moved about noiselessly except for the soft rustling of her kimono. This would be the first of many deliveries she would make throughout the evening. My mother had informed me that we would be eating up to seven different courses in our room that night. Every time the waitress entered was a seamless and effortless event, although the ritual of the food serving was quite elaborate.

Through smiling lips, the waitress spoke in a cheery, high-pitched voice Mom described later as talking out of the top of her head.

When she entered, Mom and Oshima-san drew their legs up, folding them to the side in a comfortable position. This was much less rigid than sitting on their knees with the lines of their *yukata* straight. Because they were in a private guest room, they could sit as they chose, having to assume respectful decorum only in the presence of their server. The waitress refilled their glasses with beer, gracefully using one hand, lifting her draping sleeve with the other as if she were pushing aside a curtain.

I attempted to sit Japanese-style as well, but jolts of pain shot up my ankles, forcing me to spring out of the position. This proved to cause even more cramping. The waitress waited patiently, smiled, and unsuccessfully suppressed a laugh.

Wincing, I exclaimed to Mom, "I can't get up; it hurts too much!"

The waitress's eyebrow rose in surprise at my English while Mom related to Oshima-san the concern I had shared with her earlier, after the bath, about the seven courses we were going to be served that night. The waitress and Oshima-san laughed.

"No, I said it was too much food, not that I couldn't eat it," I corrected Mom, feeling annoyed the way young girls do when their mothers treat them like children in public.

Imitating a reprimanded child, Mom puffed out her cheeks comically and widened her eyes before translating my response to the other women.

*"Anata wa kawai desu ne!"* (You are so cute!) The waitress grinned broadly behind her hand. Whenever a Japanese woman broke out in laughter or smiled larger than the controlled small smiles, her hand shot up to cover her mouth. Mom did this a lot during our visit, even though at home she laughed without awareness, often with her mouth wide open, and sometimes even slapped her knee.

The waitress asked Mom why I didn't speak Japanese. I sipped my orange drink as Mom explained that I spoke very little Japanese because we lived in America. Mom explained this to almost everyone we met. Sometimes people would ask on the subway or bus if they overheard our English conversation. They often remarked how strange it was for someone who looked so Japanese not to speak the language.

Looking directly into my eyes, the waitress said in Japanese that formal *kaiseki* can have as many as twelve courses. "She does understand," the waitress said, impressed when I replied "Really?" in Japanese.

At this, enunciating each word, she continued in Japanese, "*Kaiseki* is special food, *ne*. You will notice the food is beautiful." The waitress said "bu-ti-fu-lu" in English.

"Ah, do you know what *kaiseki* means?" She glanced at Mom, who shook her head no on my behalf.

"*Kai* means 'pocket' and *seki* means 'stone.' It is said that Buddhist priests in training tucked warm stones in their kimono pockets and rested them on their stomachs, which would ease their fasting. Originally, *kaiseki* was part of the tea ceremony ritual, where only priests and the very wealthy indulged. Now everyone can enjoy it. This is good, *ne?*"

Gracefully but firmly waving her hand at Mom and Oshima-san as if directing traffic, she said to me in a soft voice as clear as a trickling stream, "They have learned about *kaiseki* at a younger age than you, *ne*. Study your mother and aunty, *ne;* they will show you what to do."

The shoji doors opened and three waitresses entered, each holding a black lacquered tray with covered bowls of *misoshiru* (miso soup with small cubes of tofu) and a bowl of rice that would last us throughout the meal.

A waitress took what looked like a tablespoon of sake from a small-handled pot and poured it into a small cup. I knew Mom didn't like sake, but she respectfully held the cup with both hands and bowed politely to the waitress.

I was eager to start on my rice and miso soup, but I heeded the waitress's suggestion to follow Mom and Oshima-san. The waitresses brought more covered trays. They opened each one and presented it as if the dishes were the finest of their kind. With subtle expertise, our waitress showed us small white porcelain bowls containing shredded tofu skin, two trimmed asparagus spears, and a lacy tangle of daikon.

Solemnly, Mom and Oshima-san brought the steaming soup to their noses, inhaled, eyes directed upward, pondered the sources of its fragrance, and took a drink. They spent a few minutes discussing the vegetables' freshness and brightness before they finally began eating.

A small platter held snapper, yellowtail, squid, and *amaebi* (sweet raw shrimp) sashimi garnished with more tangled daikon. Next to it was a salad of squiggly wakame (sea kelp) arranged like an aquatic still life. A beige wooden bowl, one side painted with a striking black brushstroke, held a clear fish broth with one clamshell at the bottom. On its surface floated a delicate *sansho* leaf, reminding me of leaves floating down the creek in the woods near my house.

The food wasn't the only object of Mom and Oshima-san's attention, though. They also examined and appreciated each vessel. Oshima-san picked up a ceramic plate holding chilled wilted spinach and bright parboiled asparagus, carrots, and soybeans dressed with rice vinegar. She turned the plate slowly, admiring its rustic lines and feeling its rough glaze.

I too became caught up in the beauty beneath each delicate-lidded dish. I thought I couldn't eat another bite when the waitress placed *hassun* (foods originating from the mountain and sea) before us. Once I noticed the beauty of simple poached mushrooms topped with herbs stacked to resemble a shrub, and small lightly seared scallops arranged to look like a stony hill, I revived my appetite.

For dessert, I found the juicy melon slices, peaches, and plums, all picked locally and at their peak of sweetness, as satisfying as any confection.

The bath, feast, and drinks left Mom and Oshima-san as relaxed and pliable as cooked udon noodles. The maids led us back to the porch to admire the crescent moon peeking from behind wisps of clouds, while the waitresses cleared the dishes, plates, and bowls and laid out our futon beds.

Mom and Oshima-san fell asleep immediately. Chirping crickets outside our screen windows kept time to the women's soft snores as I lay awake and watched the silhouette of tree branches play across the white shoji doors like shadow puppets.

The dewy summer night smells, the cool bed linens, and the buckwheat-hull pillow that cradled my head and neck should have put me to sleep as well. That evening in the Spartan *ryokan,* with the hot spring, our leisurely dinner, its pace, and its focus on the presentation that varied from the dish itself to the position of the chopsticks, created a fissure in my consciousness and introduced me to the idea of aesthetics, a concept that would expand through the years.

Almost asleep, I jolted awake at the thought that my visit to Japan would end soon. We had two more weeks. That was half a month and plenty of time, I reassured myself. I rested my head on the buckwheat-hull pillows. Like a mantra, I told myself *plenty of time* until I sank into sleep as deep as a warm Japanese bath.

# Cold Buckwheat Noodles with Dipping Sauce
## (Zaru-soba)

*Making your own sauce is easier than you think and tastes much better than the store-bought kind. It also keeps well in the refrigerator.*

### Sauce

½ cup mirin
½ cup soy sauce
2¼ cups water
1 cup dried bonito flakes

### Noodles

300-gram package soba (buckwheat) noodles
½ sheet nori (dried laver), cut into fine threads
   (⅛ inch x ¾ inch)
4 teaspoons wasabi paste
¼ cup finely chopped green onions

*For the sauce:* Bring the mirin to a boil in a saucepan. Add soy sauce, water, and bonito flakes and bring to a boil again. Reduce heat and simmer for about 2 minutes. Strain and let cool.

If you want to serve the sauce cold, place in the refrigerator for at least 1 hour before serving.

*For the noodles:* Boil the soba noodles according to the package directions. Stir often to keep them from sticking. To check for doneness, pinch a noodle strand between your fingers. When there is no hardness in the core, the noodles are done. Rinse well in cold water and drain.

Divide the well-drained soba onto 4 plates. Sprinkle nori threads over the top.

Place a 1-teaspoon mound of wasabi and a neat pile of green onions on a small dish. Fill small, deep, cup-size bowls halfway with chilled dipping sauce. Serve all the dishes together.

Serves 4.

# Family

Back in our small room on a warm, moonless night after a long day of visiting and sightseeing, Mom told me that Obachan's real name was Chiyo. Mom often shared with me stories of adult troubles and tragedy, subjects that she otherwise would have discussed with other women friends over lunch after shopping. But living in Indiana, an ocean and a continent away from her close friends, Mom didn't have the luxury of long talks with her girlfriends. As a child, I understood that I served a special purpose as her substitute confidante. When she told me tales of sadness—real stories, not the make-believe ones I read in books—I didn't want to ruin Mom's need to express it by showing shock or dismay. I often held my face blank, devoid of emotion except for the curiosity of a good listener. Underneath, though, I would often recoil with horror and shock.

Being in the place where my mother's stories took place, I was able to visualize everything, large and looming as the screen in a movie theater. Mom revealed that Obachen was married before she met my grandfather, Sawagi, and that she had borne a daughter with her first husband. My mind saw this like a movie. I could see the young woman named Chiyo, cradling her baby girl and waiting for her husband to return from the war. Not long after her daughter's birth, Chiyo learned that her husband had been shot and killed in the front lines.

Soon afterward, her grieving in-laws forced her out of their house, prying her infant daughter out of her arms. "You're no longer welcome here. The baby is all we have left of our son. Go remarry and have more children," they demanded.

Crying, Chiyo begged and pleaded for her daughter, but the couple swatted her away like a stray cat.

Mom compared being a daughter-in-law in Japan to slavery. She described how, after marriage, a bride became practically the property of her husband's family and household, where three to four generations lived under one roof. New wives deferred to their mothers-in-law in every respect to keep the family and home running smoothly. The daughters-in-law cleaned the entire house, cooked, and washed clothes for all of its members. To maintain peace, the family system ignored the abuses at the hands of the mothers-in-law.

At the household of her first husband, Obachan was denied a second bowl of rice, said Mom, even though she was nursing her baby and needed to eat more food. Her mother-in-law's excuse was that the extra food was for men and children. Wives could go without, since they didn't do much around the house. Mom added that Obachan's treatment, at the time, was common and not even severe compared to how other women fared.

Obachan had no choice but to leave her daughter behind. Almost thirty years after I heard that story for the first time, when I gave birth to my son, I was reminded of the intensity of how traumatic it must have been for her. One afternoon after my son was born, I revisited the story with Mom.

"Did Obachan ever see her daughter after she was grown up?" I asked.

Mom thought about this before answering. "I can't remember hearing that she ever did, but I do know that Obachan outlived her daughter."

It took me a few moments before I could say anything. As a single mother with shared custody of my son, I empathized with the never-ending sadness, longing, and emptiness Obachan must have experienced with the loss of her first child, but to live in a society where she could seek no support or retribution seemed unimaginable and horrific.

Obachan got married a second time to my grandfather, a widower with two surviving daughters. The couple gave birth to a son, Takeo, and a daughter, Sachiko. Obachan's new life was a layer of past and present as she managed the household of her children and the daughters from her husband's previous marriage.

Mom had no choice but to accept her father's remarriage. She and her sister, Akiko, were raised in Obachan's household, where they were treated lower in priority than their half siblings, Takeo and Sachiko. My mother and Akiko were clothed and fed but not given the nurturing, encouragement, affection, and loving treatment their real mother would have provided.

Before I learned of Obachan's tragic past, I thought she and her daughter-in-law, Eiko, had a peaceful mother- and daughter-in-law relationship. Despite Obachan's abrupt, almost rude way of speaking to Eiko, Eiko responded cheerfully and respectfully in an overly high-pitched voice.

During one afternoon tea, Obachan told Mom, right in front of Eiko, that her son's wife's simple looks came from country stock. Eiko nodded her head in agreement, no trace of hurt or annoyance in her pleasant face. But when she cast her eyes downward, I was convinced I saw a pained look. I was stunned that Obachan would behave so rudely after her own experiences at the hands of a mean mother-in-law. It seemed as if it were a cruel legacy, passed on to daughters-in-law who perpetuated it when they become mothers-in-law.

Mom understood the complexity of these relationships and knew to keep her facial expression under check when Obachan behaved badly. She neither agreed with her stepmother, which would alienate her sister-in-law, nor defended Eiko, which would insult Obachan.

I never heard Mom speak ill of Obachan. Obachan treated me with the same attention and affection she doled out to her other grandchildren. Although she wasn't my grandmother by blood, even after I learned her real name I never felt unwelcome in calling her Grandmother.

Every morning we were in Tokyo, I helped her with the cleaning and shopping. I looked forward to those times, and I believe Obachan did as well from the way she beckoned me to join her in whatever she was doing.

At five feet tall, her physical strength and charisma more than made up for her petite stature. In my uncle's rice store, Obachan insisted on performing the menial cleaning chores as a humble mark of her high status in the household. She carried large sacks of rice tossed across her back more easily than any man could, including her son. Sometimes when both

Uncle Takeo and Aunt Eiko were too busy to watch their baby, Obachan tied her grandchild, Naochan, to her back while she scrubbed the store's wood floors.

A couple of years later, Uncle Takeo and Aunt Eiko had a second baby. Uncle Takeo wrote in a letter to Mom describing how Obachan hoisted both children, the infant on her front and the older on her back, all the while smiling and chatting to customers and ringing up their orders. Carrying a baby or a bag of rice was the same, she would tell them nonchalantly.

When I wasn't with her as she worked in the rice store, our other daily chores included picking up all the futons and blankets on the tatami-floored bedrooms and putting them away. Together we rolled the cumbersome futons into the closet, and then each of us took a corner of a blanket and met in the middle like dancers performing the two-step.

After she furiously vacuumed the floor with the smallest sweeper I'd ever seen, Obachan untied her white embroidered house smock and stepped out of her faded red slippers into comfortable cork-soled sandals. She hung her shopping basket in the crook of her arm before heading to the neighborhood fish and produce stalls to buy groceries.

Obachan wore Western clothes, but her short, pigeon-toed stride revealed a life spent wearing a kimono. Even so, with her back straight and head held high, she walked at the brisk pace of a city dweller.

One of our routine stops included the neighborhood fishmonger, whose catch of the day lay on ice in long wooden boxes. Squinting to keep the smoke from his smoldering cigarette out of his eyes, the seller lifted the lids of the boxes for Obachan. Taking her time, she checked for clear eyes and lifted the gills and poked the skin with a gnarled finger. Last she smelled the fish up close. All the while she wore a stern, unhappy look on her face as if she were about to walk away at any second. Only when the seller wrapped the fish and placed it in her basket would Obachan finally break out in a friendly smile.

At the vegetable lady's stand, Obachan perused the long, skinny, deep-purple eggplants the seller had chosen for her. Shaking her head, she handed one back. The vendor replaced it with one as flawless as the first. Obachan slowly nodded her head, as if to say, *If this is the best you can do, so be it.*

She tucked the eggplants, a bundle of spinach, and two rolls of *somen* noodles wrapped in paper into her basket, then leaned her head toward mine and, as she smiled, whispered in Japanese, "Even if a vegetable looks good, give it back for another, so the vendor knows you're paying attention, *ne?*" She smelled of sweet barley husk, sandalwood, and the universal powder smell of old ladies.

Down a quiet, narrow alley that dated to the early 1940s, Obachan ducked into a smoky gray-curtained doorway. Displayed in polished wood-framed cases were delicate pieces of *wagashi* (sweets used in tea ceremony). The milky-white, almost translucent disks were about the size of silver dollars and, like most Japanese sweets, had a casing made of rice flour with a burgundy-colored bean-paste filling. Just looking at them, I could feel how my teeth would sink into the gooey goodness, the subtly sweet rice flavor mixing with the strong, sweet red bean as I chewed.

Dazzled by the miniature selection, I scanned the treats, my eyes drawn to the shapes, pastel colors, and adornments of lines and curlicues. I was intrigued by one pastry that was lightly dusted with *mochi* powder, with ever-so-tiny green leaves on its oval base. It was named "summer wind through the trees."

The white-uniformed woman behind the counter filled
a flat box made of thin, light wood with a dozen assorted
*wagashi.* Then she wrapped the box in thick handmade paper
that she held in place by taping a single strip of clear tape confidently along the line where the paper overlapped. Obachan
said cheerfully, "Your mother said living in America, she missed
eating these pastries the most, so we will have them with tea
when she returns this afternoon."

Because her son was a rice merchant, neighbors, restaurant owners, and other shopkeepers often stopped Obachan
to chat. As she usually shopped alone, Obachan proudly introduced me as her granddaughter visiting from America when
people inquired about who I was. As she strolled through the
throng of housewives, vendors, and other pedestrians, she
talked with me and asked questions. It didn't matter that I
understood only part of what she was saying or that I couldn't
answer in Japanese quickly enough. Whenever a glitch in our
communication appeared, I would give her a smile and she
would laugh uproariously and move on to another topic.

❀

I had never been given as much undivided attention from
anyone as I was from Obachan. Because all my biological
grandparents were dead, I didn't know how good it would feel
to be enveloped in the adoration of family. After our chores or
a morning of grocery shopping, Obachan made me a typical
Japanese lunch of *oyako donburi,* hot rice served in a big bowl
topped with juicy nuggets of chicken, sweet sliced green
onions, and eggs. Other days, for a treat, she took me to the
corner convenience store to buy a small frozen pizza.

When lunch was over, Obachan and I climbed a set of narrow concrete stairs in the back courtyard that led to a platform where laundry hung on a clothesline. As we plucked the stiff, sun-dried clothes I admired the aerial view of the neighborhood. The platform's perimeter was lined with tall potted plants, but I could still see through them to a woman cooking in her kitchen, an elderly man feeding his canary, and a cat walking on a roof ledge.

Long after the laundry was folded and put in the basket, and after the sun slipped behind a building and brought cool relief, Obachan and I sat on the platform, admiring the waves of red clay–tiled roofs contrasting with the glass and steel sky-scrapers jutting like quartz crystal in the distance.

The soft, buttery late-afternoon light I saw on the roof-top reminded me of a similar hue, when the sunlight filtered through tall wheat fields in Indiana. I hadn't thought about home since we arrived. At various times during my trip, I missed Dad and my brothers, but I knew I would be home and back in my old life soon enough. And now, just as lengthening shadows signal day's end, my lengthening time here meant my visit to Tokyo was growing shorter and shorter.

It was at this time of day, close to dinnertime, when the rooms became noticeably muted, as if someone had brushed them over with a blue watercolor, that Obachan made her offering to the Shinto shrine set in a corner of the downstairs tatami room. On a small rosewood shelf sat a bowl of ashes that held a burning incense stick, a packet of incense sticks, a candle, matches, a metal cup–shaped bell with a wooden stick resting across the lip, a small dish of rice, a glass of rice wine, a dish of salt, and a photo of Grandfather in a simple wood frame.

Every day Obachan tidied up the shrine, changing the rice or replacing fruit offerings that were overripening. The wife, Obachan explained, has to eat the old dish of rice before replacing it with the fresh one. She told me this as she ate it. I saw tiny little bugs between the grains. She didn't pick them out but stuffed the tablespoon-size portion into her mouth, chewing with her eyes closed as if she were eating something sacred.

She showed me how to light the candle and incense sticks. She struck the cup-shaped bell twice with the wooden stick, clapped her hands two times, and then prayed with the palms of her hands touching, head bowed, and eyes closed. The last blow to the bell resonated, holding its note in the air. When she finished praying, Obachan blew out the candle. Perhaps it was the cool breeze through the shoji sliding doors, the tinkle of the iron chimes that hung in the doorway, or the serenity of the altar room sanctuary in the bustling house, but I felt a reassuring closeness when I looked at the photo of the stranger who was my grandfather. His unsmiling face looked down from the altar, stern and serious, yet a look of sincerity came from his eyes.

As if reading my mind, Obachan began telling me stories about my grandfather. He smoked a long thin pipe that burned pellets of strong tobacco, she said, and stored the pipe in a special silver case. From under a daybed, she pulled out a cardboard box and then carefully unraveled the pipe and the case from its remnant silk wrapping. As she talked, she rubbed the tobacco case and the mouthpiece of the pipe with the same small towel she used to mop her brow, occasionally stopping to steam the metal with her breath. The tobacco case was untarnished from constant rubbing.

"Did your mother tell you her father loved collecting fabrics?" she asked me.

Not allowing me enough time to answer, she continued.

"Sawagi didn't sew like your mother. He hoarded pieces of material and kept them neatly in cedar-lined trunks."

When he was dying of stomach cancer, she explained, he wanted to see his favorite kimono and Western fabrics, saved from before the war. Obachan didn't have to describe these materials to me. On the movie screen of my mind, I saw stiff brocade, brilliant kimono liners like slips worn under Western dresses. I saw a springtime flower bed of colors, nubby tweeds, lightweight crepe de chine, and double-sided silk satins that slipped through the fingers like water.

Obachan, swept away in the tide of her memories, spoke so quickly that I couldn't make out all of what she was saying. I concentrated and listened, hoping my mind could keep up and translate her sentences fast enough.

"There was not much we could do about his pain toward the end. He seemed to get relief from touching the material. For hours he held on to a piece of blue-and-white *yukata* (summer kimono) fabric. When he felt better, he examined the intricate weave and pattern of a silk cloth used for obi (kimono belt)." She held a piece of blue and white–patterned cloth crumpled in the box up to her wrinkled face. The fresh, bright fabric she held to her face was like a spring maple leaf against a rock worn down by a lake's constant tide. She demonstrated how he stroked his cheek with it.

Obachan described how the doctors gave him morphine to ease his worsening pain. The combination of drugs, fabric, and memories triggered hallucinations of the past. There was one fabric, Obachan remembered, a long piece of canary-yellow brocade, shimmering with woven threads of white, that struck a chord in his memory so strong that he sat up in his bed, something he hadn't been able to do on his own for weeks.

"Sawagi wanted it wrapped around his shoulders," Obachan told me.

Her eyes sparkled at the remembrance of that day. "I knew it was just the drugs, but he seemed so happy. He talked about the old spring festivals, the ones before the war when all the young girls dressed in expensive kimonos, their hair held in place with mother-of-pearl combs and spangled tassels. It was like a big wave of color."

"He called out to imaginary neighbors," she said, cupping her hand to her mouth to show me how he amplified his voice. "Those who used to stop at his rice store to chat and have a cup of sake before going on their way to dance, eat, drink, and view blossoms at the cherry groves."

Carefully, she wrapped up the polished pipe and tobacco case in the silk and neatly folded the piece of *yukata* cloth, adding, "Those neighbors were all long dead, and I knew it wouldn't be much longer before Sawagi joined them at the festival."

Obachan's haunting story remained etched in my mind. On the eve of my last day in Tokyo, I attended a summer festival. It was Aunt Akiko's idea to see the *hanabi,* a fireworks display held at nightfall at a nearby park.

The sky stretched out like silky blue-black velvet. Paper lanterns in comforting sorbet colors, strung up and down the park's cobbled sidewalk, bordered the festivities like a gilded picture frame.

Housewives and elderly women from the neighborhoods danced in groups, wearing light cotton summer kimonos, twirling their kimono sleeves or snapping paper fans open and shut as part of their dance routine. In another area, a *taiko* drum group beat rhythmically. Onlookers also wore traditional summer kimonos, some in vibrant hot pinks and intense greens resembling blinking Christmas tree lights.

A man pushed a red-canopied cart loaded with wire cages containing butterflies, crickets, and beetles of all sizes and colors. My nine-year-old cousin, Hire-chan, bought an iridescent purple beetle with sharp, scissorlike pincers, which the man placed into a small plastic cage gingerly, using long chopsticks.

Other carts sold paper fans, sparklers, sweet red-bean hard candy, and good-luck trinkets. Obachan bought animal-shaped lollipops made from brown syrup for everyone. We found a small patch of grass on a hill and licked the sticky lollipops contentedly. Mom and Aunt Akiko said they hadn't tasted these sweets since the war.

We all stopped talking to admire the fireworks as they lit up the sky with a gigantic chrysanthemum blossoming midair in a blink of the eye. Glittering greens, red, whites, and golds speckled the night sky like a jewelry display window.

Instead of watching the show, I watched my relatives' faces. I had never felt such deep contentment as I did that night, looking into their eyes, wide and upturned, reflecting the flowers of pink, blue, white, and red popping sparks. I drew in my breath and tried to capture the moment with all the details, like a net chasing after butterflies.

Aunt Akiko sat between her two sons, clapping, pointing, and exclaiming with delight as often as her boys did. Hire-chan and Haru-chan were nine and eight years old. At my first meeting with them, I tried to act mature, but soon the two boys had me playing tag and hide-and-seek. They couldn't speak English, but it wasn't necessary when we communicated mostly through laughter and physical play.

Mom and Aunt Sachiko sat hip-to-hip and talked into each other's ears. Obachan just smiled. She commented and pointed at a particularly spectacular display.

From nowhere, the familiar sinking feeling of sadness filled my stomach. I felt a lump growing in throat and my vision blur with tears.

The finality of leaving struck me like a clap of thunder and a downpour. I didn't want to go back home, yet there was nothing I could do about it. I knew I could not stay in Japan, but the thought of leaving family was deadening.

❀

The next morning I tried to pretend it was just another day, not the day I would be leaving. We had an early flight the following morning and had to leave the house in the afternoon to stay at the airport hotel overnight.

The whole family gathered for our departure. The mood was upbeat and pleasant, with an undertone of sadness. For lunch we ate *sekihan,* rice with red beans sprinkled with roasted black sesame seeds. Coincidentally, it was the same dish Mom ate with her family before she flew to marry Dad fifteen years before.

When it was time to go to the airport, all my aunts, cousins, and Obachan walked us to the curb as Uncle Takeo loaded our suitcases into the car. I swallowed the sob stuck in my throat as Hire-chan clung to and cried in Aunt Akiko's skirt. They all waved goodbye until we turned down a corner street I didn't recognize, their familiar faces disappearing for good.

The airport hotel was clean and adequate for a night's stay, but in my growing despair, I wanted to be nowhere but in the family house in Tokyo.

As I watched Mom unpack a few essentials, there was a soft knock at the door. Suzuki-san, another close friend from my mother's banking and hiking days, had taken the train from the city to the airport to join us for a bon voyage dinner. I was happy to see her and remembered that the last time I saw her had been two weeks earlier, when my visit stretched ahead like an unexplored road touching the horizon.

Suzuki-san sat in one of the armchairs as Mom organized our things. My mind went back to what it would be like to sleep in my old bed at home. How long would it take before I forgot the smell and firmness of the futon over the tatami mats, and the *shh-shh* sound of buckwheat hull–filled neck pillows that at first felt so strange to lie on and now were as comfortable as a feather pillow? Once home, would I lie awake, missing the nightly city sounds that drifted into our open shoji window and lulled me to sleep?

Without warning, I started to cry. Not modest, misty-eyed tears, but deep racking sobs that shook my whole body and made my face a puddle of tears and snot. Embarrassed, I ran into the bathroom and locked the door, pressing a towel to my mouth.

Mom spoke high-pitched Japanese into the crack of the door. "Linda, open the door. Suzuki-san made a special trip to say goodbye to us. Be a big girl and come out."

Between sobs, I tried to compose myself and catch my breath, but my voice still hitched uncontrollably.

"Linda-chan . . ." Suzuki-san took Mom's place at the door. "You poor thing. Come to dinner. Eat something. You'll feel better."

Through the door I heard whispering. Mom realized I wasn't coming out. Speaking into the door, she asked if it was all right if they went to dinner at the hotel restaurant. I still couldn't talk from my hiccupping, but I managed to let her know it was.

I sat on the edge of the bathtub, glad to be alone. I stared down at the bath mat and observed the way the threads with the letters of the hotel name were woven higher than the rest of the mat. I couldn't tell Mom I wanted to stay in Tokyo, live with Obachan, Uncle Takeo, and Eiko, and visit Aunt Akiko and Aunt Sachiko. I knew she would laugh at my foolishness and I couldn't take that, because I knew it wasn't even a possibility.

I missed Dad, and even my brothers, but the journey home forced me to examine my life in Indiana, a stark exercise for a ten-year-old. I wanted to run away from my life there, to toss it away for somewhere better without really knowing if going somewhere else would be an improvement.

My unhappiness was rooted in not knowing where I belonged. Today I understand why Mom wrote home and to her friends often. Indiana was her new home, but she knew in her heart, without question, where she belonged and where she could go if she ever needed to return to her origins. Her family in Japan stayed in the back of her mind like an anchor that kept her sane and moving forward.

I didn't know, as I perched on the cold porcelain tub and stared at the terry-cloth bath mat, that I had begun a lifelong journey in search of home. Anguish turned into a bottomless hopelessness that felt as though my chest were on the verge of being crushed.

Before I came to Tokyo, I didn't understand what family meant, or the responsibility of it. I didn't know how family could influence me and change the direction of my life or where I lived. It didn't feel like it at the time, but these new revelations and bits of wisdom were the real treasures I took home from my trip.

I wiped my eyes, blew my nose, and took in an unsteady breath, and then another, until I felt more together. I wondered what everyone at the house was doing at that moment. I would continue this exercise for months after I left. Perhaps Obachan listened to the radio while she washed the rice for the evening meal. Aunt Eiko might have fed Naochan dinner as Uncle Takeo, fan blowing fully on him, read the evening paper. I found consolation in this soothing picture, but my heart still ached. After I returned to Indiana, I understood that it was broken.

## Rice Cooked with Red Beans (*Sekihan*)

*This dish is always present during celebrations and holidays, as it represents good luck and future prosperity. The sweet rice adds just the right amount of sweetness and stickiness to the regular rice. A sprinkling of toasted black sesame seeds adds a dramatic color contrast and nutty flavor.*

⅓ cup adzuki (red) beans
2 cups water
1 tablespoon black sesame seeds
1 teaspoon salt
2 cups rice
¼ cup sweet rice *(mochigome)*

Cover the beans with water and bring to a boil. Drain and rinse with cold water. Cover the beans with 2 cups of water and bring to a boil again. Reduce heat and simmer for 45 minutes. Test doneness by pinching the beans between your thumb and index finger. The beans should be soft. Pour the beans through a strainer, reserving the cooking water. Set aside.

In a small skillet, toast the black sesame seeds on high heat for about 3 minutes, shaking constantly. Remove the seeds from the heat, sprinkle with the salt, and place on a plate.

Wash both kinds of rice together in a large bowl by rinsing and changing the water until the water runs clear. Put the rice into a rice cooker. Add the beans and the reserved cooking water; cook according to manufacturer's instructions. If using a saucepan, add 2½ cups of water (the reserved cooking water plus more, if needed), bring to a vigorous boil, reduce the heat, cover, and simmer for 20 minutes.

When the rice is done, stir the rice and beans. Scoop into a decorative container and sprinkle with black sesame seeds.

Serves 4.

Eating Pie in Tam's Kitchen

When Mrs. Dong, her son, Phuong, and her two daughters, Trang and Tam, came to Versailles in 1980, part of the large numbers of Vietnamese refugees making a new start in America, I felt as though I knew their experience. Through the years I had watched the grainy war footage on the evening news and heard the horror stories circulated by townspeople with family fighting in the war.

Government agencies settled the Dongs in Versailles, where there were no other Vietnamese families. At the time, it was a federal policy to resettle the Vietnamese in as many areas of the country as possible, so no one particular city would bear the burden of social services. There was also a mistaken hope that separating them from their own cultural groups would bring about a quick assimilation into American society.

At thirteen, I had my own selfish reasons for looking forward to the Dongs' arrival. Finally, I thought, my family wouldn't be the only Asians in town. I flirted with the idea of what it would be like to have an Asian best friend for the first time in my life. I fantasized that this friend and I would be the coolest girls in school. All the other girls would want to hang out with us, and the boys would find our darker looks more appealing than those of the blond girls.

On the first day of school, Phuong, Trang, and Tam Dong arrived to the popping flashbulbs of area newspaper photographers and an entourage of hosts. Local Baptist church members had coordinated housing, food, and clothing and arranged employment for their mother at a local casket-making company.

I caught only a quick look at them between classes. Trang was the oldest sister. The constantly tired look in her downcast eyes made her appear twenty-five rather than sixteen. She kept her chin down low so that her hair hung between her and the student spectators who gawked as she searched for her classroom.

Fifteen-year-old Phuong had a sleepy look as well, with uneven hair that looked as if it were cut with a pair of dull scissors. He couldn't speak a word of English, but everyone was disarmed by his lazy smile.

Tam was fourteen, a year older than me, with long hair and a flawless complexion. She already had a group of students wanting to help her find her classes and show her the rounds.

That day brought a noticeable air of benevolence, a sense of goodwill. Out of reflex, I expected some of the kids to make fun of the Dongs' slanted eyes, flat noses, and accents, the way I had been teased in the first grade. I braced myself but then sat back and watched in amazement, even jealousy, as even the meanest boys laughed good-naturedly when our new Vietnamese residents practically spat out their first taste of the cafeteria's macaroni and cheese lunch.

In many ways, the whole community of Versailles had taken part in welcoming the Dongs to their new home. Months before they came, community members organized clothing drives, someone donated a newly remodeled apartment, and families cleaned out attics and family rooms for furnishings. Making sure the exiled Dongs felt welcome and at home gave comfort to those who had lost loved ones in the Vietnam War. Doing a war-related charitable act gave them a sense that everything in our corner of the world would be all right.

Even though I knew that the Dongs deserved all the attention and outpouring of welcome they received, I was jealous and couldn't stop myself from wondering if their welcome would have been different had they just showed up in town as an anonymous Asian family without the cloak of world politics.

Was I the only one who thought it was strange how the Dongs smiled constantly? The first time I noticed their grins, I couldn't help but smile back. They appeared to be very happy to be here. But as the days passed, I realized the smiles didn't express their appreciation or gratitude, but rather fear. Smiles were their shield.

❁

I found out more about the Dongs firsthand one weekend afternoon a couple of weeks after they had settled into their new apartment, which was just a few blocks from where we lived. Mrs. Anders, one of our church's older do-gooders, had decided it was time to introduce the town's two Asian families to each other.

Originally, Mrs. Dong was to accompany Mrs. Anders to our house alone, but Tam came along to translate for her mother. Mom, upon seeing Tam, immediately called me out of my bedroom to join them.

As I slipped into one of the straight-backed chairs at the dining room table, Mom, seated at the head of the table, poured English tea into her best teacups. Meanwhile, Mrs. Anders described her battle with a pack of moles that had invaded her yard. When she thought no one was looking, Mrs. Anders, a stout woman with auburn wash-and-set hair, turned her head and discreetly slipped out the top plate of her false teeth so she could better taste Mom's homemade lemon cookies. She ignored the individually wrapped disks of *osembe* (rice crackers) arranged in a wooden bowl and peered down at the small dessert bowls of *anmitsu* (a sweet Japanese dessert made of *mochi*, cubes of gelatin made from seaweed, red bean paste, and sliced fruit).

"My, what's this?" Mrs. Anders muttered, wrinkling her nose when she saw the dimpled balls of *mochi* beneath the moist halo of fruit. Before Mom could answer, Mrs. Anders picked up her spoon and took bites until she was scraping the bottom of the bowl.

"Yummy," she said, primly setting the spoon next to the empty bowl. Mom never answered the question, and Mrs. Anders didn't bother to repeat it.

At that point, Mrs. Dong and Tam, who were seated across from me, immediately reached for their bowls and spoons.

Before taking a spoonful of the frosted gelatin cubes, sweet bean paste, and mandarin orange slice, Tam said, "It's been so long since I have eaten this dessert."

I didn't realize that there were different versions of this sweet throughout Asia. Mom made this dessert mostly in the hot summer months, saying the light cloudy blue of the gelatin cubes reminded her of the coolness of the ocean.

I didn't answer Tam's proclamation with this bit of information at the time, though, as I was immediately struck by how the two Vietnamese women looked more like sisters than mother and daughter. They both had petite, slender frames above which their heads towered over their narrow shoulders like sunflowers, and I saw where Tam got her full, creased lips.

Despite her youthful looks, Mrs. Dong dressed like a schoolmarm in a white blouse, somber black cardigan, gray tweed skirt, and sensible black shoes. Tam took after her mother's matronly style. Her uniform comprised red sneakers with no shoestrings (so she could slip her shoes on and off when she came home, I concluded), faded, baggy khaki pants, a white blouse buttoned all the way to the top under a red V-neck sweater, and an oversize blue-and-white plaid blazer (an item of clothing I recognized because we had passed it on to the church charity).

As I sipped my tea, I noted the complacent facial expressions that Mom, Mrs. Dong, and Tam wore, and I knew they didn't understand a word Mrs. Anders was saying as she rambled on and on. At the appropriate moments, they feigned interest with gracious nods and smiles.

Mom glared at me and nudged me with her foot under the table in an attempt to get me to interact. I knew Mom wanted me there to steer the conversation in case it got thrown off course by some misinterpreted pleasantries or lapses into awkward silences.

With a soft clicking sound, Mrs. Anders discreetly slipped her false teeth back into her mouth. "Terry, what year did you come to Indiana?"

I hated it when people called Mom "Terry" rather than by her Japanese name, Teruko, but this didn't bother Mom at all. She agreed that her Japanese name was too difficult for most people to pronounce. Whatever is easiest is best, she always said.

Mom took a second to count the years back on her fingers. "Hmm . . . umm . . . 1959." Mom shook her head at her forgetfulness.

"Now, that must have been difficult. Coming here and all." Mrs. Anders smiled encouragingly. Mom gave her a look of incomprehension.

"That must have been hard for you, leaving home," Mrs. Anders rephrased.

"Yes, very hard." My mother was using her overly pleasant voice, slightly high-pitched and melodic, the one she used around people she didn't know very well. "I couldn't speak any English."

Mrs. Dong smiled and nodded her head in the same vague way Mom did when she didn't understand what was being said.

Tam, in a low tone, translated Mom's response into Vietnamese. Tam looked at me shyly. "My mother understands most English. She's just shy about speaking."

I nodded my head. Already Tam was compensating for her mother, the way I did for mine. She was assuming the responsibilities immigrants' children automatically assume, as I did when I called doctors, the phone company, and even Dad's workplace, as if these tasks were chores like washing the dishes or feeding the family pet.

As she leaned forward to get another packet of rice crackers, Tam's long hair cascaded like a sheet of water. I was close enough to notice that she wore no trace of makeup, yet the thick lashes framing her slightly slanted eyes created the illusion of smudged kohl. Her traditional long hair with bangs complemented her heart-shaped face.

I considered how her hairstyle would work for me, but it was too late. I had recently gotten a perm so I could bend my once-poker-straight hair with a curling iron to create the soft-feathered look that was popular at the time. Rather than accentuating my almond-shaped eyes, I unsuccessfully tried using eye shadow to make them look like Caucasian double-folded eyelids. The result was badly kinked hair and raccoon eyes.

Mrs. Anders clapped her hands together loudly and wiggled her finger at Tam and me. Her smile was so big I could see the color variation between her false top teeth and real bottoms, the same size and color as white and yellow corn on the cob. "With your black hair, you two look like a couple of bookends. Like two china dolls."

Pleased, Tam looked at me and smiled brightly. I didn't crack a smile.

"I'm not Chinese, though," I said.

Stammering slightly, Mrs. Anders said, "I didn't mean China as in Chinese, I meant china like the plates because both of your complexions are so smooth."

"Oh." I wasn't bothered by my mistake. I had responded the same way when a stranger had called me a china doll. He had meant "Chinese," and in the future, when anyone made this reference toward me, I'd immediately become defensive.

To mend her error, Mrs. Anders snorted, "My skin sure didn't look like that when I was your age. I broke out awful."

Turning back to my mother and Mrs. Dong, Mrs. Anders asked, "Now, Terry, I always wondered if the Vietnamese and the Japanese are at all the same."

Mrs. Anders did a double take when Tam and Mom laughed out loud at this question. I snickered. Tam muttered into Mrs. Dong's ear, and she joined in the laughter too.

"No, nothing the same," Mom finally said after regaining her composure.

"Really? Not even the language?" Mrs. Anders looked uncomfortable. She didn't understand why they were laughing at her question, but she chuckled along good-naturedly anyway. "Well, I thought you would all be like distant cousins or something," she added, sending Mom, Mrs. Dong, and Tam into another gale of chortles. Now everyone was laughing except for Mrs. Anders and me.

They laughed to lighten a serious topic, a response lost on Mrs. Anders, who was still trying to make sense of whether they were laughing at her or with her. But instead of trying to figure it out, she continued to chatter on in an attempt to make small talk.

Finally, Mom asked Mrs. Dong a question. "What do you think about living in the United States?" Mom asked her, while pouring hot water into the teapot.

"Everyone has been nice to me and my family. I appreciate this country so much." She said it in perfect English, and I knew she must have repeated this many times. Mom had several phrases, such as, "I'll have a cup of coffee, cream and sugar, a ham sandwich, and coleslaw," that she said so often they sounded perfect, without a trace of her accent.

When Mrs. Anders excused herself to go to the bathroom, Tam and I talked about school. Mom turned to Mrs.

Dong and asked what I thought was a strange question, "Do you have rice?"

Mrs. Dong's face lit up like a marquee and she automatically answered, "Yes." This four-word question somehow closed whatever distance had existed between my mother and Mrs. Dong. Mom knew how searching for and making familiar food was a common denominator to all newcomers to America.

"For me, the hardest thing about being here is finding Japanese food," Mom said, shaking her head at the thought of it.

Mrs. Dong said something in Tam's ear.

"My mother agrees," Tam said. "And she wants me to tell you that for days we had to eat Western food and the first rice we ate was the kind sold in a box, but we had missed it so much, it was the best thing we ever tasted."

Mom smiled and nodded as she jotted down on an index card the address of a grocer in Cincinnati she thought might sell Vietnamese ingredients. She brought a brown paper bag from the kitchen and gave Tam the rest of the rice crackers to take home.

Mrs. Anders returned to the table and clapped her hands together like a wind-up toy monkey banging cymbals. "I'm so happy you all are getting along like hummingbirds at a feeder. Did I miss something?"

***

At school, Tam had all the potential—cute looks and genuine perkiness—to be a candidate for homecoming princess and even cheerleader, if she wanted. But she didn't want it. Maybe she didn't understand the status, the sheer power that American high school kids put on such things. She had left a ravaged country with nothing but the clothes on her back. As a teen who never experienced any disaster worse than running down to the basement during a tornado warning, I was baffled and annoyed by her lack of interest in being popular. Through time, I began to believe Tam might be a snob.

At lunchtime, I watched from the bleachers as the popular girls swarmed around her like sweat bees. She didn't understand the questions they asked in their fast, nasal southeastern Indiana drawl. Often she was reduced to perching at the edge of the bleacher seat, frozen, as though thinking if she didn't move, they might eventually leave her alone.

By the holiday season, the initial newness and novelty of the Vietnamese kids faded. Eventually they became like everyone who had braces or chubbiness—anything that made them different and therefore an easy target for teasing.

Before a basketball pep rally I overheard Lester Matheson leading Tam into a trap. With a half-cocked grin and a false expression of interest on his pale pimply face, Lester asked, "Tam, what do you call that," pointing up to the ceiling lights, "in Vietnamese?"

"You mean rights?" she answered, tentatively looking at everyone around her for some feedback.

"Yes, rights. That's right, rights." Everyone joined in the laughter.

I couldn't bear watching them. Mom and Dad pronounced words starting with *L* with a soft *R,* and I had many times wanted to defend them when people were alternately confused or amused by their accents. I was teased when I was much younger, too, and diligently practiced saying *R*-words the way a lisper would say *S*-words until my accent was gone.

I collected myself mentally before diving into the conversation. *Here we go,* I said to myself. I was sitting one bleacher up from Lester and Tam. I leaned down and popped my head between them. There was plenty of room, as Tam had recoiled from her persecutor.

Exaggerating a laugh, I turned to Lester and said, "Yeah, Tam may talk funny, but at least she doesn't have to use a gallon of Clearasil." It was raining outside and the bleachers were more crowded than usual. Everyone within hearing distance cracked up. Others turned to see what was going on.

I knew it was a low blow, but that's what it took to stop a bully like Lester. I knew even then, in junior high, that weak-minded boys sought approval by making fun of other people. Lester scowled at me like a miffed cat. I stared straight back, daring him to respond. He wouldn't, because we both knew that by teasing Tam about the way she talked, he was stepping into my territory.

After that incident, Tam came to me when she had questions she didn't want to ask her new friends for fear of ridicule, such as the time she walked out of the school library with a book, not realizing it needed to be checked out at the front desk.

During those early teen years, I tested my values, weighing the choices I made as I matured. I wanted to be a good, helpful kid, but the pull of peer pressure and the desire not to be different from my classmates was much stronger.

I wasn't gentle or kind when Tam came to me. I received her requests grudgingly and acted as if it were a burden to help her. I didn't want to be her protector, yet I couldn't stand by and let her be teased just because she didn't have a strong enough grasp of the language to defend herself. In Tam's interactions at school, I saw my mother's immigrant vulnerability and my own hidden struggles as an Asian in the white-bread part of America where I lived.

If I had complained to the teachers, it would have only made matters worse. Teasing was a personal battle. I had learned early on I'd rather fight back than live in daily misery.

&#10047;

When Tam first arrived in town, she was unguarded. She smiled and commented freely. Soon she began to hesitate before speaking when she didn't know the intent of her listener. She stopped saying "No problem" in her friendly, accented way because kids started mimicking her.

Even when her eyes lit up and her hand waved like a paper pinwheel to get my attention, I avoided her gaze. I pretended I was in a hurry to get to class when I passed her in the halls. The Asian friendship I had fantasized about became a reality I didn't want. I truly felt bad for Tam, but I wasn't secure enough in myself to carry the load for both of us.

Being mistaken for Tam was the final straw. Although Tam had waist-length straight hair while I had a permed shag, and although she wore a conservative blue-and-white blazer with a button-down shirt while I wore jeans and sweaters like other girls, people mistook us for each other with the excuse that our hair was the same color, or that we looked the same from behind. One woman, a member of the church Tam attended, finally had the guts, or the lack of sense, to admit to me that she thought all Asians looked alike.

I was trying to convince my peers and myself that I was as American and, more important, as local as everyone else.

I believed if I dressed the part, feathered my hair back, wore heavy eye makeup and jeans so tight I had to lie on my bed to zip them, the uniform of the girls in my age group, that I would naturally fit in.

One weekend afternoon during a visit to a mall in Cincinnati with my girlfriends, I caught a reflection of myself in a store window. For a split second, I didn't recognize the person looking back at me. I wondered who the Asian girl was.

All the enjoyment of the moment, window-shopping with my friends, was knocked out of me. I felt crushed and foolish. For the longest time, I believed that tinkering with the details of my appearance would change it all, that I would be welcomed and not judged by my outward Asian appearance. Instead, there I was—an Asian girl with blue eye shadow, wavy hair, and Gloria Vanderbilt jeans.

My last encounter with Tam took place while walking home from school on a brisk autumn afternoon. In the distance, like a spreading ink spot on gray construction paper, Tam ran toward me. She was wrapped in a navy peacoat three sizes too large. I could see her blue-and-white blazer beneath. I felt a surge of panic followed by a sick feeling in my stomach, my typical physical reaction when I saw her.

"Someone gave us sweet potato pies. Can you come over and have some?" Tam asked, out of breath, when she finally caught up to me.

As she waited for me to respond, a blast of wind swirled around us like a vortex and she burrowed down deep into the collar of her coat. The temperature wasn't really low compared to how low it would get in the coming months. The cold of a Midwest winter was unbearable for a girl who, up until then, had spent her entire life in the tropical climes of Vietnam.

Caught off guard, I tried to come up with an excuse to get out of the invitation. "I've got to go home and walk Mr. French," I explained lamely.

"I saw your mom walking the dog," she said with a confident smile. "So you can come?"

I felt my temper give way. Couldn't she tell I was avoiding her? Wasn't it obvious that I didn't want to go to her house? Straining to be nice, I reminded myself that it wasn't her fault that I was irritated.

"Just come, see where I live, eat a piece of pie, and then leave." Her hair swirled attractively around her head, like black party streamers in a breeze. Helpless, I couldn't think of any way to get out of it. I nodded my head. The Dongs lived three blocks away from my house on the first floor of a boxy two-story apartment building across from the Baptist church.

In the foyer, I automatically slipped off my sneakers when I saw the line of street shoes. Tam pulled a random pair of worn house slippers from a big wicker basket and set them in front of me. We did this as naturally as anyone else would take her coat off and hang it in the closet. There was none of the hesitation my friends showed when I had to ask them to remove their shoes at my house, a rule that always called for explanations.

Even today, I detect the same awkwardness when I tell guests no shoes are worn in my house, as if I had asked them to take their clothes off.

From the Dongs' foyer I saw cardboard boxes stacked in the hallway and in one of the bedrooms. Tam saw me glance at them and flipped open the lids, showing one full of T-shirts, another with dented pots and pans, never-been-used table linens stained from long storage, and chipped, mismatched dishware. Charities had delivered them long after the family was well furnished and equipped. Tam explained that they kept the donations because it would appear ungrateful to get rid of them. So they sat there, taking up a big share of the apartment.

The rooms were small and dark. Even with fresh paint and a few improvements, the walls had absorbed years of dampness. Their dank odor was similar to the inside of a camper kept shut all winter. The medicinal smell of mothballs from the boxes of clothing and the distinct smell of dried Asian ingredients added to the mix.

Tam's older sister and mother sat at the kitchen table, drinking tea and talking. At first, I didn't recognize Mrs. Dong's voice. She was speaking Vietnamese in a loud, strong voice, not the pensive, soft tone I had heard during afternoon tea at my house.

Mrs. Dong nodded at me as she talked. Trang waved a little hello. I smiled and waved back in response. As Trang cut the pie and served it on plates, her brother, Phuong, shuffled into the room, wearing flip-flops with his feet halfway in, making it easier to slip them off when he wanted. Phoung said something in Vietnamese before wearily taking a seat at the table.

I sat silently, eating my wedge of donated pie, a tasteless burnt-orange paste cooked in a frozen piecrust. The family spoke rapidly in Vietnamese, laughing and sparring at each other's comments. I felt insignificant and left out. At my house, Mom and Dad made it a rule to speak English if a non-Japanese speaker were present. I understood for the first time how important this would be to guests, and that my parents did this out of politeness and so as not to alienate the nonspeaker.

At first I thought they spoke Vietnamese in my presence because I was a kid, but before too long a white school friend of Phuong's stopped by, and the family acknowledged him with smiles and switched to high-pitched, soft, broken English. The boy nodded at them as he stood awkwardly in the doorway, nibbling on a piece of pie.

The Dongs went back to talking in Vietnamese after Phuong and his friend left. The ball of anger in my stomach grew so tight I thought it would rip my insides. I looked at everyone's plates. Phoung had scraped the filling from the piecrust, Trang had eaten just the whipped cream topping, Tam had taken one bite, and Mrs. Dong put her piece back on the tin pan. I had eaten all of mine out of nervousness and already regretted it. Its heaviness made the knot in my stomach unbearable.

It was useless to stay, but I felt glued to my seat. I was waiting for a break in conversation so I could announce my departure. Finally, I stood up. Tam, who hadn't said a word to me since we sat down, looked at me as if I had appeared out of thin air. Mrs. Dong nodded when I thanked her for the pie. Trang started talking again as soon as I announced that I had to go home.

Tam, sensing something was wrong, called out to me from her front doorway as I made my way down the driveway. She suggested we get together that weekend, that maybe she could stop by my house. I said something in response, but luckily my words were lost in the wind.

The three blocks to home felt like the longest I'd ever walked. A low throbbing in my right temple had replaced the tangled knot in my stomach.

As weeks passed, I couldn't put my finger on the source of my animosity toward Tam. These feelings reminded me of when my brothers and I had to join my parents' Japanese friends and their children at social dinner parties. I had played with these kids throughout our childhoods, but as we all grew older we began withdrawing from each other. At later get-togethers we barely spoke to each other.

The last place I wanted to be was around other Japanese American kids. I saw the same confusion, unhappiness, and avoidance in their eyes, and all I wanted to do was flee. I felt the same when I sat in Tam's kitchen. It took me a long time to admit to myself that it was because I was ashamed, and that I disliked Tam because she wasn't Americanized enough for me. She made me remember the insecure girl who saw her true Asian reflection in the store window at the mall.

As time passed, Tam's English improved and she excelled in school. She found a group of girlfriends, and I rarely saw her anymore. So much time and so many events had passed after she first arrived in Versailles, and our loss of interest in each other seemed mutual. Eventually, the Dongs moved west to another Indianan small town.

Occasionally I'll share this episode from my life with friends, as though talking about it somehow releases me from the guilt I still harbor. I have to bite my tongue when they tell me I should have educated the townspeople about my ancestry, or educated Tam on American culture and walked her through how things were done in the United States. But these are conscientious responses from adults who have forgotten what it's like to be young and unsure. Looking back, I see I did what I had to do instinctually. I never tell them I avoided Tam as an act of survival. When the Dongs finally moved away, I felt a sense of relief and witnessed the sweeping-away of a bittersweet memory I couldn't ever quite recall.

❀

## Fruit and Sweet Gelatin Dessert (Anmitsu)

*This colorful dessert resembles a bowl of gumdrops when it's assembled.* Kanten, *or agar-agar, is sold at most Asian food stores and health-food stores. I prefer to use the strands or blocks because most recipes call for 1 stick, or about 7–10 grams. For this dish, I referred to my mother's recipe and cross-referenced the jelly-making instructions in the Japanese cooking bible, Shuzuo Tsuji's* Japanese Cooking: A Simple Art *(Kodansha International, 1980).*

### Jelly

> 1 stick (7–10 grams) Japanese gelatin (*kanten* or
>   agar-agar)
> 2¼ cups water
> 2 tablespoons sugar

### Syrup

> 1 cup water
> 1 cup granulated sugar

### Toppings

> 4 cups mixed fresh fruit in season (peaches, pears, and
>   oranges are especially good)
> juice of ½ lemon
> 1 can *anko* (sweetened whole adzuki beans)
> 6 sticky rice cakes, optional

*For the jelly:* Line a 9-inch x 9-inch baking pan with aluminum foil. Break the gelatin into big pieces. Place in a bowl, pour in warm water to cover, and let soak for 30 minutes, or until softened.

Rinse thoroughly and wring out softened pieces into smaller pieces, then place in a large pot with water. Cook over low heat until the gelatin is completely dissolved. Add the sugar, stirring until it dissolves. Do not let it come to a boil. The liquid will have a cloudy appearance and slightly thickened consistency.

Skim off any foam that accumulates on top. Pour the hot liquid into the foil-lined pan. Let cool to room temperature and then cover with plastic wrap and refrigerate.

*For the syrup:* Combine the water and sugar in a small pan. Place over high heat and bring to a boil. Reduce heat and stir until the sugar has completely dissolved. Transfer to a bowl and let cool to room temperature and then refrigerate until chilled.

*For the toppings:* Peel and slice the fruit. Combine in a bowl and add the lemon juice. Cover and refrigerate to chill. Open the can of *anko,* place in a bowl, cover, and refrigerate to chill.

When the gelatin has firmed, cut into ½-inch cubes and gently remove from the pan by lifting the foil up and out.

Using a big serving spoon, distribute ½-cup portions of jelly cubes into serving bowls. Arrange the chilled fruit, 1 rice cake, and a heaping tablespoon of *anko* atop the jelly cubes, and then pour the syrup sparingly over the top.

Pass the remaining syrup at the table for those who want additional sweetness.

Serves 6.

# Mom's Write Hand

When I was fifteen it was cool to forge your parent's signature on excuse letters. I peeked over my classmates' shoulders as they hunched over letters intended to get them out of half a day of classes. I was not surprised when their plump, loopy cursives with circles dotting the *i*'s didn't convince the discriminating eyes in the administrative office.

None of my friends knew that I had been signing my parents' signatures and writing their personal and business correspondence, as well as school permission letters, for several years. It was my job at home, but unlike a chore such as taking out the trash, its implications were much larger. To help my parents deal and communicate with the day-to-day issues that popped up from the outside world, I assumed this adult responsibility in the third grade.

It started when I asked Mom for a permission letter so I could participate in a class trip. Looking back, I realize that it was the end of an innocent time in my hometown, in the last years before it would become no longer safe to walk home from school without adult supervision. A strong current of friendliness remained, in which folks waved to one another and some still left their front doors and cars unlocked. It wouldn't be too long before a new undertow of leeriness would emerge.

At my request, Mom first tried writing the letter herself. She brought out the good business-paper notepad and Dad's silver-and-red Parker pen from the top desk drawer and scribbled something on the vellum paper. Looking at her handiwork, she tilted her head slightly, the way people do when studying paintings in art museums. Unsatisfied, she shook her head and tore the letter into tiny pieces.

I looked away, pretending to be occupied with the ladybug patch sewn on the thigh of my blue jeans. I sensed her uncertainty and growing frustration and knew I would add to it if she saw that I was watching her.

She slid the pen and notepad forcefully across the table in front of me. "My handwriting's no good, yours better. You say in a nice way I let you go."

I slowly scooted my chair away from the pad and pen. I didn't understand how Mom could ask me to do such a thing. Like lighting the oven and smoking cigarettes, writing permission letters was a grownup's responsibility, an act that, if discovered by another grownup, would mean certain punishment.

Mom mistook my frightened look to mean that I wasn't ready to write on good paper yet. She nodded and pulled out a piece of paper from the desk garbage bin. She flipped the mailing advertisement over to the blank side. "First practice on this. Don't write sloppy," she ordered.

As if contemplating a chess move, Mom leaned forward pensively while I wrote.

"Hurry up," she said impatiently. "My TV program is coming on."

I couldn't tell Mom she shouldn't have asked me to write the letter, that it was wrong. She would think I was being mouthy and challenging. I tried to think of a way out. Dad would probably write the letter, but I hadn't seen him in weeks, as he worked the second shift at the factory and was chick sexing during the day.

When I finished with the sample letter I pushed it across the table to Mom. She dropped her chin, which made her glasses fall down almost to the end of her nose.

She peered down at the letter, read it, and smiled, then handed me the good paper. I tucked a piece of lined paper underneath it to serve as a guide in writing straight.

When I finished, she signed it, looked at it again, and unexpectedly crumpled the note and tossed the paper ball into the wastepaper basket. To waste expensive writing paper this way wasn't like Mom at all. She reused ribbon and wrapping paper from presents, and straws from the Dairy Queen, and collected stacks of thin paper napkins from fast food restaurants.

Later, when she wasn't looking, I fished out the letter from the trash basket. I saw why she had thrown it away. Her signature, written in block letters like a child's, clashed ridiculously with my slanted cursive handwriting.

I rewrote the text on another sheet of good paper. After reading it, Mom pushed the letter back to me. "Go ahead," she said, her eyes as bright as river stones. She made a scribbling motion with her hand and I signed her name to it.

I tossed and turned that night, worrying about the letter I was to give my homeroom teacher the next day. I was at the age when I thought teachers possess a telepathic ability when things are amiss.

I knew that if Miss Owen had even an inkling of suspicion that the signature was forged, she would punish me with a paddling, without asking for an explanation first.

I was convinced that all schoolteachers believed children were liars and manipulators, and pain and humiliation were the only ways to snuff out bad behavior. At the time, it was common for teachers to hang their paddle of choice on the classroom wall. Some paddles were drilled with holes; others had taped handles for a sturdier grip. Their appearance was supposed to thwart any ideas of misbehaving. Even the school principal endorsed paddling. He was a burly mustached man who strolled through the hallways and playground carrying a wooden yardstick as a prop of authority like a clipboard or whistle. I had seen kids walloped with the principal's yardstick in front of the whole school as punishment for writing fake letters. The humiliation of getting spanked in front of the entire student body was more than I could bear. My nerves were so wrecked that I was tempted to confess to the forged letter before I had even turned it in.

The next morning, in homeroom class, Miss Owen called my name.

"Linda, come up to the desk, please," she said. The front of the classroom felt as though it were a street block away. Miss Owen turned Mom's letter around so it faced me. Her head was level with mine, so close I could see her oily, enlarged pores and the brush marks trailing through her hair-sprayed coif.

"Look here," she said, pointing to the paper with a finger as wide and even as a sausage link. "Your mom put the wrong year. She put in last year."

I felt light-headed with relief and fought an uncontrollable urge to snatch the letter up, correct it, and give it back. Instead, she looked at it again. "See, I'm going to mark out the year and put in the correct one and initial it at the top. It's got to be correct for the office files." She said this more to herself than to me. It was her first year as a teacher and she wanted to do everything by the book. Miss Owen gave me a quizzical look as I stood there, "Well, child, don't just stand there staring. You can go sit down now."

She didn't even notice the big breath of air I let out.

I believed that would be the first and last letter I'd write for Mom, but a couple of weeks later, she asked me to write the same kind of permission letter for Alvin's school outing. In a panic, I told her I would get in big trouble if the teachers found out I had written and signed the letter.

Mom didn't seem to understand the magnitude of the trouble that might result. I was convinced that they would never believe me if I said my mother actually allowed me to write the letter. I was worried that Mom wouldn't be able to explain to my teacher, or my brothers' teachers, that I was the official writer of permissions in my home. But Mom was nonchalant about the whole thing, and so I acquiesced.

Annoyed, I wondered why Alvin didn't write his own letter, since it was his trip. Perhaps sensing my hesitation, Mom patted me on the shoulder, smiled, and told me that the girls in a family always wrote letters for their parents. I believed her, just as I had when she told me, with the same straight face, that eating too much *dacai*, a spicy Chinese preserved mustard green, would make me dumb, or that I'd stop growing if I put the laundry basket over my head, or that toothpaste had a little sugar in it so it was important to rinse well. I believed her because she was my mother.

Mom was a product of a traditional Japanese upbringing in which the man's needs came first, yet when she was living in Tokyo as a single, independent working woman, she tasted a life unfettered by the restraints of husband and domestic duties. Having experienced both worlds, she raised me with double standards regarding the role of women. On one hand, my mother imposed on me the restrictions and standards of the traditional role of women as she knew it, which prioritized men over women, but she would also tell me I could do anything I put my mind to. Mom didn't see that she was contradicting herself and losing credibility with me.

At home, it was my responsibility to set and clear the table and wash the dishes, while my mother waited on my brothers and father as they ate.

When I asked Mom why my brothers didn't have to help with the household chores, why they were assigned to this duty only when they were being punished for something, she told me simply that it was a girl's place to do these things. I knew this wasn't right, because I had been in my friends' homes and knew that some boys did have chores, and that they had sisters who didn't have to wait on them hand and foot. So it was a shock, like when I hit my funny bone, to hear her say this so matter-of-factly. I didn't agree with this at all, but I was too young to voice my opinion, and already I knew that a wall would instantly come down between us if I argued. I kept my views to myself for years, letting them pile up like a rubbish heap. It wouldn't be until after I was working on my own and visiting home that I would finally tell my parents how I resented the unequal treatment between my brothers and me while we were growing up. For a few moments they looked at each other in a quizzical way, and then they shrugged their shoulders and said that was the way it was back then. I wanted a more dramatic explanation. But I had to be honest with myself; I didn't expect one. Their mild honesty silenced me because I knew what they said rang true. It was just the way things were done, and there was no use trying to change what was already completed.

❋

It pained me to see my mother struggle with English as a second language. Here was a woman who grilled a steak better than any man. She comforted me when I got into altercations with other kids. She made her own pattern when a customer requested a bridesmaid's gown. She nurtured friendships for decades across an ocean and a continent. Yet speaking, talking on the phone, or writing in English left Mom with a shell of insecurity. Understandably, she was extremely sensitive and vulnerable about this shortcoming.

Each day held constant reminders. If the phone rang or someone tried to strike up a conversation, her mind froze, making it even harder for her to choose her words.

One would think that after all the teasing I had received early on in elementary school, I would have been sensitive to Mom's feelings, but at the age of eight I hurt my mother in the worst way possible.

My membership in the young girls' club, the Brownies, required Mom to have phone conversations with the other Brownie mothers to coordinate refreshments and organize activities and outings.

One evening she was speaking on the phone with one of the mothers from my troop as Keven, Alvin, and I were eating at the dinner table. We giggled into our hands every time she said "brownies," which with her accent sounded like "baloney." Keven started it first. "I'd like to take some baloney to the baloney meeting," he said. We howled and mimicked Mom right there in front of her. She didn't yell at us or react in any way, so I assumed she wasn't paying attention.

After dinner, my brothers and I went to our rooms to do our homework. Mom called me from the living room. She reclined on the sofa, watching the evening news as she always did.

I came to the sofa where she sat to see what she wanted, and she sat up and smacked me across the face.

"Don't make fun of me," she said between clenched teeth and lay back down on the sofa, turning her eyes to the television as if I weren't standing there.

The hurt I had caused Mom was far more painful than the slap. It didn't occur to me that she would feel the same hurt that I felt when I was teased. Guilt and shame cemented my feet to the floor. My mouth felt closed shut as well, and I couldn't muster the voice to tell her I was sorry.

I don't how long I stood there. Eventually I sulked off to my bedroom, my hand still held up to my cheek.

The only way Mom could overcome her insecurity was to master the English language. Caring for a house and three children and having nowhere to study English, Mom learned what she could from soap operas and other television shows.

Her general reluctance to assert herself in English stretched into the future when she delayed becoming an American citizen because she was convinced she wouldn't pass the English written exam. Finally, she took the test.

Like the crumpled letter she tossed in the wastepaper basket, she kept her naturalization plans a secret. She had lived in America for more than thirty years, but she figured if her children didn't know she was studying for the test, no one would be the wiser if she flunked it. She eventually confided in me when she asked me about one of the mock test questions, details about how the U.S. judicial system worked.

When Mom passed the test and became naturalized, it was as if her fears of reading and writing English were exorcised. She began to speak openly about the years of unhappiness and exclusion pent up inside her and how she longed to master the English language. There were no English as a second language courses in rural Indiana during the 1960s and '70s. Raising three children with Dad gone most of the time made it all the more trying. Shyly, Mom revealed that she was ashamed that she hadn't helped my brothers and me with our homework, and that, most of all, she had never read us bedtime stories.

❀

It wasn't long before I was writing all of Mom's English correspondence—thank-you notes, condolences, and short notes on Christmas cards for family friends. I gave each note, especially the ones to relatives and friends, the same attention to detail I did my class reports.

When Mom made my favorite *okonomiyaki* (Japanese pizza), it was a dead giveaway that she had a letter for me to write. She knew I couldn't refuse after eating the savory pizza/pancake of shredded cabbage, ground meat, baby shrimp, and green onions, topped with mouthwatering *tonkatsu* fruit sauce and tangy red pickled ginger.

Through time, though, I looked forward to writing these letters. I enjoyed pretending I was Mom and sharing all that happened in our home. In Christmas cards I'd jot down chit-chatty details about the costume Mom was sewing for my church program or the progress of the garden or how proud we were of the summer harvest.

Because reading the handwritten responses that came in the mail could be as difficult as writing the letter, it also became my job to read those aloud as they arrived. I couldn't help but have author's pride when recipients sent back long letters and thanked my parents for the detailed update. Since I had spent some time writing their correspondence, carefully wording their letters as I thought an adult would, it never occurred to me that the people receiving them had already figured out that Mom and Dad hadn't written them. To all of them it didn't make a difference. They were probably happy to have gotten any correspondence, but I couldn't help but feel a guilty embarrassment for my parents.

About the time I turned twelve, Mom had me make doctors' and dentists' appointments by phone. If a bill needed to be straightened out, she had me call the utility companies. She even had me make important family emergency phone calls, such as the time I had to notify Dad at work that Keven had burned his face after an accident with the alcohol lamp from his chemistry set, or the time Alvin busted open his knee after wrecking his bike going down Busching Hill.

Often the person at the other end wasn't receptive to the idea of talking to a child. During one call with the water company, as I tried to give the account number, the woman on the other end of the line said, "Honey, are you home alone? Put your mom or dad on the phone."

"No, my mother ..."

"Well, put her on the phone then, dear."

"But ..."

"Listen, young lady, this isn't a joke. Put your mother on right now."

I held out the receiver to Mom. I saw a spark of apprehension cross her eyes. Mom took the receiver.

"Ha-llo?" she said. Listening carefully, she looked at the ceiling and then read the account number aloud. Talking through a smile and trying to sound pleasant, Mom slowly explained what was wrong with the bill. Abruptly, she handed me back the phone.

"Hello?" I said. I heard a sigh on the other end of the line.

"All right, honey, what is it that I can help you with?"

After a year and a half of this, I began to resent the letter writing and phone calls. When I came home and saw another list of phone numbers my mother wanted me to call, with notes scrawled out in her childlike handwriting, or found the writing paper and good pen waiting for me alongside my afternoon snack, inside my head I'd get hysterical. *Write your own damn letters! Make your own phone calls!*

I invariably picked up the pen or the phone receiver, believing that by completing these jobs I somehow protected my parents from the random ignorance and rudeness of people who didn't have patience for those who couldn't speak English well. As an American-born child, writing letters and making phone calls wasn't a difficult task, but knowing my mother couldn't do it, or was afraid to, and that she depended on me made it a weighty responsibility.

Slowly, through time, it magnified my parents' deficiencies. I saw my mother in the stark light of dependency, weakness, and vulnerability in a way that a child shouldn't have to. I started skipping breakfast to avoid hearing Dad sound out each syllable as he read aloud from the newspaper. It was yet another permanent reminder that my family was different.

※

One afternoon after a shopping trip in Cincinnati, I learned that I couldn't shelter my parents the way I had hoped. We had stopped at a large supermarket chain on the way home. Mom and Dad headed to the meat department to buy ground pork. Keven and Alvin went to browse the science fiction and rock music magazines while I checked out the makeup section to look at the nail polishes and smell the shampoos.

"What?!" a woman's voice boomed.

My stomach muscles tensed when I distinctly heard Dad stammering and then the woman shouting, "What are you saying?!"

My vision felt acutely bright and clear as I followed the voices as quickly as I could. I arrived just as the woman behind the meat counter threw up her hands as though she were giving up on something broken. She was the grandmotherly-looking type, with a white apron covering a huge chest that thrust forward like a robin's and a round Kewpie doll face with several chins. Beneath a white cotton cap, her Tabasco-red hair was set in tight, shiny ringlets. Thick, candy-smelling cologne sold in the locked glass cabinets in the cosmetics aisle clashed with the gamy smell of raw meat.

Smothering and familiar, jolts of anger and guilt took the place of my stomachache.

"What's going on?" I asked. A tall glass refrigerated case displaying the cuts of meat stood between us. I made an effort to speak as slowly as I did when dealing with bills over the phone. If I talked too quickly, I'd start to slur my own *R*'s as *L*'s, something that often happened when I got nervous or spoke too fast, having grown up listening to my parents' accents. I worked to fix this tendency by practicing enunciating my words while I watched anchorwoman Jane Pauley on *The Today Show* before school every morning.

But here at the meat counter, the adrenaline pumping in my veins made it difficult to talk slowly. The pained expression I saw on Dad's face made me angrier. Mom peered out from behind him, her arms crossed as if protecting herself. The way her face softened with gratitude when she saw me pushed up my anger another notch.

Dad turned slightly away from the woman and explained under his breath, in Japanese, what was going on. Hearing him, the woman's eyes glazed over, and I wished Dad had told me in English.

He waved at the meats in the case. "All he wants is some ground pork. It's usually in the case, but it's not here today," I explained, trying to raise as much nonchalance in my voice as I could muster. There were other customers milling about, waiting to be served.

"I'll have to grind some up special," she said, sighing, talking straight to me and ignoring my parents as if they had disappeared into thin air.

As she pushed the meat through the meat grinder, the counterwoman said cheerfully, "Your father kept saying, 'Poke, poke.'" She laughed. "I had no idea that he was trying to say 'pork.'"

I didn't even look at her when she said this, diverting my eyes to the bright redness of the meat and the pale, puckered skin of the headless chicken carcasses. I fought the overpowering urge to reach across the counter to find out how hard I'd have to shake her to make her ringlets jiggle.

Mom smiled and laughed, a reaction she had when she was nervous. Dad appeared to have taken solace in the fact that I had intervened and felt better enough to ask a question about the beef. Like a baby startled from sleep, the woman shouted in an alarming way, "What?!"

"Whaad? Whaad?" I cawed, mimicking her Midwestern drawl. I savored the way her eyes widened and rolled with indignity. I felt that familiar, satisfying hot electricity tingling all over me. I wanted to get revenge, to make her feel the stab of humiliation my parents had.

The control I had struggled to rein in was completely gone. "What is your problem?" I yelled, waving my hands, "Don't you understand English? Won't you just *try* to *listen* to what he's saying before screaming 'Whaad? Whaad?!'"

I stopped when I saw how nothing was registering in the woman's eyes. It was like pounding my fists on a solid metal door. It was no use.

I took a deep breath and looked around me. A mother and father and their young son walked by slowly, staring. An older woman wanting to buy some cold cuts looked at us, reconsidered, and walked the other way. Keven and Alvin finally emerged from the magazine aisle. I wondered how long they had been hiding between the aisles before deciding to make an appearance.

"What's all the yelling about?" Alvin asked. We all ignored his question.

The woman slid the paper-wrapped meat toward us and turned her back.

I swallowed hard several times, trying to dislodge the imaginary fish bone in the back of my throat. The meat paid for, we walked through the automatic doors, as if in a trance, out to the parking lot.

The white sunshine made me squint and cover my eyes. I hated my parents more than I hated the woman behind the counter. I hated them for not fighting back, for allowing her to push them around. I hated them for always bowing down, for letting the other person be right.

My eyes welled with tears. I didn't dare sniff, though my nose was stuffed up. It took all my energy to keep my face from scrunching up. I tried to get my mind off crying by imagining I was wearing a mask.

In the car, all I wanted to do was lie down and sleep. But first I wanted to crawl underneath something, such as a blanket. A cave or a closet would have been even better, somewhere dark where I could sleep until I felt normal again.

During the drive home, Dad told Keven and Alvin his version of what had happened in the store. With much astonishment, he described how they didn't understand what he said, no matter how many times he repeated himself. Alvin stared out the window, listening. Keven flipped through his *Rolling Stone* magazine.

They were probably relieved they hadn't been involved, just as I would have been. This incident at the meat counter reminded me of our appointments with the dentist.

As a youngster, I had plenty of cavities in my teeth, but our dentist reserved his Novocain for extractions only. Even when I felt the raw electric pain of the drill bit rubbing back and forth on my tooth, I didn't cry. I just suffered through it and focused on the eventual end of the drilling and the knowledge that I wouldn't have to sit in the dentist's chair for another six months. It was all about getting through it and away as soon as possible.

I joined my brothers in looking out the car window, but without seeing the square green and brown patches of farm-land that passed by. I watched my own distorted pale reflec-tion in the window. The sunshine made my eyes water again, but I didn't cry.

## Japanese Potstickers (Gyoza)

*It's important to thoroughly mix the filling for several minutes so the flavors can be absorbed into the meat. I find squeezing the meat with clean hands the most effective and fun way to accomplish this. Serve the gyoza with a traditional dipping sauce or Furiya's Gyoza Dipping Sauce (recipe follows).*

½ pound ground pork
1 cup finely chopped napa cabbage
2 green onions, chopped
1 garlic clove, minced
1 tablespoon ginger, grated
¼ cup sake
2 tablespoons soy sauce
1 teaspoon sesame oil
dash of salt and pepper
1 package of 3½-inch-round dumpling wrappers (see Note)
1½ tablespoons vegetable oil

In a large mixing bowl, combine well the ground pork, cabbage, green onions, garlic, and ginger for about one minute. Add sake, soy sauce, sesame oil, and salt and pepper and mix well for about 5 minutes.

Place the individual wrappers on a flat surface. Put a tablespoonful of pork filling in the center of the wrapper. Seal the dumpling by moistening the edge lightly with water halfway around the round wrapper. Fold the edges together and press down firmly.

In a nonstick skillet heat the vegetable oil over high heat. When a small piece of wrapper sizzles in the oil, lower the heat to medium high. Place the dumplings in rows so they are touching closely. When the edges begin to dry, about 3 to 4 minutes, add water so the dumplings are one-third covered. Cook until the water evaporates.

Using a spatula, lift the *gyoza* out by rows. Flip the *gyoza* over, brown side up, onto a plate or cookie sheet. Keep warm in the oven. Cook remaining dumplings as directed above.

Makes approximately 30 *gyoza*.

*Note:* Dumpling wrappers are sold in Asian groceries and refrigerated sections of some supermarkets and are generally sold in 12 oz. packages.

### Traditional Gyoza Dipping Sauce

    1 part rice vinegar
    1 part soy sauce
    chili oil, to taste

Combine ingredients. Serve with *gyoza*.

### Furiya's Gyoza Dipping Sauce

    ¼ teaspoon Colby's dry mustard paste
    1 tablespoon soy sauce
    1 teaspoon rice vinegar

Combine ingredients. Serve with *gyoza*.

## A Taste of the Big Apple

I always envied the abundance of relatives I encountered in my friends' families. Language, culture, and the Pacific Ocean kept me from getting to know my mother's side of the family as well as I would have liked to. Aside from my trip to Japan and an occasional phone call, I would have no further contact with them, except through my parents. I wouldn't see them again until more than twenty years after my first visit. Our closest relatives living in America were Dad's older brother, George, who lived in Brooklyn, and his sister, Jane, a New Jersey resident.

From an early age, I remember Dad phoning his siblings every Christmas. And it was one of these holiday phone conversations that initiated our first family visit to my Aunt Jane's home.

Driving was the most economical mode of travel for my parents as airplane travel at the time was financially unrealistic for a family of five, plus a dog. In the usual fashion of our family vacation travels, my brothers and I were herded out of bed and into the station wagon hours before sunrise. Dad wanted to stay on schedule and arrive in New Jersey by evening, so we lunched on rice balls at roadside rest stops instead of stopping for lunch at Howard Johnson or a fast food restaurant.

I was seven years old that Christmas, and I had never met Aunt Jane in person. I had only seen photographs of her, which didn't do her justice. In person she was the most glamorous woman I had ever seen. She was an Asian version of Lauren Bacall. Her shoulder-length bob was parted on the side, and it softly sprang up in a lazy wave. Her fingernails were short and painted red. An eye-catching turquoise stone in a simple gold setting, a purchase from one of her trips to Turkey, dangled on her ring finger.

Perhaps sensing my awe, Dad whispered that she used to carry a leather satchel with a secret drawer in the bottom to stash her jewels for safekeeping, and that once he'd witnessed her pull open the drawer and dress herself in jewels before they'd attended a play together. In spite of his frugal ways, Dad smiled proudly when he described the sable coat and diamonds she wore to the grocery store.

She and her husband, Yoshio, lived on a prosperous tree-lined street in Linden, New Jersey. All the houses on their street were neatly lined up next to each other like books on a shelf. Out back was a small fenced-in yard with plastic-covered lawn furniture.

The house was decorated with beautiful printed wallpaper. Our house in Indiana was sprawling by comparison, but my aunt's house was richer in detail. The shiny dark wood side tables and pristine upholstered chairs and sofas in traditional floral prints reflected the fact that her children had grown up and moved out. In every room there were beautiful things to marvel at: the cut-glass mirrors, lamps with intricately painted vase bases, toile-covered footstools, and clusters of porcelain animal figurines. Our living room was furnished with a dented coffee table and a lumpy sofa from too many pillow fights. Even in Aunt Jane's bathrooms, the wallpaper was a colorful candy stripe and there were small, snowy-white hand towels with flowers embroidered on them and soaps molded to the shape of shells in the glass soapdish, instead of our frayed towels and battered Lifeguard soap.

In the evening, as the house became enfolded in the indigo-blue winter darkness, Aunt Jane went from room to room, switching on the lamps. The filmy gray tendrils of cigarette smoke, the soft, spicy scent of Yves St. Laurent's Cinnabar, and the sound of tinkling ice were her constant companions.

We came to visit during a long weekend before the Christmas holiday and couldn't have picked a colder, snowier time. My brothers and I remained indoors and watched more television than we were allowed to at home. The adults spent most of the day getting into long conversations over cups of coffee, then green tea. Occasionally the idea of going into the city or taking a drive to see some point of interest would come up, but nothing was ever instigated, or it became too late to go. During cocktail hour on the first night of our visit, Aunt Jane turned to me. "Linda, tomorrow we'll make chocolate chip cookies together, okay?" Aunt Jane spoke English in the same high-pitched tone she used when speaking Japanese. Mom used this high-pitched voice when she spoke Japanese around other native speakers. She had pointed out other women who did this on different occasions and said it's achieved by imagining your voice is coming out of the top of your head. Although it sounded exaggerated and unnatural to my ears, in Japanese culture it is considered feminine and attractive.

The following morning I woke up with anticipation, expecting to see butter softening on the kitchen counter, a mixer, measuring cups and spoons, and a bowl out and ready. The morning passed into noon, however, without mention of the cookie-making. Sandwich-making stuff came out, but no ingredients for chocolate chip cookie batter were to be found. By late afternoon, when there was still no mention of the cookies, I knew it wasn't going to happen. I didn't feel comfortable saying anything to Aunt Jane, but I still wanted her to know that I was disappointed. I found Mom in the living room and crawled over to where she was sitting, whining about nothing until she asked me what was wrong. When I told her, she promptly took me in to the kitchen, where Aunt Jane was making tea.

"Jane," she said, using her high-pitched voice, "Linda is sad that you all didn't make cookies today."

My aunt seemed genuinely embarrassed by her forgetfulness and apologized profusely. She put her beautifully groomed hand on me and promised we would do it tomorrow. I nodded my head eagerly, allowing myself to get my hopes up high.

The cookies were forgotten again the next day. But this time I was more hurt than disappointed, and I didn't want Mom to know that I had been duped again. I also had a feeling that Mom would get angry at Aunt Jane. I was a lucky child who hadn't experienced a lot of disappointments up to that point in my life, and the letdown certainly took the sheen off my aunt.

On the third night of our visit, we sat at the dinner table in that satisfied state of contentment after Aunt Jane had served a traditional Japanese meal of rice, miso soup, tofu, thin slices of rare sirloin marinated in soy sauce, and ginger. Unlike the traditional dynamic at my house, where Mom cooked, cleared, and cleaned up after a meal, Uncle Yoshio cleared away the plates, put the coffee on, and set out the dessert without being asked. While Uncle Yoshio was in the kitchen, I saw Mom lean in and quietly ask Aunt Jane if her husband minded cleaning up.

She answered, "Of course not. I cook, he cleans up. It's only fair." Mom nodded her head in understanding, which I took to mean that in my aunt and uncle's household, this setup was more a function of her will than his.

During dinner, the conversation was engaging and intimate. We were leaving the next morning and my parents and aunt and uncle were feeling generous and sentimental with each other, the way guests and hosts do before departing. They reminisced about the past, and Dad and Aunt Jane shared funny and touching childhood memories.

As Uncle Yoshio cleared the plates, the bold smell of brewing coffee awakened the room. Dad looked down at his hands folded in front of him and smiled to himself. Mom slowly and carefully folded the cloth napkin, replacing it neatly at her place setting. Even my brothers and I were basking in the warmth of the family setting.

Aunt Jane reached for my father with her gaze and said, "Ichan," using his childhood name in a small voice I had never heard before. "It's nothing to worry about, but I have a doctor's appointment next week."

Aunt Jane hesitated a moment before pulling down the collar of her blouse. She tapped a lump the size of a golf ball embedded below her clavicle. The light from the dining room chandelier made her neck resemble plucked chicken skin. She said she was having it examined the following week.

A heavy silence fell upon the dining room. Mom attempted to hide her surprise by being nonchalant and saying it was probably nothing. Dad agreed it was a good idea to get it checked out. Uncle Yoshio insisted Aunt Jane not worry about it.

As everyone spoke, Aunt Jane continued to massage the knot with her pinkie and ring finger while pinching a smoldering cigarette between her index and third finger. Taking a deep breath, she said confidently, "I'm not worried."

The exchange among my adult relatives left me troubled in a way that I didn't understand at the time. It was the first time I had been privy to the fears surrounding sickness and death, topics that my parents never shared or discussed with me. Several days after we returned to Indiana, Uncle Yoshio called and informed us that the test on Aunt Jane's lump came back malignant. She had advanced lung cancer. That week was the first and last time I ever saw Aunt Jane.

❀

A couple of years after her passing, when I was eleven years old, we went to Brooklyn to spend the Christmas holiday with my father's brother, George, and his family.

They lived in a big brownstone on State Street near downtown Brooklyn, close to the Abraham & Strauss department store. Their home had tall double doors and big, spacious rooms with fireplaces and lofty ceilings. Aunt Milly decorated the first-floor living room with comfortable, antique-looking furniture, worn Oriental rugs, and tall plants that emerged from large urns.

Floor-to-ceiling hardback, paperback, coffee-table, and leather-bound books crammed the library. Its hardwood floor was barely visible under the stacks of old magazines and newspapers, work papers, music cassettes, and LPs. Every inch of space had something on it, even the lumpy brown sofa, which was covered with dog hair and occupied by Hansko, an odiferous three-legged German shepherd. Their home bespoke scholars, readers, and big thinkers.

My three cousins, Sumi, Sonja, and Signy, were strangers to me. I was nearest in age to Signy, who was thirteen, the same age as Alvin and a year and a half older than I. The last time I had seen Signy I was eight, when our families met for a vacation in Alexandria, Virginia. At the time, Signy was a Judy Blume–reading, Yahtzee-playing youngster. So I was surprised that Christmas in Brooklyn to find that she had turned into a sophisticated adolescent who admired Flemish artists and drank sweet milky coffee.

I envied my cousins' striking mixed features. They had their Japanese father's dark eyes and full lips and Aunt Milly's Scandinavian nose and heart-shaped face. All three of them had Cher-like long, straight black hair that framed their faces gorgeously.

Despite our similarity in ages, my cousins appeared far more chic and worldly in their urban uniform of battered, baggy trench coats and army fatigue pants. They possessed the same silent, confident gaze I'd seen on models Gia Carangi and Janice Dickinson in the pages of *Vogue*. My urban cousins ate doughnut-shaped bread called bagels and even managed the subways by themselves. An early snowstorm fell that winter. I remember vividly following Uncle George as he led us to see the city sights: the Statue of Liberty, the Rockettes at Radio City Music Hall, the World Trade Center, Macy's, and Rockefeller Center. His back, encased in a green army jacket, provided my visual marker against the backdrop of gray buildings, moving columns of pedestrians, and sidewalks bordered with old snow scabbed with dog urine and feces.

I wondered what they must have thought about us, their country cousins. I couldn't help but watch my cousins' every move, the same way the hillbilly children who lived deep in the backcountry did when they came into Versailles with their parents once a month to grocery shop. I'd observe those children, the way they stood in a stupor at the curbside, shoulders hunched, staring at us town kids with fascination.

Compared to the rusticity of my rural breeding, my cousins' colorful lives, details of which were frequently disclosed to us by Mom, dripped with sophistication. I could scarcely fathom their big-city existence, which included things like movies, plays, and travel abroad. They possessed an elusive luster that I found both dazzling and intimidating. Rather than making my brothers and me feel an affinity toward them, as was Mom's intent, this information served only to make us feel like culturally deprived simpletons.

❦

After that Christmas holiday in Brooklyn, I didn't see my city relatives for another five years, until the summer following my fifteenth birthday. This next visit came about purely by accident when Dad phoned Uncle George on the anniversary of Aunt Jane's death.

Uncle George asked to talk to me on the phone and I was flattered. Usually he spoke only to Dad. He asked me about which authors I was reading and how I had done in school that year. When he asked me what I had in mind for the summer, I didn't exaggerate when I told him I wasn't doing anything. I was signed up for a driver's education class to receive my permit and planning to take baby-sitting jobs. I suspected that summer would be no different from summers past, when the days muddled together like melting ice cream on warm pie. Afternoon showers marked the time and broke up the monotony of the midday heat. I was resigned to this schedule and knew nothing different.

Dad got back on the phone with Uncle George after he'd asked a few more questions of me. When Dad set the phone down in its cradle, he looked at me and said, "You will spend two weeks with your Brooklyn relatives this summer." Just like that. Uncle George apparently thought I needed a change that summer, a chance to see how my city family lived. My uncle always did spontaneous things like that. He had sent us the workbooks *Learning Hiragana* and *Learning Katakana*, which turned out to be the reason I went to Japan with my mother. Another time he sent a boxful of assorted origami paper and how-to books. Even though Mom had taught us all the art of paper-folding, the box of paper was something new and exciting for my brothers and me to practice with.

I remembered how Uncle George had taken my brothers and me aside during that Christmas visit and emphasized the importance of seeing the world. His descriptions of the places he had been sounded magnificent—the Nile in Egypt, the Kabuki theater in Japan, the hot springs in Finland.

We had nodded in agreement, but my brothers and I knew that his suggestions were as impossible as building a rocket ship and blasting off to the moon. We didn't have the heart to tell him that Mom and Dad saw things in a different light. Their worries revolved around staying healthy, working, and paying the bills. Our way of life was slow, simple, and uneventful. With no surprises. We had no options because there were no choices.

So the opportunity to spend two weeks without my brothers in Brooklyn the summer before my junior year of high school was more than I could have ever hoped for. I couldn't contain myself about my new summer plans. I started bragging excitedly to all my friends about my upcoming adventure. I was met with silence, faint smiles, and far-off looks when I informed them I would be flying on an airplane. Like me, they knew next to nothing about Brooklyn, or New York City, for that matter. But when I boarded the plane—my first solo trip—my feelings of being grown-up were replaced with doubt. I wanted to turn around, get off the plane, and tell my parents that I had changed my mind, but I couldn't face their disappointment.

It was late afternoon when my plane landed at LaGuardia Airport. My fears subsided when I caught the welcoming sight of Uncle George and Aunt Milly waiting for me at the gate. In worn T-shirt, jeans, and sandals, Uncle George was heavier-set than Dad and sported a scruffy salt-and-pepper goatee. Aunt Milly had long, wiry silver hair pulled back in a fluffy ponytail. A longtime yoga practitioner, she was wiry and agile. During my visit, she often assumed the lotus position on the subway or in downtown parks.

My aunt and uncle used public transportation, and so we took a train, the subway, and a bus to get back to their house in Brooklyn. They didn't own a car. Uncle George had gotten rid of the one they owned for the occasional trip out of the city after he got in an accident in which he almost careened off the Brooklyn Bridge. He'd lost the use of one of his eyes, which was now permanently closed.

When we arrived at their brownstone, Cousin Signy met me at the door. She surprised me when she planted a kiss on both my cheeks. "That's how the French greet each other," she explained. Signy, like Alvin, had just graduated high school. While Alvin would be attending Indiana University, she was starting school at the Sorbonne in Paris the following fall.

As Uncle George, Aunt Milly, Signy, and I stood in the foyer, I found myself staring at Signy. The last time I had seen her she had hid behind fringy bangs and worn baggy, olive-green army surplus clothing. Now she had the delicate, praying-mantis appearance of a ballerina. Her head and hands appeared bigger than the rest of her lithe, lanky body. She wore her coffee-colored brown hair in a hard chignon at the base of her neck. The fitted cropped top and baggy, earth-toned wraparound pants exaggerated her elongated stature even more.

My pink polo shirt, dark-blue Gloria Vanderbilt jeans, white sneakers, and boyish short haircut appeared bland and unstylish in comparison.

Aunt Milly shooed Signy and me out of the house, wanting us to get on our way into Manhattan, where Signy was meeting a friend for dinner. My aunt waved at us from the vestibule as we headed to the subway. I looked down again at what I wore and wished I had worn something more stylish. Except, I realized, I didn't have anything more stylish.

"What's the name of the festival in your town again? Zucchini festival or something like that?" Signy asked me once we got to the restaurant. She was twirling her drinking straw and looking at me intently. Ever since we had left the house, I had been distracted by all the things to see: the colorful groceries with striped awnings, the graffiti and racket of the subways, and the people of every race and profession.

The restaurant Signy had chosen was the famous New York City landmark Serendipity 3 on the Upper East Side, near Bloomingdale's department store. Signy and I would learn from Aunt Milly almost a decade later that Uncle George had worked on the restaurant's wood detailing, one of the many odd jobs he held in the 1950s. I couldn't even think straight as I looked around at the decor—with its jewel-colored Tiffany lamps, black-and-white floors, and large ornamental pieces, such as a metal horse and a huge clock that hung right behind Signy's chair. I was also distracted by Signy's friend, Lynn, who was already seated and sipping on a soda when we arrived.

"Are you talking about the Pumpkin Show?" I asked, trying not to stare at Lynn.

"The Pumpkin Show, yeah, that's the one." Signy broke out in a smile, and her eyes softened at the recollection of the name.

I was mesmerized by the fact that Lynn was African American. I tried to control myself, but I couldn't stop staring at her. I was hoping she couldn't tell that she was the first African American I had ever sat down and had a conversation with in my entire life. In fact, the only contact I had ever had with African Americans was seeing them on the streets or working at stores or restaurants.

I thought this as I told Signy, "It's just a fair with rides and games. At the end of the week, there's a contest for the biggest pumpkin." My voice trailed off.

I left out the fact that, in Versailles, there was nothing that rivaled that particular autumn festival. Not to mention it was my favorite time of year. The grounds surrounding the courthouse square were carpeted with blazing autumn foliage, the air scented with the intoxicating smell of funnel cakes, corn dogs, fallen leaves, and pipe tobacco. But how could Signy and her friends understand any of these things? She had never been to Versailles. We were, after all, practically strangers. I also decided not to mention how much I and everyone else in town looked forward to the event every year. Visitors came from all over the county, even from as far away as Cincinnati and Indianapolis, to visit the fair. There was once a reporter from Chicago who came to write a story about the biggest-pumpkin winner.

"Lynn," she said, turning to her friend. "These pumpkins are gigantic." Signy had a lilt to her voice that reminded me of the way Audrey Hepburn spoke in *Breakfast at Tiffany's*. She also had a way of making elegant sweeping gestures with her long hands. If people at home had talked this way with their hands, they would have been asked if they were swatting flies. At first, her mannerisms seemed so exaggerated to me, I thought she was showing off. But the more time I spent with her, the more I realized that it was just how she spoke and expressed herself.

Signy continued, "On her way to Fordham College, Sonja stopped at Linda's parents' place in Versailles. They took her to the festival. Sonja said the pumpkins were the size of armchairs and the colors were unbelievable shades of sienna and ochre." I remembered when Sonja had stopped in town on her way to college. She was driving a U-Haul truck. Dad got a kick out of how all the locals stared at her in her surgical scrub pants and tie-dyed tank top as we strolled past the rides and game booths.

I had never heard fancy words such as "sienna" and "ochre" before, but I figured she meant orange. Signy made the pumpkin show sound rustic and charming in a way I had never considered. For perhaps the first time in my life, I saw how amazing it actually was to see the large pumpkins weighing up to 350 pounds, all gnarled and bumpy like the canyons of Arizona.

I was busy watching the way Lynn reacted to my cousin's descriptions of things she had never even seen when I heard Signy use the word "JAP-y."

"What did you say?!" I shrieked. I choked on my soda and gave her a smile. More calmly I repeated, "What was that?"

Signy proceeded cautiously. "I was telling Lynn how this girl we both know was acting JAP-y." My face burned hot. I must have been flushed. Signy and Lynn exchanged looks.

Signy's face suddenly relaxed with awareness and she smiled, "Oh no, it's not what you think. Here 'JAP' means Jewish American Princess. You know? Spoiled, pampered."

"Oh, yeah, right," I said, waving my hand as if to shoo away any concern, even though I had no idea what she was talking about. I tried to laugh at the misunderstanding, but my nerves were jarred from the embarrassment. I had never heard the phrase because I had never met anyone Jewish before, either.

I was relieved when our bacon, lettuce, and tomato sandwiches arrived. Sensing my self-consciousness, Signy announced, "Lynn and I are very glad you're here. Usually, we never have an excuse to eat here. So we only come when we have visitors in town. The BLTs are our favorite. And we have to order a banana split."

My sandwich was as thick as a dictionary. The pieces of toasted bread were the size of dinner plates, and they were stuffed with at least a half pound of bacon. The tomatoes didn't even come close to comparing to Dad's delicious homegrown variety, but the sandwiches were impressive nonetheless.

"What kind of bread is this?" I asked, savoring its buttery taste.

"Challah, I think," Signy said, emphasizing the "ah" at the end. I wouldn't come across that bread again until I moved to California many years later. I remember biting into the soft dough and its slightly sweet flavor transporting me back to my first evening in the Big Apple.

I listened as Signy and Lynn talked about their upcoming plans for college. Lynn would be attending Brown University to study playwriting. At the time, we had no idea that she would go on to become an award-winning playwright; all I could think about at that moment was the fact that I had no idea where Brown was, or what kind of school it was, and I found myself again envying my cousins' urban sophistication.

When the banana split arrived, we made a small dent in the sweet mountain of ice cream with our long-handled spoons. I racked my brains for something witty or thought-provoking to add to the conversation, but the only topics that came to mind were snippets of town gossip and vapid, boy-crazy anecdotes.

To my relief, Signy suggested we walk to the Paris Movie Theater next to the Plaza Hotel after dinner. Since she was going to school in France, she wanted to train her ear to the language by watching her favorite movie, *Diva,* a film whose intrigues revolved around a bootlegged opera tape and a cast of Parisian characters.

Once we were comfortably seated in the theater, I found that rather than experiencing the excitement of watching my first foreign film, I felt a relief at having a moment's respite from feeling so awkward and out of place. During my visit, I covered up my feelings of inadequacy by pretending the new experience was something I had actually done before. In hindsight, I wasn't fooling anyone.

In the darkness of the cinema, I was able to process everything that had happened that day. The excitement about and anticipation of my journey that had built up during the previous weeks had faded completely. Having finally arrived, I saw for the first time that I was as uninteresting as a shovel. In those first few hours, I felt the creeping apprehension that I didn't belong, and I was overcome with the tug of homesickness for the familiarity of the small town I had left behind.

❀

The homesickness stayed with me well into that first night. I slept on a futon mattress laid out on the floor of Sumi's old bedroom. I tried to envision what my friends were doing back home, but I couldn't because of the noise coming from the room next door. Burkhardt, a struggling vibraphone musician from Germany, was boarding in Sonja's old bedroom. I heard him opening and closing a bureau drawer well past the time we had gotten ready for bed, the floorboards creaking with his every footstep.

Before I had tucked in for the night, Aunt Milly, a knowing sparkle in her eyes, gave me a night-light. "In case you wake up in the middle of the night and can't see," she told me. As I lay there wide awake in the semidarkness of Sumi's room, my eyes adjusted enough to read the titles of some of the books on the shelf. I saw none of the raunchy romance novels I read;

Sumi's shelves were filled with classics in French and German and contemporary literature, most of which I had never heard of. Like the downstairs library, Sumi's room was stacked from floor to ceiling with books, except that they were layered two deep in the shelves and crammed sideways along the tops of the books. They were arranged so precisely that they seemed to be an extension of the exposed red-brick wall.

Lulled by the muffled street sounds outside and the comforting hum of an electric fan that stirred the warm air, I thought about the similarities between my father and Uncle George. In appearance, they shared the same Charlie Brown round head, family paunch, proud broad shoulders, and deep, jolly laugh. But my uncle spoke as articulately as an English professor, while Dad sounded as if he were in his first semester of studying English as a second language.

There were many times during my girlhood when I despised my country upbringing. But the times this would become overbearing occurred away from home and around my peers, such as the week I spent at a math camp where I met girls from much bigger towns who had seen and done more than me. I began to complain about it more vocally as I got into my teens. Mom never voiced it, but I think she too missed the culture and excitement of the city. When I hemmed and hawed about the unfairness of being stuck in the country with nothing to do, instead of explaining that this was where Dad could find work and where we were settled in school, she would snap, "Stop complaining. When you finish college and get a job, you'll never have to return to Indiana."

Uncle George met Aunt Milly in New York City, where they later married and settled. Dad was still in Japan during those years. Anti-Japanese sentiment prevailed during those postwar years, making it difficult for Uncle George to find work. To make a living, he took up cabinetmaking and carpentry. In the 1950s, he fell into the beat scene and explored his interest in architecture, literature, dance, art, politics, and psychology.

In the 1970s he became involved in left-wing political groups with beliefs that went against the status quo. He dabbled in journalism and writing, whether for corporate marketing, political publications, or letters to the editor criticizing an article line by line.

When Dad's U.S. citizenship was reinstated, he arrived in New York to reunite with the siblings he hadn't seen in decades. From there, Dad was drawn to the Midwest because he said the city made him sleepy, while the countryside revived him.

The country and the city where my father and his brother respectively chose to settle reflected their varying personalities, like a watercolor and an oil painting.

My father and uncle would turn out to be the two most influential men in my life. Initially, that summer in the Big Apple was a shock. And though at times I resisted it, I slowly opened and thrived on the new tastes, smells, sounds, and sights I was experiencing during my city visit. When I left, I took away elements that would ultimately determine the way I perceived myself and the direction my life would take. My uncle's invitation to the city that summer was the greatest gift I could possibly have received as a young person.

After college, I would leave Indiana for a very long stretch of time and live in cities all over the world, until, like my father, I felt a deep physical yearning, akin to remembering an old loved one, to return to the quiet and the stillness of a small town, that place where I could sleep like baby.

During my stay I followed my aunt, uncle, and cousin around wherever they went. I tagged along behind whoever wanted company, like a string attached to a balloon.

I went with Uncle George on his weekly trip to buy groceries. He didn't go to a big supermarket chain that sold everything like my family did; in fact, I never once saw a supermarket during my stay. He visited small, out-of-the-way shops with old hardwood floors and specialty food items, such as cheeses and artisan breads.

When we passed a butcher, I asked Uncle George shyly if I could have meat for dinner one night, something I sorely missed in their mostly vegetarian household. He laughed and nodded his head yes.

Aunt Milly was a strict vegetarian. Red meat, whether used in Japanese or Western cooking, was a dominant part of my diet. I loved it all: thick, rare steaks; *tendon,* a Japanese dish of thin slices of simmered beef and eggs over rice, teriyaki-marinated pork chops, meat loaf, with pearls of white bread, coated with ketchup, and, of course, hamburgers. I was defenseless before Aunt Milly's arguments on the virtues of vegetarianism and felt guilty when I asked for meat, but I couldn't ignore the craving. Even though Uncle George participated in his wife's vegetarianism, sometimes he indulged in red meat. That night we both feasted on thick rib-eye steaks. Topped with sautéed mushrooms and onions, seared crisp on the outside, fleshy pink and leaking red-tinged juice on the inside, the marbled rib eye was the most delicious piece of meat I had ever tasted. Uncle George appraised me at the dinner table as

I cut into my steak and chewed, and an expression of complete understanding swept across his face.

As a practicing vegetarian, Aunt Milly, of course, wanted the people she loved to turn to vegetarianism. Except for a short lecture during a subway ride, though, she didn't impose her beliefs on me. She understood that I came from a different upbringing and that my diet, albeit Japanese, included red meat.

Like my craving for a steak, I was also unable to shake off some of my naive country habits. One morning, on our way to the subway that would take us back to Brooklyn from Signy's exercise class on Manhattan's Upper East Side, a man on the street said he wanted to show me a card trick. I walked over to where he stood, and he flashed a picture of a naked woman looking at herself in a mirror. Signy yanked me away and pulled me after her until we got to the next corner. Before she said anything, she dug in her bag for a cigarette and matches.

"Look, Linda, you're going to be here for what, another week?" She inhaled the smoke deeply and held her cigarette like I'd seen actresses do in the movies. Her upturned eyes then softened as she tapped the ash from her burning cigarette. "If you hope to survive even that long, I want to give you one word of advice."

I looked at her expectantly.

"Walk with purpose, that's all. Walk like you know where you're going. Because if you don't, every freak in this city will know you're new here and bug you." She took a final drag from her cigarette, not even halfway finished, and dropped it on the sidewalk. With her powerful ankle, Signy turned the ball of her turquoise-colored pointy-toed flats into it with the confident, businesslike attitude of someone twice her age. She pulled out the band holding her long brown hair up, then gathered it all up again and twisted it back into a neat bun.

The unspoken hint that the freaks would bother her for being with someone like me lingered between us like the smoke from her cigarette. "But I don't know where I'm going," I answered honestly.

"No one has to know that. Just act like you do and you'll be fine. And another thing," she said, flicking a speck of tobacco from her tongue. "Could you stop saying hi to everyone?"

⁂

The city Furiyas constantly debated, or "discussed." Uncle George and Aunt Milly loved to argue any issue and they encouraged their daughters to join in.

On one occasion, in the middle of a particular discussion they were having about something I knew nothing about, I tuned out Uncle George and Aunt Milly and withdrew into my own thoughts. Unexpectedly, Uncle George turned to me in midsentence and asked what I had to say on the subject. My mind froze. Shamefaced and embarrassed, I shrugged my shoulders and mumbled, "I dunno."

"Sure you do," Uncle George said crisply. "You've got to have an opinion."

His voice softened. "Believe it or not, there's no right or wrong answer, just a viewpoint. It's how you organize what you're going to say that makes it compelling and, more important, convincing." Uncle George leaned back in his chair and laced his hands behind his head as if he were giving me directions on how to get to the newspaper stand down the street.

"See, when you don't have an opinion, that's when people corral and hustle you around and push their views on you." He nodded his head at me.

This talk was all new to me, but I loved it and drew energy from it. I had been with the city Furiyas for only a few days and found myself caught up in their exuberant, experimental approach to life. They guided and shaped their own lives, not the other way around. I wished my parents talked to me the way Uncle George did, the way he nudged me to think outside the perimeters. I had no formed opinions because I had spent my life daydreaming, listening, being told, and being led. I jiggled along like a hula-girl doll stuck on a car dashboard.

I realized I would remain a child for as long as I lived under my parents' roof. Mom and Dad neither asked for nor considered my thoughts on any subject. They saw their children's skill at arguing a point as unnecessary, disrespectful, and a sign of mouthy back talk, the characteristics of a troublemaker.

They wanted me to listen and learn from what people told me and never question whether the information was right or wrong. Despite my American upbringing, Mom pushed the customs she grew up with onto me. When I was ten, she gave me this advice in Japanese: "If someone offers you food or drink, decline it."

"What if I'm hungry or thirsty?"

"You must still decline three times as a sign of politeness. Accept it, hesitatingly, on the fourth time," she explained.

I threw out this rule early on, and I particularly saw how poorly it served me during my first year of college. It took me only one time, when my dorm mates and I pitched in on a pizza and I declined seconds to be polite, to realize that after

turning down a first offer, a second one was not likely to follow. In America, no means no. No one asks you three times for
anything you initially pass up.

It was a frustrating lesson for Mom to learn that her
cultural rules didn't apply in American society. We got into
squabbles in which she'd exclaim that my behavior would never
be acceptable in Japan, to which I answered triumphantly, "It's
a good thing we're not living in Japan." She would give me
dirty looks in response but said nothing.

As each day passed in Brooklyn, I became more familiar
with the city Furiyas and felt more and more at home. One
warm, breezeless night, after visiting Sumi and her husband,
Maurizio's, coffeehouse, Caffe Ritrovo, on Hudson Street at
Barrow in Greenwich Village, Uncle George and I met Signy
for a late-night snack at Panchito's on McDougal Street.

At ten at night, the sidewalk was packed. There was so
much to see in the neighborhood. People were sitting and
talking on the stoops, and patrons filled the restaurants and
bars. I walked quickly, trying to keep up with Uncle George's
long strides, doing a double take at two women making out on
the hood of a gold Buick. My uncle didn't even notice them
as he boasted about the restaurant's tortilla wrappings. He
described them as authentic and told me that you know this
when they come with the threads of corn silk still in them.
I felt at ease enough with Uncle George to tell him that
having grown up around cornfields, I didn't think tortillas
with threads of corn silk were such a great thing, to which he
gave a big belly-laugh.

A basket of tortilla chips and salsa, ceviche, thick burri-
tos, and quesadillas oozing with cheese arrived just as Signy
joined us. Uncle George poured me a frozen margarita from

a large pitcher. The refreshing citrus drink was so tangy and different from anything I'd ever had that I didn't know it contained tequila.

I was enchanted by the festiveness of the strumming and singing of the strolling guitarist, the walls strung up with colored Christmas tree lights, piñatas dangling from the ceiling, and the pale yellow drinks in the icy wide-mouthed glasses. I had no idea that this decor was typical of Mexican restaurants. To me, at that time, it was as exotic as visiting another country.

That night at the Mexican restaurant, Uncle George asked me what my routine was like in Versailles. By this time the margarita was making me feel relaxed and loosened my tongue. My face was red and hot to the touch. Until that night, I had never tasted a margarita before and didn't dare bring up the fact that my parents wouldn't approve. Unlike my hometown, where everyone was in everyone else's business, I knew that my parents would never hear about this. Perhaps it was the festive evening, the time I had already spent with my relatives, or the drink, but for whatever reason, my true feelings, emotions, and resentments I had never voiced before poured out like rice grains spilling from a hole in the bag.

I described the random and unexpected racial teasing and slurs that left me quaking with anger, not at the offender, but at my parents, who raised me in a town where we didn't belong.

Uncle George appreciated my insights, and I knew my subject. And like ice that breaks at the start of a spring thaw, once the words began to flow, so did my long–pent-up emotions.

I told Uncle George and Signy how I had always felt distant, like an outsider, even though I was born in the same hospital and had attended the same kindergarten, elementary, junior high, and high school as my peers. How I spent a lot of time thinking and planning what I could do differently but never got it right.

As I spoke, Signy occasionally nodded her head compassionately or glanced at Uncle George to see his reaction. If I had noticed a frown, furrowed brows, or any sign of skepticism, I would have dropped the subject immediately. But the way Uncle George rubbed his chin and nodded his head vigorously several times made me think that he understood, which encouraged me to continue.

When I finished, he said quietly, shaking his head, "Well, that's really sad to hear." It was simply put, but somehow I liked his response better than gasps of astonishment. That night, for the first time since I had arrived, I slept through the night.

I felt shy around my uncle and my cousin the next day, afraid I had revealed too much. I hid out in the library, where I watched the videocassettes Uncle George had taped of the James Clavell *Shogun* miniseries.

Afterward, I went to the second-floor kitchen, a room just as cluttered as the rest of the house. The sink held a constant stack of dirty dishes that soaked in cold, gray water. The stove top, speckled with coffee grounds, displayed a working collection of espresso pots and coffee presses.

An asparagus pot, salmon poacher, metal dim sum steamers, drum-size stockpots, colanders, and strainers hung from silver hooks on the wall or poked out of a cupboard space that already overflowed with bags of bulk grains, beans, and boxes of flours, spices, and other dried ingredients. Charlie, the resident mouse, scratched around inside the topmost shelf.

I found a spot to sit at the long pine table after moving aside the newspapers, dishes, and mugs, and brushed away the crumbs left from that morning's breakfast.

Uncle George made homemade Chinese food for the family that night. It felt safe to sit in the kitchen because it wasn't just the three of us that night. Burkhardt popped in and nibbled on chopped vegetables before disappearing to make a phone call, the mile-long phone cord dragging behind him like a tail. Hansko, the three-legged German shepherd, hobbled around on the floor and waited for food to drop. Sumi came by when she heard that her father was cooking Chinese. She and Signy talked loudly over each other while John Coltrane played on the stereo. With a wine bottle in hand, Aunt Milly responded to her daughters' chatter as she wove around Uncle George and searched for a wine opener. All the while, Uncle George paced back and forth from the wood-topped island to the stove as he transported vegetables and chopped meat in his cupped hands.

Uncle George was infamous for making a big production when he cooked. He liked to run the show, which meant he made a bigger mess out of what was already a mess to begin with. His biggest pet peeve was people who came between him and the stove, and he was known to chase unsuspecting guests with a metal spatula if they got in his way.

Like a warlock referring to his book of magic potions, Uncle George stroked his beard as he consulted a dog-eared, grease-stained Chinese cookbook that lay open on the table. He then threw fistfuls of bean sprouts, red and green peppers, bok choy, and shiitake mushrooms into a wok. Here and there, he added squirts of dark liquids from red-labeled bottles and thick, lumpy sauces to make the flames dance and spit. Next to him, hot vapors puffed from a bamboo steamer.

I held my breath as I sank into the comfortable security of family. Here I observed the same qualities of closeness I had always envied in my friends' families. I was in it then, and I tried to grasp the moment in my mind and cling to every detail frantically in an attempt to mentally preserve it. I sat quietly and listened, watched, and absorbed it all with a stupid grin on my face.

"George told me you really opened up last night," Aunt Milly said as she gently eased the cork from the wine bottle. She said it as caringly as possible to keep me from feeling embarrassed.

I glanced at Uncle George as she continued. "It's hard enough being a young lady nowadays, but even more challenging, I'm sure, for a Japanese American young lady in the Midwest."

My heart swelled, despite the fact that I didn't like people feeling sorry for me.

"We discussed your situation and agreed it would be a good idea if you enrolled at New York University before you graduate from high school. That is, if that's something you might consider."

"I would love to go to school here," I stammered. "Thank you so much." It was as though I had received an unexpected gift of a lifetime. I was excited and hesitant at the same time—excited because the prospects of it seemed as crazy as my going to Mars, and hesitant because it was uncertain and too good to be true.

We all paused as Uncle George made his way toward us carrying several big oval plates, the kind used at Chinese restaurants. He had heaped them with sautéed green beans smothered in aromatic black-bean sauce, two versions of a home-style tofu and vegetable dish, one with pork, the other without, salt-and-pepper deep-fried prawns, and sliced beef with oyster sauce.

"Well, it's an excellent school," Aunt Milly said, tickled by the awed expression I must have been wearing. "You'll get so much out of it socially and academically. And, of course, you will stay with us. Your parents won't worry so much if they know you're under our roof." She tapped the tabletop with her fingertips, looked around, and smiled. "It's settled, then."

I couldn't stop smiling as we ate. Signy and Sumi made endless suggestions about what I should do my first year in the city. I nodded, delighting in the gentle care and sincere interest they gave me. I finally felt I could have something interesting to offer. I reached for another serving of the crispy prawns, heads intact, that Uncle George had cooked, and placed more of the tofu and pork on my plate. I made sure to spoon the velvety brown sauce atop my mound of fluffy rice. The tender green beans, evenly coated with salty bean sauce, snapped perfectly when I bit into them.

After dinner there was no more talk about school. Aunt Milly moved us seamlessly into dessert, dishing out wedges of Junior's of Brooklyn cheesecake, a New York–style baked cheesecake that uses cream, eggs, and cream cheese to enhance its rich smooth consistency. I had never tasted baked cheesecake. Mom made hers from a recipe printed on the Philadelphia cream cheese box. Junior's was dense, creamy, and rich, like soft chunks of toffee.

I was midway through the cheesecake when it began to dawn on me that Mom and Dad would not agree that my going to school in New York City was a good idea. When I talked to Mom on the phone that night, I didn't mention Uncle George and Aunt Milly's idea. I wanted to savor the possibility of living and studying in New York City before it was spoiled by their response. I knew deep down that, like my brothers before me, I was expected to apply and attend an in-state university with lower tuition my parents could afford. A private, out-of-state school with high tuition would surely be out of the question.

I tried to comfort myself by reassuring myself that Mom and Dad wouldn't let an opportunity like this slip away. My Tokyo-born mother had described the exciting pulse of the city, where anything and everything happened, convinced that's where I'd be headed one day. I couldn't say so aloud, but I was almost certain that, with Uncle George and Aunt Milly behind me, my parents would accept the idea.

About a week later, the night before I flew back to Indiana, Signy took me to my first white-tablecloth restaurant, a treat from Aunt Milly and Uncle George. Wise Maria's was an Italian restaurant with one seating a night, which served a small ball of citrus sorbet in a cordial glass between courses and where the waiters called me "Miss." As I sipped a cappuccino awkwardly, smoked my first cigarette, and talked with Signy about city living, I relished how far I had come.

Midmorning the next day, I watched the end of *Shogun* in the family library. I thought I was the only one awake when Uncle George came in, carrying several rolled-up newspapers under his arm.

He stood near the television for a few minutes, watching the miniseries in silence. Gingerly, he rubbed the eye he had damaged in the near-fatal car accident and then took the papers and sat behind the desk. As he skimmed the headlines, he asked if I was looking forward to living in New York. I said I was.

"You know it will require a lot of work," he said. "Changes like this don't happen overnight, but it'll be good for you to finally get out and away from the country."

"Before you know it, you'll become a real New Yorker." I waited for him to say more, but he didn't. He turned on his desktop computer and began tapping at the keyboard. Before I left for the airport, Uncle George promised me he'd call and talk to Mom and Dad soon about my attending school in New York.

Returning to Versailles, I experienced the glimpse of nostalgia I would feel when I left the very hometown I dreamed of fleeing. Like an old tarnished coin made shiny again, my former feelings of indifference and boredom were replaced with a new appreciation of the Americana so many New Yorkers I talked to admired. It didn't seem like such a bad place to come from.

I kept my plans to move to New York to myself, not sharing them even with my best friend, Tracy. I couldn't wait to spill the news and imagined the expression on her face when I revealed my secret.

I told and retold Mom what I did, saw, and ate in New York. I'd throw in a "When I go back, I'm going to . . ." in the hope that I'd better prepare her for Uncle George's call. At this, she'd only respond in an annoyingly chipper voice, "I'm happy you had a nice vacation."

Several times I almost blurted out my intentions. I wanted to impress upon her that it wasn't a passing frivolous experience. I was really going to live there, but I told myself not to spoil the plan. I had to wait for the right time and place.

As Uncle George promised, he called a couple of weeks later. As I listened from the living room as Dad spoke to him from the dining room, a warm, nervous giddiness bubbled inside me. *This is it,* I told myself.

"Yes, Linda had a good time in New York," Dad was saying. ". . . Yes, she graduates high school in two years. . . . Yes, she talks about New York all the time now." I rounded the corner to catch him in a laugh, followed by a frozen smile, and then an immediate frown. "That's a very expensive college, isn't it?" The tone in his voice turned more solemn. "That's nice that you would let her live with you. . . . Right now we don't know . . . probably in Indiana . . ."

I stuck my head all the way through the doorway to get a good look at Dad's reaction. He shook his head slowly and looked up at the ceiling. "Okay, well, thank you very much for taking care of her. Talk to you soon. Bye."

My father looked at me as he hung up the phone, but then he addressed his comments to Mom, who had been cooking in the adjacent kitchen. "George called about sending Linda to a university in New York." Mom let out a "ho, ho, ho" sort of laugh. It was her astonished, incredulous laugh. I hated it.

I had hoped Dad would be jovial, but I could see him fuming the way people do when put in a bad spot. Doubt began crawling up my spine. I remained where I was in the doorway.

Finally, Dad looked directly at me with piercing eyes. "Do you know how much it costs to go to New York University? We can't afford it. What is George thinking? What are you thinking?"

Shaking his head, he said sternly, "If you want to go to school in New York, get a scholarship. You were only in New

York for two weeks. You don't live there. No way," he said to me. Then, he turned to Mom again and began speaking in rapid-fire Japanese, which seemed to emphasize the preposterousness of the situation. As if I couldn't understand what he was saying, he said, "Can you imagine what would happen to her if she lived in the city by herself?"

At this, I blurted out helplessly, "But Uncle George said I could live at their house." They both gave an exaggerated "ho, ho, ho" laugh again, and I felt like screaming.

My hopes slipped away like sand pulled under my feet by the surf's tow. "But Mom, you always told me everything was better in the city, that I would love living there! You told me before I went to visit Uncle George that it would be a good experience."

"If you want to live in the big city, first you finish college, get a job, and then move," said Mom. Dad nodded his head in stoic agreement. The subject was closed.

With each word, the lightness I had been floating on for the past several weeks evaporated. I had returned to the reality of small-town life, and I saw clearly then that the rarefied world of the city Furiyas was never mine to have in the first place. In my bedroom, I scolded myself for being so stupid to let my expectations soar so high. I was a fool to believe I could escape from the country Furiyas' life and step so easily into the world of my city relatives.

Time passed and wore away my dreams. I let go of the idea of attending college in New York. I knew someday I would leave Versailles, but it wasn't going to be immediately after high school.

I was twenty-three when I made it back to New York for a visit. I had since graduated from Purdue University and gotten

an entry-level job in Washington, D.C., with a local com-
mercial real-estate developer. I took the train to Penn Station
one winter weekend. Aunt Milly met me, but Uncle George
couldn't join her. His health was weak; he'd been diagnosed
with cirrhosis of the liver.

The fleet-footed, constantly on-the-move Uncle George
I remembered became winded just walking a few steps. He
talked in short, wheezy gasps, no longer able to hold his own
in a conversation because he couldn't catch his breath. Despite
his poor health, he refused to stay home, doggedly going out
even if it took him hours to get around what used to take him
thirty minutes.

✤

Three years later, shortly after I moved to San Francisco,
Uncle George called to say how proud he was that I had
a syndicated column in Japanese American and Canadian
newspapers, about growing up in a Japanese family in the
Midwest. He was thrilled that I had made it to the Bay
Area, and reminisced about his youth in Sacramento and
how he and his buddies had often traveled to San Francisco.
There was so much I wanted to share with him—questions
about writing, how he got started, how I might break into
freelance writing—but it was hard to hold a conversation.
Uncle George broke down into racking coughs throughout the conversation, and I didn't want to keep him on the
phone very long.

We maintained correspondence after that first phone
call, though, when he requested that I send him a few of my
articles. A week later, the clippings came back, bleeding from

the many comments he wrote out on the side margins in red ink. He had gone through my columns line by line and made comments on everything, including research sources, grammar, and sentence structure.

For about a year and a half after that, he regularly typed letters on a manual typewriter. Then he became busy with his last big project, a campaign to broadcast sumo bouts on television in New York City. Not long after that, he passed away at the age of seventy-eight.

His letters are dear to me, not just because they are filled with pride and words of encouragement I needed at that early stage as a beginning writer, but for their bravado and strength, and for the unwavering voice of the uncle I remembered from my trip to New York City as a wide-eyed fifteen-year-old.

He died right on the cusp of when we might actually have had the great conversations he'd encouraged of me those evenings around the dinner table at his home in Brooklyn. It occurred to me that now I could have "discussions," and that I'd be able to hold my own about our two great loves: food and writing. At first, his letters were a source of inspiration to me, but now, years after his death, I often skim through them just to absorb the eloquence and larger-than-life presence preserved in his typed words.

# Chinese Home-Style Tofu

*This traditional Chinese recipe uses a variety of vegetables. Make sure they are cut the same thickness as the meat. Boiling the tofu is important to keep it from breaking apart easily. You can use a leaner cut of pork if desired. I prefer something with added fat for flavor and tenderness.*

2 cups + 1 tablespoon vegetable oil
12-ounce box firm tofu
½ cup all-purpose flour
½ pound pork loin or boneless rib
1 tablespoon ginger, grated
2 green onions, chopped
1 teaspoon soy sauce
¼ teaspoon chili sauce
½ cup water
½ cup shiitake mushrooms, sliced
½ cup canned sliced bamboo shoots
½ cup green bell peppers, cut to ⅛-inch slices
1 tablespoon cornstarch mixed with 2 tablespoons
    water
1 teaspoon sesame oil

Heat the two cups of vegetable oil in a deep sauté pan or wok.

Slice tofu lengthwise and cut into ¼-inch-thick slices. Fill a medium-size saucepan three-quarters full with water. When water boils, add tofu slices and cook for 4 minutes. Remove and allow to cool. Dredge the slices in flour and then fry in vegetable oil until golden brown. Blot on paper towels and set aside. Drain frying oil from pan.

Slice pork into ¼-inch-thick slices. In a wok or nonstick sauté pan, heat remaining vegetable oil over high heat. Add pork slices, stirring well, until slices begin to turn pale in color. Add ginger, green onions, soy sauce, chili sauce, and water. Lower heat to medium high and stir well until fragrant, about 1 minute. Carefully add tofu, mushrooms, and bamboo shoots, folding into the mixture carefully. Allow to cook over medium-high heat for about 2–3 minutes.

Stir-fry the green bell pepper slices and then stir in the cornstarch-water slurry. Drizzle with sesame oil before serving.

Serves 4.

# The War Bride's Husband

Mom and Dad were on friendly terms with the neighbors and the parents of my brothers' friends and my friends. They kept a vigilant eye out when one of the families across the street left for vacation. During planting season, Dad doled out advice on the best way to deter pesky moles and scare away deer. When it came to food and language, though, there were too many cultural obstacles, and no invitations came out of the frequent screen-door visits and back-fence chats.

Through the Cincinnati chapter of the Japanese American Citizens League, a national organization for Japanese and Japanese Americans, they met other couples like them, immigrants who came to America in the '50s and early '60s, along with a handful of second-generation Japanese Americans.

We'd often schedule our twice-monthly trips to Cincinnati to replenish our inventory of Japanese food to coincide with social gatherings like birthdays, anniversaries, and seasonal Japanese holidays, as well as small potluck dinners and barbecues, where Mom's delicious dishes and Dad's garden vegetables, homemade pickles, and homemade tofu were met with great anticipation and appreciation. It was fun for all of us children as well. With our parents deep in conversation and centered in the living room, we got a rare opportunity to gorge on sodas and sweets.

Often I fell asleep on the long drive back to Versailles, waking occasionally to see the reassuring silhouettes of Mom and Dad in the front seat and the front headlights cutting through the velvety darkness.

In my teens I became mindful of the conversations the adults had and the shared experiences that brought them together. I knew nothing about the Japanese American internment, and I was in high school by the time I really began to understand how it affected me as a first-generation Japanese American. As a child I had no idea that during World War II, days after the bombing of Pearl Harbor, President Roosevelt signed Executive Order 9066. Under this order, 110,000 Japanese, more than half of them American citizens, were viewed as a threat to national security and relocated to camps that were guarded by armed solders.

My parents talked openly about how they survived World War II, but their experiences were different. My father was a Japanese soldier in Manchuria, my mother a teen in war-torn Tokyo. They had heard of the internment of the Japanese Americans when they were in Japan, but they learned the details of it from their new Japanese American friends when they settled in the States.

Growing up, all of us kids had heard the adults talking about World War II when we played together at the potlucks.

They made references to the internment experience, but no one ever expanded upon it enough for me to understand.

The first time I overheard the word "internment," I thought it was some kind of recreational camp, like a summer camp with cabins and planned activities. Through time, the pieces of conversations I patched together brought to light the fact that it was something far more grave.

At these Cincinnati Japanese American Citizens League events, personal details flew around harmlessly as a fly, but often they had the impact of a bee sting. Once, during a leisurely dinner, when some guests were still eating and others sat politely in front of finished plates, the conversation turned toward the problems one of the younger couples had experienced when they bought and moved into a new house.

During a pregnant pause, Mrs. Uno, the wife of one of the first couples my parents met through the organization, a woman who was always trying to look on the bright side of things, observed that at least they hadn't had to rush to pack like she did when her family was interned, when they had less than a month to put their life in order and were allowed to take only what they could carry.

Elderly Mrs. Yamashita, who kept quiet much of the time, mostly nodding or shaking her head at what was being said, blurted out that she took a hatchet to her cabinets.

Her eyes, usually rheumy and watery, became as hard as the ax she had used. "I'd rather have destroyed them myself than sell them for nothing," she said, before reverting to her nodding.

Silence fell over the party. The people around the table looked off, deep in their own thoughts. The solemnity was broken when the men cleared their throats and the women started clearing the dishes. I could tell by my parents' neutral expressions that they felt they couldn't comment on the conversation.

At another party, I sat on the kitchen floor petting the family dog, invisible to two women who were deep in conversation, one washing the dishes while the other one dried.

"Remember the dish towels in the camps?"

"Dish towels? They were old rice bags!" said the one who dried, sharing in the irony of the mutual joke that made light of the grim conditions they faced in the camps.

"Well, before they were dish towels, they were washcloths, before that hand towels, then bath towels." They broke out in laughter.

"If there was anything left of a dish towel, they were cut into strips and made into mops." They laughed even harder.

The woman who washed dabbed at the tears that ran down her face and added, "I hope I never see another dish towel again," which sent them into another fit of hysterics that faded to a long silence. Eventually, they saw me at their feet. Their laughter made me smile, but I still didn't understand.

Even when I did study the internment in high school, my teacher didn't shed much light on the topic. And my high school history book gave only a sliver of a paragraph to the event, at the end of the chapter on World War II. The American public learned more about the Jewish Holocaust than they ever did about the Japanese internment, despite the fact that the former happened on their own soil.

In the sixth grade I saw the TV movie *Farewell to Manzanar*, the story of a Japanese American family's internment ordeal in Manzanar, California, after the bombing of Pearl

Harbor. It was only then that I understood what I had heard at those League events all those years.

My heart ached as I watched men paint images of racial slurs on the sides of houses after the United States declared war on Japan. Soldiers herded the men, women, and children onto trains as families left their homes and businesses indefinitely. I was shocked by the anti-Japanese sentiment and I couldn't imagine what life was like in the camps, or what life was like afterward for all those people who had been held prisoner in and by their own country.

The suspicion and anger that Japanese Americans encountered after Pearl Harbor was much worse than anything I had experienced in my young life, yet I understood the utter helplessness and anger they must have felt. As I watched the movie, I felt an intense, numbing sadness and hopelessness, like discovering an untold secret about a close friend.

I received a taste of this injustice my junior year of high school, in history class, when the class lectures moved toward the bombing of Pearl Harbor.

My eleventh-grade history teacher, Mr. Hudson, talked about the atomic bomb dropped on Nagasaki and Hiroshima. Sitting on the corner of his desk, he rattled off the number of American soldiers killed in the war and the number of Japanese killed after the bombing of Nagasaki and Hiroshima. I squirmed a little in my seat and wished he would move on.

He paused and sipped his coffee, letting the enormity of the number sink into our young minds.

As I stared, Brad Monroe pointed his finger at me as if he wielded a pistol. "Bang. Kill 'em all." A big grin spread across his face.

I felt my face flush bright red. The green of the chalkboard and the matte gray of the metal desk grew more intense as I tried to focus. I wasn't sure if I had imagined or lived that moment. I waited for Mr. Hudson to set Brad straight or initiate a discussion or, even better, wield his adult authority the way I thought teachers were supposed to.

I locked eyes with Mr. Hudson the way a drowning person would with someone on dry ground. I pleaded silently for him to equalize the situation, but still he said nothing.

I could feel the tension in the room as my classmates waited. Mr. Hudson looked away as he stood up. For a moment I thought maybe he hadn't heard what Brad had said.

Mr. Hudson grimaced and lifted his chin. I saw his Adam's apple jump as he jerked the knot of his necktie tighter. Under his breath, as clearly as the town siren went off every day at noon, he said, "Yup."

I felt the heat of my classmates' eyes burn into my back. Defiantly, I scanned the room and made eye contact with each person who stared at me. It took every ounce of inner strength I could muster, but I knew I had to do it. My girlfriends, including Tracy, looked back at me with pity. Others met my gaze as if to push me to do something, say something, perhaps to delight in the tension. I knew the few who smirked agreed with Brad, and part of me wanted to slink down in my chair.

I squared my shoulders and faced forward in my seat until the almost audible silence subsided. Time had slowed down. Even though the whole thing happened in seconds, the time felt magnified fourfold. When the class bell rang, I dashed out the door to my locker. Tracy looked at me as if she had seen a ghost.

"What was that all about?" she asked.

I tried to sound nonchalant. "I have absolutely no idea."

I didn't complain to anyone, not to my parents or to the school administrators. If Mr. Hudson didn't help me, why would anyone else?

I tried to shake off the incident by convincing myself that the history of war between Japan and America really didn't affect me, and that what had happened was just small-town ignorance at its worst. But still, a naive part of me, one that looked up to authority figures such as teachers, withered away as a result of that classroom incident.

I told myself that one day I would leave this town and never return. Similar incidents occurred as I got older, such as the time I was working as a cashier and a war veteran who lived in Versailles called me a stupid Jap bitch, reinforcing my motivation to one day get out.

When my brothers entered high school, they stopped going to the League dinners and parties and told me that doing nothing was better than hanging out with our parents and their friends. Mom still insisted that I go, but more often than not I'd wiggle out of it with one excuse or another. What I didn't tell her was that I didn't want to hear about what happened during the war anymore, and that I wanted to keep the history of World War II between the pages of my history book.

❀

I should have stayed home the day I went to the last potluck dinner I'd ever attend. I was sixteen, much older than the children who were obligated to be there because they were too young to stay home alone. It was an Indian summer afternoon, when the sunshine shimmered between the autumn trees and created a breathtaking canopy of auburns, oranges, browns, and yellows.

My parents' longtime friend Mrs. Uno organized a surprise party for her husband. When we arrived, people were already gathered in the small split-level house. I had been in the Unos' house many times before; as a kid I'd run through the hallways and rooms, but now the space felt miniature and cramped.

The men congregated around the television in a small, dark room already gloomy with its banged-up black Naugahyde sofa, creek water–green shag carpet, and brown paneled walls. A basketball game played on a small TV set in the corner. The women milled about the kitchen. At first they busied themselves unpacking the food they had brought. Then whatever dirty dishes were around were washed, dried, and put away.

By the sink, Mrs. Uno lined carrot and celery sticks on a platter while she kept an eye on the driveway and anticipated Mr. Uno's arrival from playing golf. The chaos of a house full of guests didn't distract her from her favorite pastime— gossip. "Inoue Barnes went back to Japan this summer," she told the women.

"I heard she goes back every year," Mrs. Tanaka replied, stirring adzuki beans and rice with a wooden paddle.

"I don't know her, but how nice to go back to Japan every year." Mom sighed as she set a kettle to boil on the stove.

"Inoue's husband is very kind to her," Mrs. Uno continued. She leaned in to the group of women and whispered nonchalantly, "Her husband is colored." Mom and Mrs. Tanaka sucked in their breath.

"Mr. Uno's returned. Everyone hide!" Mrs. Uno hissed. She grabbed the vegetable platter and placed it on the dining room buffet before hiding behind an armchair.

Mr. Uno, his skin as dark and wrinkled as the leather of his golf bag, acted genuinely surprised when he walked in and the group sang "Happy Birthday" and "For He's a Jolly Good Fellow." Mr. Uno grabbed his chest as if he'd had a heart attack, and the men laughed and slapped his back at his good humor. His big smile showed the shiny gold caps on his teeth.

More people arrived with drinks and covered dishes, which were quickly removed from their plastic containers and arranged on decorative dishware.

Suddenly, the back door banged open. "Dagnabit, I thought we would never find this place!"

"That must be Thomas and Mochiko," Mrs. Uno said with a laugh. "Come in, come in," she said in English and held the door open.

Thomas was one of only a few white men at the party. Like the rest of the crowd, he was in his late fifties. He had small ferretlike eyes and reddish hair slicked back to expose a receding hairline. By now, many people sat and stood in the doll-size kitchen, and Thomas's protruding Buddha belly knocked against the heads and shoulders of those seated around the kitchen table. The buttons at the bottom of his plaid shirt strained and revealed his white ribbed undershirt.

"Mochiko didn't write the address down correctly. Next time," he said, towering over his wife, "I'm going to make you git out of the car and find the place your damn self."

For a second, the people in the kitchen stopped what they were doing, looked at one another, and laughed uncomfortably, not knowing whether he was serious or joking. Mochiko wore a blank look on her face of neither anger nor acknowledgement.

"There, there now, you made it, so have a drink, mingle, and enjoy yourselves," Mrs. Uno cooed. "Debbie Yamamoto made her famous Japanese fried chicken." She steered Mochiko by the elbow to an empty spot at the counter.

"Hey, ho, any beer?" Thomas asked, suddenly turning jolly.

"Help yourself to the ones in the refrigerator."

"I think I'll just do that."

As he pulled the tab off a can of beer, he stuck his head into the TV room. His cheery voice became stern again. "I wanna watch the game."

He tapped the can with the nail of his index finger and grunted to Mochiko. "Bring another one of these in fifteen minutes." She nodded. She hadn't uttered a single word yet.

When Mochiko left the kitchen, Mrs. Uno stood close beside me as I unpacked a Tupperware container of *omanju,* an assortment of Japanese sweet bean pastries someone had brought and left on the counter. On a thick wooden dish I set my favorite *daifuku,* soft, sweet white *mochi* balls surrounding red bean paste and dredged in *mochi* powder. *Ocha-manju* was similar but made with green tea–flavored *mochi* and dusted with a brown soy powder, giving it a sweet, nutty taste.

Mrs. Uno worked next to me, feeding bits of information in her practically unaccented and clear English about the guests—nothing inflammatory, yet nothing boring either.

I almost preferred to hear these women speak Japanese rather than English. Their Japanese intonations and jesting were pleasant to the ear. They spoke English loudly and in blunt stabs. I wondered if this was their interpretation of how English should be spoken.

"You know, Mochiko is from Mizawa. She married Thomas after the war." I looked at her but did not understand her point. Mom sometimes informed me about people's hometowns, too, as if it somehow explained a character flaw. Mom was proud of her city origins. Once I understood this, I reminded her that I was from the country and hoped no one judged me because of that. I wasn't confident enough to say this to Mrs. Uno, though.

When it was obvious that her comment didn't register with me, Mrs. Uno leaned the same way she had before and clarified, "Mochiko's a war bride."

"What's that?"

Her response was comic. She did a double take and bugged out her eyes, indicating that I hadn't been raised to learn the right things. Her eyes scanned the kitchen, checking to see if anyone was close enough to overhear the conversation. She shrugged her shoulders and decided not to explain further, as guests were still getting ice and wrapping napkins around chopsticks. She picked up the tray of sweets. Before she scurried off, she yelled over her shoulder, "Ask your mother to tell you more about this."

❁

I found Mom and Dad in the back yard a little while later. They were standing by the grill and talking with some new guests who had just arrived. I had never noticed it before, but the group was divided between two contingents, the Japanese couples and the mixed couples, which consisted only of Japanese wives and Caucasian husbands.

Mrs. Uno announced from the porch that the buffet was ready. I was hungry, more out of boredom than anything. Mom joined me in the queue, curious to see what items the other guests had brought. In truth, the only thing that I had looked forward to about the party was the food. What remained wonderfully the same about these potluck get-togethers was the buffet of Japanese comfort foods.

Next to the small bowls of Dad's homemade *tsukemono* (pickled cabbage) and spicy red kimchi were cold dishes, such as red and white salad, a mix of julienne carrots and daikon tossed in sweetened vinegar and white sesame seeds. Someone had made another salad of coarsely chopped iceberg lettuce, celery, and red peppers beaded with miso-ginger dressing.

The savory choices included Japanese fried chicken, chicken pieces marinated in soy sauce and spices and fried to a crisp golden veneer. A potluck favorite was *gomoku* sushi, or five-item sushi, a rice dish topped with layers of shredded shiitake mushrooms, burdock root, snow peas, and pickled ginger. It resembled New Year's confetti.

In the center, surrounded by side dishes of vegetable tempura and fried rice and white rice, was a *jubako*, a four-tiered lacquered box. It was neatly lined with *inari-zushi*, or vinegar-flavored rice stuffed in fried tofu pockets, and *futomaki* (fat sushi roll). American dishes lined the table as well—potato salad and deviled eggs, and for dessert, apple pie.

"The *maki* looks good. Have some," Mom said. I looked around us to make sure no one was within earshot of eavesdropping. I held out my plate and quickly asked if she knew what "war bride" meant.

"Why do you ask?" Mom was agile as she used the top clean end of her chopsticks, the customary way of serving oneself food from the buffet.

"Mrs. Uno said one of the women here was a war bride. She wouldn't explain it to me and told me to ask you instead." I heaped fried rice on my plate, taking another look to see if anyone was approaching.

"There is more than one woman here who is a war bride, and Mrs. Uno shouldn't be starting ideas in your head and not finishing them," Mom mumbled under her breath in Japanese. "She talks too much."

As the guests started lining up for food, Mom said nothing more until we found a spot where we could eat by ourselves, in the chrome-and-vinyl chairs in the yellow wallpapered kitchen. The rest of the guests had congregated around the choice eating spots—the breezy back yard or a sunny, secluded corner in the television room.

She spread her napkin on her lap, something she remembered to do only when she ate out. After she glanced around to make sure no one was coming or going, she told me, in English, "After Japan surrendered in the Second World War, GIs like Thomas helped in the reconstruction."

She spoke in English to avoid being overheard by the other Japanese women, who would eavesdrop more easily if she spoke in Japanese. "Some of those men found Japanese women different from girls at home. Some Japanese women found American men better than Japanese men. The two fall in love, but some girls' families had trouble getting food. The soldiers gave them candy bars, food from PX, money to buy white rice, all hard to get right after the war. My father made sure I stayed away from GIs. I was only a teenager, not pretty enough. If they gave me candy I take it, but I wouldn't smile or talk with them like some other girls. To be seen with them was bad. 'Hunger better than that,' my father told me."

She stopped to take a bite of the fried chicken. Reverting to Japanese, she exclaimed, "Did you taste Mrs. Yamamoto's chicken? It's delicious. Here, take this piece."

She pressed her grease-stained fingers daintily on her napkin and continued, "People were jealous and hungry, bad mix. Neighbors watch and never forget. Date American GI, girl's reputation gone." Mom made a cutting motion in the air with her plastic knife. "Probably never can marry a Japanese man. Many girls married and went to America with their GIs, but the poor unlucky ones were left behind when the soldiers went back to their wives. So many babies were born with no fathers. Very sad time, wartime."

Now I started to understand the relationships between the Japanese women with American husbands. I had seen these older couples all my life and never given it a thought, except that their marriages seemed unconventional. By the time I was in my teens, I realized that I was attracted to Caucasian boys. I had never been in a social setting where I had the opportunity to meet Asian boys, and seeing mixed couples put me at ease, showing me that Japanese-Caucasian couples were acceptable.

Just then, Thomas, Mochiko, and another couple came to the kitchen table to join us. Chairs scraped the floor as they put down paper plates and plastic drink cups and settled themselves. As the Japanese wives got acquainted with Mom, my ear was drawn to the conversation between Thomas and a portly Caucasian man too old to be wearing the sparse gray ponytail tied at the back of his head.

After they sat down, I overheard that the ponytailed man and his wife had just moved to Versailles from Columbus, Ohio. The men had only just met, but as they talked, they learned that they shared many things in common. Both had been stationed in Tokyo right after its surrender. The two exchanged information about their regimens and duties. "I saw some action, but by then the war was over," Thomas said.

"Yeah," the ponytailed man agreed. "The best thing that ever happened to me was being sent to Japan."

They both slapped their knees and laughed as they reveled in their private joke.

"Remember that alley in Ginza, the one with all the girls who danced with their shirts off, Mochiko?" Thomas tapped his wife on the shoulder the way he had tapped his beer can earlier. Up close I saw the beauty beneath her fine lines, droopy eyelids, and dyed black hair. Mochiko, normally relaxed and affectionate, jolted to attention at the mention of the strip joint in Ginza.

"I don't remember," she laughed nervously. "That was almost thirty years ago." Mochiko's eyes darted as she looked uncomfortably at the women around her, who politely looked away.

Thomas turned back to his new friend and continued, "Whatever the name of the place was, it was crazy—the girls, the booze." He drifted off, shoved an egg roll in his mouth, and licked at his fingertips with wet smacking sounds.

The ponytailed man answered wistfully as he cracked his knuckles. "Yes sirree, it sure was a different time."

I peered around, amazed that no one reacted or protested what these men so brazenly discussed. They continued and reminisced about the nights they caroused the whorehouses in Tokyo, while the Japanese women chattered on, seemingly unfazed, about the best Cincinnati grocer from whom to buy Japanese food.

The vulgarity of the men's discussion, transpiring right in front of my mother and the two other Japanese women, weighed down my chest. Suddenly the air in the room felt stuffy and oppressive. I looked around to see if the windows were open, but instead I saw Japanese women's faces as indecipherable as a blank wall, their voices much too cheerful and high-pitched.

Just as Thomas remarked that he adored Korean women the most, Mrs. Uno strolled into the kitchen.

Thomas looked directly at Mrs. Uno and intentionally caught her eye as he continued, "I like their pretty long hair, and they're fun, if you know what I mean." He chuckled loud and deep in his chest. Mrs. Uno picked up a bottle of soy sauce and retreated.

I was both repulsed and intrigued by the men's conversation. *How far will they go*, I wondered, *before anyone reacts?*

Here was an ideal setting to put a man like Thomas in his place. I knew he was creating tension and discomfort that no one wanted to confront. The other guests avoided the kitchen, and the women diverted their eyes when they entered. The will to act coursed through my veins until suddenly I hit a stumbling block that unleashed doubt. Was I being too rash? Would my reaction embarrass my parents in front of their friends?

My hesitation set off a passivity within me I had always thought I lacked. I had come to loathe the stereotypes of Asian people as being subservient and passive, even though I saw it in my parents. I strove to avoid it, often going out of my way to prove I wasn't like that.

When I shopped at the malls in Cincinnati, I often caught people staring at my family and me. At first I thought I was just being paranoid, but I'd catch their reflections in shop windows when they thought I hadn't seen them. At this, I'd turn around and glare at them until they skulked away. When I voiced my indignation to Mom after one such occasion, she brushed it off cheerfully: "They look at you because you are so pretty."

At this, I stared at her blankly. She really believed what she said and thought it would make me feel better. Didn't she see that everyone in the mall was white? I wanted to shout at her that they stared because we were Asian. I'm sure my brothers noticed, but they never said anything. I was the only one who reacted.

The light faded westward in the autumn sky while Mom still talked with Mochiko. Thomas finally ate in silence. His ponytailed buddy and his wife had moved on to another room. The buzzing in my head had quieted. I was still doubting myself, thinking I had overreacted to the men's conversation. Boys at school talked boisterously about the girls they liked, I reasoned. Wasn't this the same thing?

Mochiko got up from the table. Thomas shoved his empty beer can into her hand. "Get me another one. This time I want it cold."

My stomach dropped. I didn't want her to leave Mom and me alone with him. Up to that point, I had avoided conversation with him and wanted to leave it at that. *What am I afraid of?* a voice in my head asked.

I wanted to leave but thought it was impolite to abandon my mother and leave her alone with Thomas. I somehow believed I could shield her from his crass ways. I failed to recognize that they were the same age, and that my mother was a savvy woman who could see right through him.

A woman I didn't know set a plate of Japanese pastries on our table. I smiled up at her, hoping I might engage her in conversation so she would stay and my mother and I wouldn't be alone with Thomas. But she was busy passing out the sweets, and she quickly left the room. Out of nervousness, I took a small bite from one of the *kurimanju*, a sweet bean paste baked in a light roll-like casing. The smooth, creamy sweet swirling around in my mouth reminded me why it was my favorite Japanese sweet.

My sensuous enjoyment of the dessert caught Thomas's attention. Before I knew it, he had scooted his chair closer to my mother and me. He asked me in his slow, squeaky drawl where I lived, what school I went to, and what my favorite subjects were. Mom eyed him warily as she enjoyed the pastries. Mochiko returned with his beer.

I answered his questions politely as he leered at me as he drank in a big swig of beer. Seeing him up close, I couldn't take my eyes off the way his Adam's apple bounced up and down with each swallow. A trickle of beer streamed out of the corner of his mouth. He wiped it away with the back of his hand. He licked his full lips, darting his tongue out slowly and languorously like a baby discovering how it worked. He moved his fingers together as though testing to see if they were sticky.

"Well, you wouldn't believe what I was doing when I was just a few years older than you," he said, setting the can down on the table. A beer flush crept up his neckline. His eyes shone brightly.

"I was dodging the goddamn Japs. Yikes," he lowered his voice and cowered his head in mock fear. He looked around.

"Better watch what I say around here." I turned to see if Mom and Mochiko would react to this. They said nothing, which seemed to fuel his confidence.

I wanted to shake Mom, to break her unreachable silence. Several unsuspecting guests had come into the kitchen to make tea and throw away a stack of used paper plates. I searched their faces and saw, as quick as a candle flicker, a look of distaste. *Thank goodness*, I thought, *I'm not the only one.*

"After the Japanese surrendered, I was in charge of making sure food supplies and provisions were coming. Bobby, who was sitting over here, was in a different barracks. Where did he go?" He looked behind him as if Bobby would pop out from behind his chair.

"Anyway, we did the same thing in different districts. I was twenty-one, in shape. Didn't have this," he said, patting his belly. "Those geisha gals there in Ginza loved me," he muttered, smiling to himself. I squirmed and looked down.

Mochiko wore a resigned smile as her husband pulled out a small black-and-white photograph from his billfold. It was taken back in the 1950s when they first met. Her hair was curled in a coiffure and she wore a dark printed dress with puffy short sleeves. She was perched on the lap of a thinner, younger Thomas, her arm dangling around his neck. From what I knew of the culture and the times, and all the pictures I had seen in my mother and father's photo albums, where everyone stands close, never touching, a Japanese woman sitting on a man's lap was not considered proper.

He leaned toward me and purred, "Why don't you grow your hair out? I love Japanese women with long black hair." I could have kicked myself for hee-heeing nervously, and I could have strangled Mochiko when she turned away from us and started another conversation with Mom.

"You're such a pretty Japanese doll," he continued, emboldened by our silence. Without any warning, he reached out and gave my shoulder a tentative squeeze with his doughy soft fingers.

I could feel the intent behind his touch as I recoiled. My strong talk and willfulness had left me. Thomas had violated my personal space, but in my panic, I didn't know what to do. If I had been with friends, I would not have hesitated to create a scene. But in my parents' world there were hidden implications, hurt feelings, and bruised egos. I was at a loss. I glanced across the room and caught a reflection of myself in the mirror of a tall wood curio cabinet. My eyes shone with the controlled fear of a dog that wants to get away from a stranger. In the mirror I saw the identical mask of resignation I had seen on Mochiko and my mother and many of the other women that afternoon. As the cloying sweet beans coated my mouth like chalkdust, I realized I would do nothing, and he knew it.

The voice in my head had grown stronger, insisting that I not make a scene. *Don't embarrass your parents in front of their friends. Keep quiet. Don't be impolite. Others come first. Nobody likes unpleasant people who don't smile.* All the teachings I had heard while growing up transpired at once and immobilized me like a fly caught in a spider's web.

Thomas scooted closer. His beer breath and Aqua Velva burned my nostrils like gas fumes. His animal paw came nearer.

Anger replaced my complacency; I knew in my heart that I hated this man. He was no different from first-grader Raymond Neilley, who did his dance while he called me Chink, or the meat-counter lady with the shiny red curls who bellowed "Whaad, whaad?!" or the pimply-faced Lester Matheson who made fun of Tam Dong, or Mr. Hudson as he stood motionless after one of his own students had pointed his finger at me as if it were a gun.

I saw all of them in Thomas. Without thinking, I pushed back my chair. Everyone jumped at the screech as the chair scraped against the linoleum.

Looking back, I believe my parents would have championed me if I had rebuffed him, or that the other adults in the kitchen would have guarded me from him if I had reacted as I wanted to. But no amount of rumination through the years has convinced me that, at the time, I was brave or confident enough to stand up to him.

That day marked the beginning of the long, slow journey of accepting my Japanese identity. For years I replayed the scene in my mind and asked myself why I was so petrified. The person I thought I was—strong-minded, opinionated—was crushed that day.

In the back seat on the drive back to Versailles, I was silent. The inside of the car was warm and comforting. The weather had turned cold, and the dark, steely blue-gray cast to the sky foretold a long winter ahead. Dad and Mom discussed the food and the people and exchanged gossip. Dad had stayed outside by the grill the entire afternoon.

I couldn't bear listening to the casual chatter any longer. I leaned forward and poked my head between the two of them. I asked Mom if she heard the way Thomas was talking about Japanese women and why she sat there immobile next to him the entire time.

Mom turned from the front seat and looked at me curiously. Laughing, she said, "What's wrong with you? He's just an old GI."

"Did you hear him when he said 'Jap'? No one did any-thing or said anything back to him." I shuddered when my parents both laughed at this. I envied the ease with which my parents reacted to racism. They lacked the indignation and anger that ran through my veins like poison.

As he drove, Dad looked at me from the rearview mirror and said, "Sometimes it's best just to let history be forgotten." Now I knew why he had remained outside, away from the kitchen.

Mom waved a plastic sandwich bag with four *kurimanju*. "I know you like these, so I brought some extra home."

The sight of the round flaky pastries brought back images of Thomas—his soft, putty-looking fingers and the way he licked his lips constantly. A disgusting sweetness coated my mouth and left an aftertaste. I didn't care if I never tasted another sweet bean pastry again.

## Chestnut Pastry (Kurimanju)

*A Japanese version of a moon cake, these treats are smooth and thin on the outside and creamy and sweet on the inside. The name is derived from the shiny chestnut color of the pastry. Beware: They are as addictive as cookies.*

### Glaze

> 2 egg yolks
> ½ teaspoon mirin
> ½ teaspoon soy sauce

### "Chestnuts"

> ½ cup shortening
> 1 cup sugar
> ½ cup buttermilk
> 2 eggs
> 4 cups sifted flour
> 1 teaspoon baking soda
> ½ teaspoon salt
> 2 cups sweet bean paste (recipe follows)
> ¼ cup poppy seeds

*For the glaze:* Mix together the egg yolks, mirin, and soy sauce in a small bowl. Set aside.

*For the "chestnuts":* Preheat the oven to 375°F.

Mix together the shortening, sugar, buttermilk, and eggs in a bowl. Add the flour, baking soda, and salt and blend well.

To form the sweets, flour your hands and gather the dough into a ball. Knead and roll the dough into a 3-inch-diameter log. Cut the log into ¾-inch-thick slices. On a floured work surface, flatten each slice into a ½-inch-thick circle with your fingers. Place 1 teaspoon of the bean paste in the center of each circle.

To form each pastry, gather up the edges of the dough around the bean paste and pinch to seal, being careful not to tear the dough. Holding the pastry smooth side up in the palm of your hand, roll it with the fingers of your other hand to form a ball, then gently flatten the top. Transfer to a baking sheet.

When all the pastries have been formed, generously brush top and sides with the glaze. Sprinkle a few poppy seeds in the center of each. Bake for about 15 minutes, or until the tops are golden brown.

Makes about 12 pastries.

### Sweet Bean Paste (An)

> 1 pound adzuki beans
> 2½ cups sugar
> pinch of salt

Remove any stones and debris from the beans. Rinse the beans; place in a large saucepan and pour in water to cover. Bring to a boil, reduce heat to medium, and cook for about 1 hour, until the beans swell and wrinkles disappear.

Drain the beans and then add fresh water to cover by a few inches. Bring to a boil, reduce heat, and simmer for about 1½ hours longer, adding more hot water as needed, making sure the beans are always covered with water as they cook.

Remove scum from top of water as needed. The beans are done when they can be easily mashed. Drain the beans in a colander lined with a dish towel. Gather the ends of the towel and squeeze out the water.

Transfer the beans to a food processor or blender and process until the beans become a smooth paste.

Place the bean paste in a large pot, add the sugar and salt, and cook, stirring constantly over medium heat until the sugar melts into the beans. Keep stirring until you reach the desired consistency—when you can see the bottom of the pot for about 10 seconds.

Remove from heat and let cool, stirring occasionally. Store in a covered container in the refrigerator.

Makes 5-6 cups.

At the Heart of a Black Walnut

s a young teenager, I remember feeling stunned by Dad's pat comment "Sometimes it's best to let history be forgotten."

When I played back that incident in my mind then and now, I wonder, *Didn't it look strange to any of the adults present to see a sixteen-year-old girl recoiling from a grown man's inappropriate gestures? Didn't they catch my looks of distress as they dashed in and out of the room?*

It wasn't like my parents to make a scene, but I had expected and hoped for outrage when I described what had happened afterward, in private. Instead they laughed off Thomas's lecherous behavior, brushing aside the racist comments and disrespect. By this time, I was accustomed to making excuses for their insensitivity and lack of acknowledgment, but this situation was serious enough to me that I couldn't allow it to be brushed off so easily.

I laid most of the blame on my mother for not interven-
ing, and although Dad wasn't in the house when it happened,
his response to the incident when I relayed it to him after the
fact was just as hurtful. Their apathy left an indelible mark on
my heart and a quiet devastation in its wake. It was a huge
blow to what little pride remained, and I wouldn't recover it
for a decade. From that experience dawned my realization that
I alone would be the only person I could truly count on. Sadly,
this wasn't a surprise. Except for the language they spoke to us,
their personal stories, and the food we ate, my parents didn't
instill in my brothers and me a strong sense of pride in our
ethnicity, or even the determination to stand up for ourselves.
We had to learn that all on our own, as they did.

I knew Mom was deeply proud of her origins, but she
kept it to herself, showing it in the most subtle of ways—such
as not giving up her Japanese passport for more than thirty
years, or in the dignified way she described the construction
of a kimono. Most of what I learned about my parents' culture was taught to me through Mom's cooking talents and
Dad's enthusiastic appetite. It was only at the dinner table
when I was a child, and later in the kitchen, that I experienced an absolute peace and connection with my Japanese
heritage. Each bite, taste, cut of the knife, and addition of
ingredients was solely my own experience that couldn't be
diminished or belittled.

❀

As a child, away from the dining room table, I was ashamed
of the uneasiness I felt toward my Japanese ethnicity. I hated
feeling this way. My outward Japanese appearance was a facade

toward which I held secret animosity, a constant condition I didn't know how to deal with.

What happened with Thomas wasn't my first run-in with the hard emotions of helplessness, or with the knowledge that my parents wouldn't come to my rescue, but it was the spark that set off an avalanche of questions about why my parents were the way they were. I asked myself what had happened in Mom and Dad's past that made them ambivalent about their own heritage; what had made them actively choose to not teach their children their culture and instill pride in them?

I remember how Mom and Dad often bantered back and forth about their lineage. Mom teased him about his peasant youth growing up in the countryside, and Dad would always retort that she was an uppity city girl. There was a long period when my brothers and I were in elementary school, before Mom and I went back to Tokyo, when her deep frustration about living in a small farm town cast a desolate shadow in our home.

For Mom, growing up in the rice store owned by her father exposed her to that food staple of the Japanese diet in the same way a French baker might instill in his child the love of the perfect baguette. At an early age, she learned its importance to the Japanese diet in the way the customers were mindful of every grain of rice they were paying for. After all, in Japan rice is served with each meal of the day.

Mom was dependent on Dad for almost every aspect of her existence—travel, communication, and finances. He drove her to appointments, errands, and the grocery store, all of which had to be done before midafternoon when he left for work at the factory. During the spring and summer, when he moonlighted sexing chicks at the hatcheries and had to catch

up on his sleep before heading to the factory, Mom walked
to the small grocery store in town. Because she couldn't drive
herself to the nearest big city store, she settled for its limited
offerings. For example, Mom would sometimes use yellow
onions instead of green onions, though they are a staple in
miso soups and other Japanese dishes and add a crisp, clean
flavor and bright green color. But rather than substitute dried
spaghetti pasta for Japanese noodles, Mom would make her
own fresh *udon* noodles from flour and water.

I remember one ill-fated attempt when Dad tried to
teach Mom how to drive at the Vocational School parking
lot while my brothers and I were at Sunday school. When
we got out of church, I saw them parked at the curb, sitting
silently in the car. Mom looked out the side window and Dad
wore a grim look on his face. She refused to say a word to him
all day. Her fate had been sealed that day—she would never
learn how to drive.

Midwinter was the worst for her. Weeks passed, cooped
up in the house, when the only people she saw besides us were
the occasional customers for sewing jobs she took on the side
to make extra money.

If she wasn't sewing, she watched television, her only
other companion, from which she learned what little English
she could. As the days shortened, so did her temper. Trivial
things set her off. It could be a frustrating phone conversation when she was trying to straighten out a bill, or disappointment at Dad if he couldn't take her grocery shopping
in the city, or discovering she lacked an ingredient to make a
particular recipe. She paced furiously back and forth between
the dining room and kitchen, her arms crossed tightly across
her chest, speaking Japanese so quickly that I couldn't keep

up. Then she would storm off to her bedroom, slamming the door behind her. An hour or two later, she had no choice but to come out to make dinner. Her unhappiness filled the house like thick, heavy incense.

At first I believed that Mom's unhappiness was only about her longing for her home city of Tokyo. She always talked about growing up in the city—the shops, culture, bookstores, and easy travel by subway.

But I learned differently one late fall day, when I was eight years old, just weeks before Thanksgiving. I couldn't find a winter coat I liked in the stores in Cincinnati, so Mom insisted Dad drive us all the way to Chicago to shop at Marshall Field's department store. Dad argued that he didn't want to drive the six-hour trip when we'd recently made a trip there to buy Japanese food.

Mom turned pale as cream and said to Dad, "My mother died when I was twelve. I had no one to help me choose my clothes or take me shopping. It got worse when my father remarried. I was the oldest, but my half brother got everything—the rice business, the house. If my mother hadn't died when she did, my life would have been different. If my mother had lived, she would have made sure I was connected with the proper Japanese husband at the right age." She raised her voice, "Not someone living in the *inaka* (countryside) who is too selfish and cheap to take his own wife and daughter to the city!"

That next weekend, Dad drove us to Chicago.

That was when I realized that Mom was still grieving for her mother, that her unhappiness was about much more than being homesick. Because her mother died so early on, Mom wanted to make up for all the experiences she had missed with her own mother in her time with me. From going to the movies to making cookies together, I knew, and she constantly told me, that the simple things we did together gave her great joy.

Her mother was bedridden and sickly for most of Mom's life. She died of heart failure when Mom was twelve. That same year, Mom's infant brother died from digestion complications, and her ten-year-old brother died of dysentery. From the original family of six, only Mom, her father, and her six-year-old sister remained.

A couple of months before tragedy hit, Mom's family vacationed at a seaside resort in northern Japan, a trip that was destined to become one of her fondest memories. Her mother was at her most energetic and everyone thought she was on the mend. She bought Mom an orange scarf for the occasion and took the children to eat the local delicacy of juicy sweet clams steamed in sake, a dish that Mom would later associate only with the sorrowful time that followed.

Mom was abandoned again only a year later, when her father remarried, and then again when her stepmother gave birth to Uncle Takeo and Aunt Sachiko. In Japanese families, new births seal the half siblings' priority. After those births, not only did Mom and Aunt Akiko have diminished importance, but they received little in the way of motherly affection or attention from their stepmother. So Akiko wouldn't feel the wretchedness of abandonment, Mom cared for her like a mother, doling out affection and attention as her father slipped deeper into his new family.

If these hardships weren't enough, during World War II death and the threat of it were a constant in Mom's everyday life. At an age when girls were supposed to be preening in the mirror and daydreaming about boys, she confronted her own mortality daily, taking cover when the air raid siren sounded.

The bombings were nothing new to her. Two previous houses she and her family had lived in were destroyed. At school they prepared her for survival, giving her a rucksack heavy with provisions: water, dried food, a candle, matches, and a whistle.

The surrender of the Imperial Army in 1945 and the end of World War II turned life as every Japanese knew it upside down. While her only surviving sister and her father's new family fled to relatives' tea farms in the countryside, Mom chose to stay by her father's side during the final, devastating bombing of Tokyo, for fear she might lose him.

Their shop survived the bombing, and her family was one of the lucky few to have a roof over their heads after it was all over. Infested with lice and scabies and unable to find drinking water, she and her father went for days without eating while peasant farmers sashayed in the streets wearing rare expensive silk kimonos they had bartered from the rich for a few sweet potatoes. Neighbors walked like ghosts, picking through the rubble, searching for something, anything, to eat. The neighborhood police chief, once respected and even feared before the war, went from home to home begging for a cup of rice, still wearing his tattered uniform.

❀

When she was in her early twenties, as the country was making the transition to reconstructing its government and economy, Mom got a job in a bank. There was still little food available in the grocery stores, and though some restaurants were open, customers brought their own cooked rice.

At the time, all reputable women lived with their parents until they married. So with her disposable income, Mom indulged in her love of clothes. She hired a tailor in the fashionable Ginza district who made stylish suits and dresses in imported fabrics.

Besides learning how to cook, iron, and clean, all Japanese women were required to master a skill in the arts as part of their preparation as future housewives. Mom's friend Oshima-san was a talented calligrapher, and Aunt Akiko knitted beautiful blankets. Her love of fashion inspired Mom to sign up for night courses at a tailoring school, where she learned how to draw patterns and sew outfits straight off the pages of fashion magazines.

During the day, Mom worked as a teller, and at night and on the weekends she attended classes in tailoring. When I started elementary school, people started noticing the clothes she made for me. Soon she was earning pin money and satisfying her creativity by sewing dresses and pantsuits for the working women in town and making alterations on band uniforms, prom dresses, and store-bought clothes.

She worked on the dinner table with her hefty Singer sewing machine. She spread out the cut fabric, a big plastic box of notions and threads like a painter's palette, and a sewing box that overflowed with tissue patterns and special tools for pulling hems and marking cloth.

To her, sewing traditionally, the way she had learned it in tailoring school, was an art. And, as with any art, mastery required toiling into the wee hours, folding, ironing, stitching an accordion pleat, and practicing a stitch until it looked machine-sewn. It also entailed blisters on the middle of her ring finger from pushing in the needle so many times, and seeing double after hours of close handiwork. There was no excuse for sloppiness. She was a perfectionist, and if everything wasn't correct or uniform, she'd take out her stitches and redo them.

Back in Tokyo, as a single working woman juggling a day job at the bank and schooling at night, Mom picked up a persistent cough. She woke up coughing up blood and was diagnosed with tuberculosis and thereafter quarantined to a yearlong stay in a sanitarium. During that year, she became so weak she couldn't sit up; she had to be pushed around in a wheelchair. Her long, jagged coughing fits were so deep that her entire body jerked with each breath. She knew many people who had died of tuberculosis and believed this too would be her fate.

She was lucky, however. During a time when most people who contracted tuberculosis died from it, she was able to obtain a newly approved serum through her friendships and connections at the bank where she worked.

When she was released from the sanitarium, she regained the strength and stamina lost while bedridden by taking up hiking and skiing.

Mom loved the mountains and took up nature photography. She took every opportunity to hike and ski. Flying down the slopes as fast as she could, her year spent near death began to seem like a bad dream.

Ironically, in Indiana, she came to hate the sight of falling snow. During a storm, the flakes fell so heavily that the street lamps turned into glowing orange orbs that pulled her into their dark grip. For her, snow meant that she would soon be barricaded in the house, stuck with a monotonous housekeeping routine with nowhere to escape to.

I was in the second grade when I began to notice the long naps Mom would take every day when Dad left for work. In the winter, these naps became more than just an hour's rest, often stretching to three- to four-hour slumbers. I remember coming home from school in the the semidarkness of midafternoon to find Mom asleep in bed.

It was bewildering entering a dark, silent house. In the beginning I felt alarmed at the possibility that something had happened to Mom. Then a sense of relief came over me when I saw her bedroom door closed, confirmation that she was asleep and not in danger.

Mom didn't know that while she slept, my brothers and I took turns sneaking soundlessly up to her bed to watch for any stirring or some sign of life, convinced as we were that she might suffocate under the heavy blankets. My seven-year-old imagination got the best of me as I contemplated what life would be like if Mom died.

Mom often woke up at dusk when the sky outside was an inky indigo blue. To this day, that particular dark hue gives me the sinking feeling of melancholy and helplessness that I felt then. Looking lost and vulnerable, Mom emerged from the bedroom all groggy, her hair flat on one side, pillow creases crisscrossing her cheek and forehead. My brothers and I didn't dare complain about her sleep habits. We'd wait patiently, curled up on the couch with our knees to our chests in the darkened living room, our faces illuminated white by the screen of the TV, like little birds waiting for their mother bird to feed them. We were hungry for dinner but didn't want to show it, since Mom often woke up in a foul mood.

As much as we loved Mom, we also feared her wrath. She had little patience when my brothers and I fought. My parents, mostly my father, believed in sparing the rod, but my mother didn't refrain from an unexpected, lightning-fast smack on the side of the head when we didn't listen or obey quickly enough.

Some evenings, the act of making yet another dinner was such a burden, and the lure of sleep so irresistible, that she'd come into the kitchen, set out three dishes, a pack of luncheon meat, a bag of chips, bread, and a jar of mayonnaise on the dinner table, and go back to bed without saying anything.

However, I can't recall a day, even when she was sick, when Mom didn't make Dad's lunch. Some of the men Dad worked with ate the same sandwich or bought the same hamburger every day, but every day Mom prepared a Japanese-style *bento* dinner for my father to take to his second-shift job.

I wondered if Dad noticed Mom's general unhappiness during the winters when she was tightly cloaked in her despair, or if keeping her problems to herself was just another unspoken part of their marriage deal.

I understand now that Mom was keeping herself together the best she could at the time. In the midst of her despondency, she got through each day by accomplishing what she had to to be productive. Dad was working and making money. He required her focused attention and care. When he left for work midafternoon, she was off the clock.

Many years later, I asked Dad if he ever noticed Mom's depression. He looked genuinely surprised. When he said that he was working a lot during that time, it indicated to me that maybe he did know and just didn't want to remember those times.

The fine print of their deal probably included an unspoken agreement that they would address a problem when it became a problem. In Dad's eyes, Mom was fine—keeping the house clean, the clothes washed, him and the kids fed—so if Mom didn't complain about it, which he knew she was too proud to do, there was no problem. And being the perfectionist she was, ripping the seams that were not sewn correctly, she accomplished what she needed to, despite her suffering.

In my early teens, as my brothers and I graduated from high school in turn, Mom's long naps and months of depression lessened and seemed to disappear altogether, even come winter.

During a weekend when I was home visiting my parents from Washington, D.C., from my first job out of college, I asked Mom about her winter bouts with depression. It was after a dinner of my favorite Western dish, a chuck roast marinated in sherry.

As we washed and dried the dishes in the kitchen, I ventured, "Mom, do you remember all the naps you used to take in the wintertime when I was a kid?"

Her face scrunched up, "I don't remember."

"Remember, you'd sleep for hours after Keven, Alvin, and I came home from school? I always thought you were sad about something. Were you?" I had learned that it was best to go the direct route when discussing things of the past with her.

I caught a split second of recognition flicker across her face before disappearing just as fast.

"No," she said, rigorously wiping the plate. "I take a nap all the time. Started when I had tuberculosis and was in the hospital."

I swished the soapy sponge across the slick dish surface, offering a quiet moment for her to speak. It was met with silence and I knew that this fragment of her history was best forgotten.

❁

Dad once told me that after he experienced starvation, hunger, by comparison, was bliss. But he didn't tell me that if someone suffers in this state for too long, even after gorging on a feast, he will never feel completely full.

The summer when I was thirteen, I was watching the blackbirds helping themselves to the fruit of our old mulberry tree and nose-diving into the black walnut trees outside my bedroom window. From there I also saw Dad, in the mis-shapen straw hat he always wore when he gardened, his head bobbing as he foraged in our trash cans.

"Look at this!" Dad shouted to my mother, who stood at the kitchen window directly below my own. He held up an oily heel from yesterday's ham. He popped it into his mouth while unwrapping a limp wedge of tomato from a piece of newspaper.

Mom yelled back, "Stop that! What will the neighbors think when they see you eating from the garbage?"

"You can make a salad with this!" Dad responded. He held up threads of cucumber skins the way kids do when they want to show their parents seashells they find at the beach. Mom slammed down the window so hard that I expected the sound of shattering glass.

Later, I asked her why Dad was eating food she had thrown away in the garbage. At first she looked away, and then she let out a sigh and shook her head. "Your father was a POW. He'll eat anything. He's never full."

Sometimes at night, I awakened to the sound of moans coming from Dad's bedroom. I clenched my body tight until the noise diminished to soft whimpers, then to the even snoring of deep slumber. I learned to stop asking him if anything was wrong the next morning, since Dad would always deny he'd had a nightmare.

He never talked about his nightmares, but the details of his war days and years spent in a POW camp must have fed them. Over many dinners, starting when I was around eight years old, and always during a weekend off from work when he was at his most relaxed, particularly after a glass or two of sherry, Dad retold his war stories. He regularly told the same stories, but each telling held a different gripping detail or horrific scene.

Dad wasn't telling us these stories to make us feel pity for him or to scare us into being better behaved. In fact, although he never came out and said so, I know he spared us many more horrible details than we could imagine. In some way, telling his stories must have served as a form of therapy or release that helped him to forget the events that haunted him.

Over Japanese-style salted salmon and grated daikon radish, I learned that in 1943, when Dad was only nineteen, he was drafted into the Japanese Imperial Army. It was during his junior year of college, in Dairen, Manchuria, west of Japan and southwest of Russia, which had been occupied by the Japanese since 1931.

His university schooling landed him a lieutenant's title. When his regiment was asked for volunteers to study Russian, he was the only man to raise his hand. He knew this skill would raise his value in the regiment, but he did it mostly to get out of six months of physical training. After his linguistic training, the army sent him back to Manchuria.

At that time, Russia and Japan had been at odds over the control of Manchuria for decades, beginning with the yearlong Russo-Japanese War of 1904, when Russia lost control of Inner and Outer Manchuria to the Japanese.

During one singularly memorable dinner, a summer meal of stir-fried garden vegetables, homemade tofu, and shrimp, I covered my ears with my hands to keep from hearing Dad's vivid description of the days leading up to the Russian invasion of Manchuria and the evacuation of Japanese civilians. He told us how he saw women leading their small children along the roads, carrying bundles of belongings and babies tied to their backs. They were trying to reach the Chinese–North Korean border to charter fishing boats to take them to Japan.

Food supplies were no longer coming through and civilians were starving. Dad saw mothers so exhausted they couldn't tell that the babies on their backs had died. As he described this experience, my brothers and I sat there, our eyes and mouths gaping.

Maybe he couldn't stop himself, but Dad told my brothers and me, just kids, how fear and panic set in the soldiers around him. Mom had to tell me to stop eating so fast. I was shoveling the rice, vegetables, and seafood into my mouth while Dad talked, unaware of how and what I was eating, engrossed in the same way I would be if I were eating popcorn at the movie theater during a scary movie.

Knowing their defeat was inevitable, some of the Japanese soldiers used their last grenades to blow themselves up. The soldiers always kept one for the option of suicide over surrender. Dad saw human limbs scattered around the battlefield—some hung in trees with fingers still curled around the grenade clips. Dad told us of the day he too grasped his grenade clip, preparing to pull it as he heard the approaching Russian gunfire. At twenty-two, his will to survive, even if it meant potential death in a POW camp, was stronger than his will to kill himself. Something in his being refused to die lying on the battlefields of Manchuria.

The Russian army captured Dad in the beginning of the winter of 1945. He and the remaining Japanese soldiers were transported by rail, on cattle cars, from Manchuria to Talbov, Russia. Moscow was five-thousand miles away. Many soldiers, including Dad, had gone into battle during the summer or fall and did not have winter clothes.

"I must have been healthy, because other men would fall asleep beside me and never wake up," Dad said, taking a bite of shrimp.

He survived on watered-down soup and an occasional bowl of rice gruel. If any of the prisoners came across horse dung, they carefully picked out the undigested soybeans and passed them out as if they were candy drops. Once a week they were allowed a pan of water to use for washing. Twice Dad contracted malaria.

During his imprisonment, it was common to move prisoners to different locations unexpectedly, which involved days of walking with no food, water, or sleep. Sometimes they were blindfolded to confuse their sense of direction. "We could have walked around the camp in circles for all we knew," Dad said, shaking his head sadly.

Dad kept his knowledge of Russian a secret for one year, translating to his fellow prisoners what the guards had planned for them. During the three years of his imprisonment, from 1945 to 1948, Dad built roads, did farm work, cleared woods, and performed other manual labor all over Russia. Even though the war was over, the Russians were in no hurry to report their captives, preferring to use them as laborers in the interim.

I was long finished with my stir-fry when Dad told us about the morning the Russian guards roused him and other prisoners at daybreak to move to another camp. He was twenty-five years old at that point. He was blindfolded and made to walk for several days until Dad smelled the ocean. Constant hunger had sharpened his sense of smell. During their imprisonment, Dad and the other prisoners had made a guessing game of what the guards were eating from the odors wafting from their barracks. When the wind blew from a certain direction, he could make out the mouthwatering aromas of cooking meat and baking bread drifting toward him from the nearby village like music.

When a soldier removed Dad's blindfold, he found himself standing at the end of a pier. He didn't know it, but he was facing the Sea of Japan. The Russians were removing the metal shackles from his ankles when a dinghy approached. A Japanese soldier reached out his hand, pulling him and the other prisoners aboard to take them to a ship bearing a Japanese flag. They pulled away from the pier, toward the Japanese ship. It wasn't until an exhausted Dad saw a Russian boat headed the other way, carrying haggard Russian POWS, that he realized he had survived the war.

Dad had shared other stories just as heartwrenching and tragic, but on this evening, I gravitated toward a child's vulnerable space of tiredness. I couldn't articulate the despair I felt for his experience. Instead, I burst into tears at the table, not just shimmering eyes and muffled sniffing, but all-out sobs and strings of snot. Mom and Dad looked at me sympathetically but didn't say anything.

My father's reality was a child's worst nightmare—with his mother dying, being sent away to another country, adopted by strangers to be their servant, and serving time in a POW camp. In my mind, I stockpiled the fears and anxieties that his experiences stirred in my imagination.

Many times before that night, I had fought the urge to cry by focusing my thoughts on something else while he told his stories. When I felt my eyeballs strain and fill with hot tears, I quickly considered how long it would take to put a lawn-mower engine back together, or what Tang was made of. To actually cry was to acknowledge that Dad's ordeals were much more brutal, stark, and real than I cared to admit.

"There, there," Dad said finally, patting my back heartily as I cried in my hands, ashamed of my tears but unable to stop. He and Mom laughed uncomfortably, as my parents often did when I cried, and said soothingly, "It was not so bad. Don't be sad. That was a long time ago."

Dad was quiet for a few seconds, recognizing he had said too much. He bolted up as if something suddenly occurred to him and said brightly, "Look at me now, I'm fine!" Mom smiled at this, relieved at this response.

❖

My entire youth was filled with Mom and Dad's stories. I saved all of them in my mind, taking bits and pieces here and there until I accumulated a big tangled ball of delicate silk thread, enough to weave a tapestry of their history.

I didn't have a clear understanding of this after the experience I had at the party with Thomas. What I wanted was for my parents to respond as they had when I was eight years old and sobbing. I wanted my father to pat my back and say, "There, there." But as I separated and examined the strands of their individual histories, I started to wonder if they believed that I was already old enough to fend for myself the way Mom had fended for herself after the death of her mother and remarriage of her father, and Dad had in the POW camps. This was life as they knew it.

This realization wasn't a satisfying notion at the time. As a young woman, I thought my parents' ability to forget their past was a cop-out and a weakness. As years passed, and as I was tempered by my own life experiences, I grew to admire and find inspiration in their humility. Rather than wallow in their own self-pity or allow their anger to overwhelm them and their families, my parents always opted to rise above their pain. They did not allow themselves to get pulled under by disappointment and resentment, like some former internees of the Japanese American concentration camps I have met, who sadly lived with bitterness for the rest of their lives, or like the middle-aged World War II vet who told me that he hated all "Japs."

The divergent path my life was taking, as well as my growing understanding of my parents' history, helped me to forgive them for the abandonment I felt after the Thomas incident. I grew to admire Mom and Dad's bulletproof optimism, comparing it to an armor that grew impenetrable and more splendid through the decades. Their tenacity reminds me of the tough inner shells of the black walnuts that fell from the tree in our back yard. Deep in the crumbling greenish-black husk, smelling of pine and staining the fingers with a sticky sap, a hard shell protects the soft nut within. Life had given Mom and Dad every reason to hate it, but somehow, through it all, they drew strength to protect and nurture themselves in whatever way they could.

At sixteen, I couldn't understand the way my future would unfold in front of me, or be sure that spinning my own threads of experience would help my character become as resilient and stellar as my parents'. But I was beginning to realize the importance of protecting the sweet, untouched meat of my spirit, buried deep down like the heart of a coarse black walnut.

## Short-Necked Clams Steamed with Sake

*Fresh clams should smell like the ocean and be tightly closed. To avoid toughening the clam meat, it's important to carefully monitor the cooking of the clams. Remove the clams from the heat after they have just opened.*

1 pound short-necked clams in the shell
½ cup water
½ cup sake
3 tablespoons chopped green onions

Scrub clams under cold water to eliminate any dirt from shells and then rinse clams in several changes of water until water runs clear. To eliminate any grit inside shells, soak clams in a solution of 3 tablespoons of salt in 4 cups of cold water in the refrigerator for 20 minutes. Drain and then rinse.

Place the clams, water, and sake in a shallow saucepan over medium-high heat until the liquid begins to boil, and then lower to medium and cover. Cook until clams open their shells, about 3–4 minutes. Discard any unopened shells.

Put the broth and clams in a deep serving dish and sprinkle with green onions. Serve immediately.

Serves 4.

## Savoring Memories

For months after the traumatic incident with Thomas at my parents' friend's house, I tried to grasp what had happened, replaying the afternoon over and over in my mind.

I hadn't felt so shaken and vulnerable since that first year of teasing in elementary school. As a youngster, rather than succumbing to the cruelty of my schoolmates, I instinctually and unconsciously embraced the power of self-preservation. As a sixteen-year-old, I had become tempered by the decorum of politeness and manners and ensnared in my teenage self-consciousness. I found myself following the passivity of my mother and the other women I'd grown up with, and I allowed Thomas to talk and paw me in a way that left me feeling violated and filthy. In the end, this left me fearful that I didn't know who I was after all. All the years of bravado and big talking seemed embarrassingly false.

I was blind to it, but I had so much to be proud of regarding my heritage: my mom and dad's colorful history, the family I had in Japan, and the food and culture of my ancestral line. And yet the pride I should have felt was buried like a small

jewel box at the back of a deep closet. I came to a painful con-
clusion that I had known for some time but could never admit
to myself, let alone say out loud. Except for a few treasured
childhood experiences, such as my trip to Japan and learning how to write hiragana and katakana, growing up Japanese
American in a rural farm town was saturated with emotions
that made me feel as if I didn't truly belong and that I was on
the outside looking in.

I felt suspended between two worlds I didn't belong in—
the American culture where I spent my entire girlhood and
the Japanese culture that matched my physical features but
not my upbringing. The connection I had felt to my Japanese
nationality during my visit to Tokyo had long faded.

Both my parents possessed the first-generation-immigrant
mentality; even though Dad was an American citizen by birth,
he was culturally Japanese. Mom and Dad assumed the role of
keeping below the radar and not wanting to draw any attention to themselves. They shared priceless family stories with
my brothers and me. These stories, as powerful as they were,
only left me more haunted and vague about who I was. We
had to form our own interpretations. I was given a slight nudge
toward pride in our Japanese ancestry, but not the shove of
inspiration that children need.

I wasn't at all proud of the stark conclusions I was making about who and what we were. It is useless to ponder the
possibilities, but I couldn't help but wonder the difference it
would have made had I grown up surrounded by a strong Japanese American community. I wouldn't experience my first
taste of Asian American pride until I moved to San Francisco
in my midtwenties. I remember feeling giddy and exhilarated
by the large Asian American community. It was liberating to

be free from the sneaking feeling that I stood out, something I had felt constantly everywhere that I had ever lived before. I envied the groundedness of the Asian Americans I met who had grown up in the Bay Area. I joined all the Asian events and community groups that I could. But even being in the supportive environment that I craved, sometimes I felt like a stranger among all the Asian Americans who appeared so at ease.

But back in Versailles, I still had to complete high school, and I had yet to connect with that part of me that could learn to be at peace with who she was. At the time, I was questioning my life, but guidance from my high school mental-health counselor was not an option. In the end it came down to the fact that after all the years I had spent lashing back and trying to get the last word, I was done fighting. I was prepared to do what before had been unthinkable—flee. I would leave Indiana behind as soon as possible and find out what it meant to me to be Japanese American.

My plan was to finish high school as close to the top of the class as possible, which I hoped would get me into a good university. If anything, Mom and Dad had been successful in instilling in me a strong work ethic because of their fear of an uncertain financial future and job security. For as long as I can remember, Mom and Dad pounded into my head that a college degree would be my ticket anywhere.

Because sports took away from our studying time, my parents didn't allow my brothers and me to participate in any organized athletics. I had no extracurricular activities on my school record. That year I auditioned and got into my high school's all-girls singing group and the band's flag-girl corps. I signed up for all the college-bound courses and was accepted into Purdue University. It wasn't New York University, but I was a step closer to my goal.

I was twenty-one years old when I came home for a visit from college one fall weekend. It was my senior year, and I felt an overwhelming urge to spend time with Mom and Dad. I had spent the entire summer working at an internship in Fort Worth, Texas, where Keven had moved for a job two years before.

As I sat down for lunch with my parents, I was overwhelmed by the familiarity of my surroundings. It felt the way it had when I was in kindergarten, just Dad, Mom, and me. Since I had gone away to college, a lot of time started passing between visits. But Mom still did her tango between kitchen and dinner table, and she refused to sit down so she could serve us fluffy tempura-battered shrimp, smelt, onion, zucchini, and eggplant fresh from the hot oil.

One bite of her homecooked Japanese food was as comforting as a night of sleep in my childhood bed.

"A new market opened in Cincinnati. It sells everything," Mom gushed. "Japanese and Chinese vegetables, soy sauce, even miso paste. They have big fish department, bigger than the Japanese store in Chicago. We ask which day the delivery comes, then go so that we get it fresh."

With a flourish, she set a dish of thinly sliced tuna and salmon sashimi on the table. I pinched a piece of the red raw fish between my chopsticks. The cool texture and subtle fish flavor melted in my mouth. It was as good as the fish we had eaten so long ago at the sushi bar in Chicago.

I was delighted when Dad told me he had bought Japanese cabbage at the local grocery store to make *tsukemono* (pickled cabbage). The days of counting boxes and rationing

Japanese ingredients were behind them. I felt both sadness and relief that Asian ingredients and fresh fish were more easily available at last. My parents were freed from the constant restraints of searching for Japanese ingredients. But behind this happiness was a sense of something lost. The passing of time and changes in routine represented the closing of a particular period of my youth.

As I popped a crunchy piece of *akashiso* (red Japanese basil) into my mouth and savored its pine-mint flavor, Dad told me about the vegetables he had cultivated that summer. He described the trial-and-error process he had gone through when he grew bok choy, the triumph he felt when he saw the first sprouts of *myoga* (young ginger), and the disappointment of growing stubborn *nagaimo* (sticky yam). Despite years of successes and pitfalls, he was proud of his back-yard garden and how full of Asian vegetables it was.

To my embarrassment, hot tears blurred my vision when Mom served a whole broiled rainbow trout and *yakibuta* (roasted pork loin), two of my favorite meals from childhood. I wiped my eyes hastily and scolded myself for being silly, and then I fanned my face with my hand with exaggeration, pretending the sashimi with spicy wasabi paste caused my watery eyes and sniffles. I was still just as shy and ashamed to cry in front of my parents as when I was a child. I kept my eyes down until I regained my composure and concentrated on the crisp silver and brown charred skin of the grilled whole fish. I peeled it away in long satisfying strips, the way Mom had taught me long ago. As I was about to dunk the fish in a sauce of spicy grated daikon radish and soy sauce, I realized Mom hadn't checked my fish for stray bones as she once did, even as recently as when I was in high school.

Now, almost fifteen years later, I asked shyly, "Mom, aren't you going to check my fish?"

Mom smiled as she recalled the old ritual. She reached toward my plate of fish with her chopsticks and then stopped, waving the dish away. "No, you're big girl now. It looks clean from here. Good enough to give to your own children."

I smiled as I recognized that she was acknowledging that I had made it safely to adulthood without choking on a fish bone. Content, I turned my attention to the row of pork slices swimming in a puddle of luscious soy sauce, garlic, brown sugar, and sake marinade. Dad and I both loved the end pieces best.

I had a habit of saving my favorite for last, savoring that best morsel for the end. The anticipation of those last bites, to me, made the meal all the more enjoyable, the eating version of the way I collected memories to enjoy later. I would wait until the end of my meal before claiming the coveted end pieces of the tenderloin.

Just as I was about to reach for them with my open chopsticks, Dad helped himself. I sat back flabbergasted and hurt as he dipped the slices back and forth in a heady mixture of hot mustard and soy sauce. I looked at Mom for support, but she shook her head. This was between Dad and me. My jaw fell open when he ate the first piece with no remorse.

As he was about to eat the second piece, he said, "I used to eat like you, the best for last. After being in the POW camp, when you never knew the next time you would eat, I changed my thinking. Eat your favorite first." He waved his chopstick at me. "If you wait too long, it won't be there to enjoy." Then, with a teasing twinkle in his eyes, he placed the last pork loin back on my plate.

I looked at it and then looked at Dad, who wore the same expression of wise calmness as always, though I had never had a name for it before. For a moment I looked at him through squinted eyes, thinking about the way he shared that wisdom with me. As usual, what he was telling me had nothing to do with food, but something bigger. I smiled to myself before taking the savory meat nugget in my mouth. It was, as always, delicious.

Our conversation closed as quickly as a changing tide, turning toward my summer internship and my final year at college. Then we all fell to silence as we gave serious attention to our food. The rhythm of eating took over. I surrendered to the familiar chimes of chopsticks that clinked against rice bowls and the sipping sounds as we drank our miso soup.

It struck me at that moment that eating had been my family's communion. We communicated not through direct words, but through actions and food. When I left for college Mom didn't tell me she would miss me with tears. Instead she packed a box of rice balls into my pile of belongings. Why did it have to be so hard to talk to them? Why couldn't I tell them that the most important lessons I learned came from their history and stories? I wanted to share with them the excitement I felt as I was nearing my college graduation. I wanted them to know that I understood that leaving home hadn't been an answer to my questions, but that it had led to bigger ones. But my thoughts remained unspoken.

For the moment I was swaddled in the comforts of home, and I was seized by panic at the thought of leaving it all. I began my mental collecting, but this time I tried to capture it all by making a final sweep, like a fisherman casting out yards of netting. I tried to freeze the images and sounds I had seen all my life—the soft haze that veiled the lawn in the inky-blue early morning, the song of wind chimes and the screech of a bluebird, and the bands of gold and white the evening sun cast onto the living room floor.

I sat back and thought about my singular goal since having turned sixteen. I had worked toward the goal of leaving Indiana without a thought to what I would do once I reached it.

That night back at my parents' kitchen table was my first inkling that no matter where I lived in the world and no matter what people saw, the small-town country girl from Indiana would always be part of me. At the time, I still hadn't done enough or seen enough places to accept the fact that an Asian face would be all that some people would ever see in me. This bothered me tremendously back then, and I didn't have the foresight to know that someday it wouldn't bother me anymore.

That night, as I reviewed the memories I had hoarded through the years, Dad's words at the dinner table resonated like a temple bell. "Enjoy the best first," he had told me. Enjoy the moment.

This message was his way of setting me free, giving me a bow and arrow. For Mom and Dad knew that the time was fast approaching for me to shoot my arrow skyward and to venture off to wherever it might fall.

The young girl so determined to move away from her past couldn't see that someday she would spread out all the images she had collected during her girlhood in white-bread America—a collage of Americana and Japanese—and gaze at them fondly, proud that she grew up where and the way she did. Ultimately I would want that for my own son, though that was still years down the line. At the time, my goal was to flee. It wasn't until three years away turned to five, and then to ten, and then to twelve that I had the courage to examine the memories I had carried with me all those years and allow myself to feel and savor the legacy of my parents, their stories, and the shared love of food and cooking. My inadequacies and anger ebbed through the years; rising in their place were humility and strong values that guided me, like a falling arrow, toward a place where I could finally let go and treasure and honor the uniqueness of my childhood and having grown up in a Japanese household in America's heartland.

## Roasted Pork Tenderloin *(Yakibuta)*

*The marinade for the tenderloin, as mouthwatering as it is, isn't recommended as a dipping sauce. To make a good dipping sauce, use English hot mustard, such as Colby's powder, with soy sauce. Any leftover slices can be frozen and added to ramen soup.*

- ¼ cup soy sauce
- 2 garlic cloves, minced
- 1 tablespoon minced ginger
- 1 tablespoon brown sugar
- ¼ cup sake
- ½ teaspoon sesame oil
- 1½–2 pounds pork tenderloins (1–2 loins)

Mix together the soy sauce, garlic, ginger, sugar, sake, and sesame oil in a glass baking dish or plastic storage container. Put the pork in the dish and turn to coat with marinade on all sides. Let marinate for at least 1 hour or, for best results, cover and refrigerate overnight.

Preheat the oven to 425°F.

Remove the pork from the marinade and place in a roasting pan. Roast, basting every 15 minutes, until the internal temperature reaches 150°F on an instant-read thermometer (inserted in the thickest part of the meat).

Remove from the oven and let cool to room temperature before slicing.

*Optional:* Heat the marinade until it boils and pour over the pork before serving.

Serves 4.

## Acknowledgments

To those who believed in my story from its infancy, mere words cannot express my eternal gratitude for your unwavering support. Aaron Wehner, Dianne Jacob, Carole Bidnick, Brooke Warner and the team at Seal Press, Michael Bauer, Miriam Morgan, and Lesli Neilson.

My big brothers, Keven and Alvin.

Kelly Garcia, Ann-Janette Watson, Signy Furiya, Mildred Furiya, Gillian Hally, Sharon Harkness, Jeffrey Harkness, Jeanette Ferrary, Marybeth Williams, Betty Fagan, Mark Fagan, Heidi Van Horn Feng, Catherine Struble, Daryl DeVries, Grace Liu, Ceil Bouchet, Anita Ritchie, and Thao Nyugen.

To all the readers in the Bay Area who have followed my *San Francisco Chronicle* food column through the years.

And Manfred Ichiro.

SCOTT BRIGHTWELL

## About the Author

Linda Furiya has been writing about ethnicity and food since 1992, when she wrote a monthly newspaper column about growing up Japanese American in Versailles, Indiana. Later she moved to Beijing and wrote about food and travel. She also lived in Shanghai, where she completed classes in Chinese cooking. Furiya returned to the United States in 1998 and began her bimonthly column on Asian cooking for the *San Francisco Chronicle* two years later. She continues to freelance for the *Chronicle*, writes, and teaches cooking and food classes in Vermont, where she lives with her son and wirehair dachshund. She is a graduate of Purdue University.

# Selected Titles from Seal Press

For more than thirty years, Seal Press has published groundbreaking books. By women. For women. Visit our website at www.sealpress.com.

*Dirty Sugar Cookies: Culinary Observations, Questionable Taste* by Ayun Halliday. $14.95, 1-58005-150-2. Ayun Halliday is back with comical and unpredictable essays about her disastrous track record in the kitchen and her culinary observations—though she's clearly no expert.

*Stalking the Wild Dik Dik: One Woman's Solo Misadventures Across Africa* by Marie Javins. $15.95, 1-58005-164-2. A funny and compassionate account of the sort of lively and heedless undertaking that could only happen in Africa.

*Mexico, A Love Story: Women Write about the Mexican Experience* edited by Camille Cusumano. $15.95, 1-58005-156-1. In this thrilling and layered collection, two-dozen women describe the country they love and why they have fallen under its spell. Also available, *Italy, A Love Story: Women Write about the Italian Experience*. $15.95, 1-58005-143-X and *France, A Love Story: Women Write about the French Experience*. $15.95, 1-58005-115-4.

*Intimate Politics: How I Grew Up Red, Fought for Free Speech, and Became a Feminist Rebel* by Bettina F. Aptheker. $16.95, 1-58005-160-X. A courageous and uncompromising account of one woman's personal and political transformation, and a fascinating portrayal of a key chapter in our nation's history.

*Incognito Street: How Travel Made Me a Writer* by Barbara Sjoholm. $15.95, 1-58005-172-3. From the founder of Seal Press comes this eloquent coming-of-age travel narrative about her beginnings as a writer.

*Es Cuba: Life and Love on an Illegal Island* by Lea Aschkenas. $15.95, 1-58005-179-0. This triumphant love story captures a beautiful and intangible sense of sadness and admiration for the country of Cuba and for its people.